COLD CASE JURY

AN UNSOLVED TRUE CRIME
YOU DELIVER THE VERDICT

MOVE TO MURDER

BY ANTONY M. BROWN

SECOND EDITION

NEW ERA OF COMMUNICATIONS

CONTENTS

ABOUT COLD CASE JURY
BEST SERVED COLD

I agree with George Orwell, who famously lamented the decline of the English murder. He thought original murders were virtually extinct by the first half of the 20th Century, and that brutality had replaced ingenuity in pursuance of the ultimate crime. Gone were the days of assiduous poisonings, carefully laid traps and mysterious killings without apparent motive. These were now the preserve of thrillers, movies and, of course, dear Aunt Agatha. Fact had lost its frisson to fiction and reality was left somehow diminished.

There is a quality to a bygone murder that seems to set it apart from its modern counterparts. It was an era of etiquette and arsenic, of afternoon tea with a spoonful of malice. Modern Britain is too open, too honest even, to create the social conditions of the past that drove some to commit murder, often with an insidious craft that flummoxed the authorities of the day.

This last point is important. Like revenge, a venerable murder is best served cold. Unsolved. These are the intriguing cases that have several plausible solutions and have bequeathed us enough evidence to let us debate what probably happened. These are the masterpieces of murder, to quote the title of an Edmund Pearson book, the dark art that would be hung upon the cold walls of a Tate Criminal Gallery. These are the cases for the Cold Case Jury.

Does this mean that these crimes were perpetrated by the Machiavellis of murder? No, an unsolved crime from Orwell's golden age of murder does not imply its criminals were more deviously clever than today's. Undoubtedly some were, but the truth is that many of these cold cases would be solved by today's higher standards of professionalism and scientific methods of detection. Even the assassination of President Kennedy in 1963, arguably the most analysed murder of the last century, spawned a vast conspiracy theory industry largely because of a flawed autopsy. Whether this was by malign influence or honourable incompetence is a quicksand best avoided here. My point is that, had the autopsy retrieved the bullet fragments from the President's brain, subsequent forensic analysis would have revealed the type of gun that terminated a presidency that bright November day and the shadows of doubt, as well as an industry, might have disappeared.

So, am I re-investigating these cold cases, unearthing fresh evidence or presenting new theories to shed new light on old crimes? Sometimes, yes, but my overriding goal is to present the reader with an interesting case for which the verdict is open to doubt. My task is to take the reader back in time to witness the events leading up to a violent or suspicious death; reconstruct how it occurred according to the different theories; and present evidence to the reader as in a real court. I hope to bring these crimes back to life, showing how the drama might have unfolded, emphasising the timeless interplay of the people involved and presenting the historical stage on which they acted. In reconstructing a cold case theory I prefer to use narrative's present tense – dialogue. Some of it is verbatim, drawn from trial or inquest testimony. The rest is more a work of imagination, yet always governed by the facts and theories of the case, connecting the evidential dots by plausible lines of narrative.

I hope I am also an impartial advocate – the Cold Case Advocate, if you like. My aim is to show the strengths and weaknesses of each theory, and then you have your say. I'm hoping you will give your verdict on the Cold Case Jury website. Over time, an overall verdict of the Cold Case Jury will emerge for each case.

My final task is to present my views on the case. But my view is only one. The verdict always lies with you, the jury.

PREFACE

The second edition of *Move to Murder* adds an additional theory, a significantly enhanced evidence file, new reconstructions and new analyses. This reflects more detailed arguments for and against Wallace's guilt that have emerged since I first started writing the book over four years ago. This is necessary because, of all the cases in the Cold Case Jury series, the Wallace murder is the most complex and, even now, fast-moving. For example, no fewer than three books on the case were published in 2021, including this edition.

One of the most significant changes in this edition is the introduction of modern forensic opinion, largely instigated by The Julia Wallace Murder Foundation website {see Part Three}. In the first edition I accepted the position of John MacFall that Julia Wallace was killed while she sat on the armchair in her front room. Having heavily criticised all of his other findings, and despite misgivings even about this, I thought I should maintain MacFall's opinion on this matter because it was accepted in court. This was a mistake. Almost certainly, Julia Wallace was first struck while she stood to the right of the fireplace, and this significantly affects the reconstructions and possibly your verdict.

The Wallace case is the most debated in the Cold Case Jury series with six possible theories about how Julia Wallace was murdered. There is a neat symmetry: in three William Wallace is innocent; in three he is guilty. As members of the Cold Case Jury your first task is to decide whether you believe Wallace is innocent or not and then select your preferred theory.

Once again, the result is in your hands.

Antony M. Brown, *September 2021*

PREFACE TO THE FIRST EDITION
WITHOUT EQUAL

The American crime writer John Dickson Carr wrote that there are few real-life murders that compare to the "tidy, clipped maze of fiction". Crime fiction, unshackled by the realities of detective work and the imperatives of justice, almost always has the better stories. After all, a novelist is free to conjure up a richly layered plot, and choreograph the clues and drama for maximum effect. Real crime is rarely so neat, or perpetrated with such forethought. Rather, the typical murder is incited by our worst emotions. Perhaps we should take a measure of comfort from this, preferring raw spontaneity to the deliberate cunning of the thriller writer.

There are always exceptions. And occasionally there is a case so remarkable it is seemingly without equal; a case that appears to have been scripted, except that it embraces the wrinkles and oddities only real life provides. One such case is the Wallace murder, which the novelist Raymond Chandler described as "unbeatable" because the body of evidence can be interpreted in different ways, each seemingly as plausible as the others. Crime writer Edgar Lustgarten agreed, calling it a "murder in a class by itself".

When I started writing the Cold Case Jury series I wanted to include *the* classic unsolved murder case. The Wallace case is a real-life Agatha Christie. So, as soon as I began writing my first book, I had already started researching this one.

The result is in your hands.

Antony M. Brown, *September 2018*

PART ONE

THE STORY

This is the true story of the murder of Julia Wallace in Liverpool in 1931, one of the most puzzling unsolved crimes of all time.

Look to nothing, not even for a moment, except to reason.
Marcus Aurelius

1. THE SET UP

The year is 1931. King George V is on the throne and Ramsay MacDonald, the leader of the Labour Party, is in Downing Street. Britain has a population of 45 million, the average hourly wage is a shilling and a pint of ale costs a little less than that. Fewer than half of all homes have a radio, and regular television broadcasts from the BBC are still five years away. The economic slump that has swept the world like a virulent disease is at its worst, and Britain has not been spared. One out of every five adults has no job.

The place is Liverpool. The city's population is at an all-time high. Over 800,000 people are crammed into the teeming metropolis, most living in endless rows of back-to-back houses. Like many industrial cities of the North, it is taking the brunt of the depression. Poverty and deprivation stalk the subdued streets like a pack of wolves. North of the city centre is Anfield, a district synonymous with the ground of Liverpool Football Club, a middling team in the English First Division. Within this urban labyrinth is Wolverton Street, an unremarkable cul-de-sac, comprising two terraces of red brick houses, each with two polygonal bay windows stacked upon each other.

Near the end of the street, on the left, is No. 29. It has a dark front door with a fanlight above. Its tall windows are veiled by thick, grimy net curtains. This is the home of William and Julia Wallace. It will be the scene of a murder, but this is not the place where our story begins. A little over 200 yards away northwest across the chimney-topped roofs of similar houses in similar streets, a confluence of three major roads forms a triangle of land bordered by well-tended flower beds. At its apex, standing like an idle sentry at the end of Lower Breck Road, is a telephone box. Although they are still a novelty, there is nothing special about this particular one – it has cream concrete walls, a pyramidal roof and a glass-panelled green door with the sign "Public Telephone. Open Always".

The date is Monday 19 January. In the chilly morning, the sleeping city comes alive: men in heavy coats and boots tramp their way across the cold cobblestones; trams whine as they plough through the streets, ferrying workers to factories and offices; and drivers of throaty motor cars honk their horns amidst the echo of clopping hooves and jangling reins. A solitary steamer glides eerily down the River Mersey like a ghost ship. Not so long ago there would have been a flotilla of cargo-laden vessels jostling for a berth. That was before the Depression. Yet, like wildebeest returning to a dried-up waterhole, dockers in their thousands continue to arrive at the docks in the hope of finding work, or to report for the dole.

During the day a persistent drizzle turns to sleet. Everything feels cold, damp and dreary. The weather does not improve as the grey skies darken and the day slides into evening gloom. The humdrum of daily routines continues. Across the city, lampmen light up the streets and workers begin to think about the trudge home. The school day is over and hundreds of grubby-faced and dishevelled children fill the streets, playing kick-about and hopscotch. The older ones begin their rounds of delivering milk and the *Liverpool Echo* to doorsteps.

Night falls. In countless houses, matches are struck to light fires and gas lamps, and housewives cook dinner on the range while their husbands read a newspaper unfurled across the kitchen table. *The Times* carries a brief report that, for the first time, Germany is exporting more goods than Britain. For the head-shaking middle class, the statistic is an unwelcome reminder that an empire is waning. The working class are already more intimately acquainted with the effects of this: they face the hardship wrought by unemployment and the social decay fathered by it.

The time is 7:15pm. A man in a long overcoat and grey hat walks along Lower Breck Road, his breath condensing in the night air. Fighting the cold and sleet, he keeps his chin tucked into his upturned collar and hands thrust into his coat pockets. He moves briskly through the dappled shadows, his gaze downward. The sound of his heels snapping on the pavement is the only conspicuous sign of his presence. As he passes under the diffused spotlight of a gas lamp, his figure is illuminated fleetingly, but his hat and coat collar hide his features, and then he is lost again to the darkness. We never glimpse his face; his identity forever veiled in doubt.

He soon reaches his destination. Without looking up, he pulls open the glass-panelled door and steps inside, the icy chill joining him in the telephone box. He closes the door and stands motionless in the gloom, the only lighting from a nearby street lamp. He taps the interior light bulb above his head, but to no avail. He rummages for coins in his trouser pockets, and pushes two pennies into the slot at the top of the metal coin box. He unhooks the trumpet-shaped receiver and presses it to his ear. He hears a click and a woman's voice asks, "Which number please, caller?"

He leans towards the mouthpiece mounted above the box. "Operator, connect me to Bank 3581." A pause. The line crackles.

"Connecting you now, sir."

The caller hears the ringing tone and waits for his call to be answered. It is about to trigger a series of events that will soon result in a brutal murder.

*

The murder of Julia Wallace in January 1931 remains unsolved to this day. She was bludgeoned to death in an apparently motiveless and frenzied attack. Her husband William stood trial for her murder, and was found guilty, only for the verdict to be quashed on appeal. No one else was arrested, let alone brought to trial. The case quickly went cold, but it has never been forgotten; criminologists and crime writers are drawn to this tantalising whodunit like fish to a brightly coloured lure.

Scores of books and articles have been published about the case. Many commentators think William Wallace was innocent. Others believe that he was guilty all along, claiming he made the call from the telephone box to create an alibi before dispatching his wife with an iron bar. Over the decades since, six major theories have been advanced to explain the slaying of Julia Wallace.

In Part One, I will take you back in time, reconstructing how events unfolded, with different versions of how the murder might have occurred. Key points of evidence will be introduced and discussed. In Part Two, you will see original evidence – including witness statements, post-mortem reports and police documents – some of which are being published for the first time. These can be read along with the narrative in Part One (the relevant exhibit number is placed in curly brackets in the text) or afterwards, or a mixture of both. Finally, in Part Three, I present my view of the case. But it is your opinion that matters. As in a real court of law, the verdict always rests with you, the jury.

Who most likely murdered Julia Wallace? As a member of the Cold Case Jury, this is the question on which you are invited to reach a verdict. Read the story, look at the evidence and select the most plausible theory that explains the killing. I hope you will enter your verdict at the Cold Case Jury website, where you can also see a poll of how your fellow jurors have voted. The result should be a fascinating verdict in the court of public opinion on a murder that thriller-writer Raymond Chandler described as an "unbeatable" mystery.

Before the clock is turned back to 1931, you need some essential background. William Wallace is the spider lurking at the centre of this tangled web. Whether he was a victim of this crime or its perpetrator, the case can only be unlocked by understanding more about his life, his interests and his relationships.

*

On 29 August 1878, William Herbert Wallace was born in Millom, a small iron-mining town in the historic county of Cumberland (now Cumbria) in northwest England. He was the eldest of three children, born two years before his brother, Joseph, and five before his sister, Jessie. As a boy, he appears to have been blessed with above-average intelligence but cursed by the limitations of his family circumstances. His father, a part-time insurance agent and printer, held the traditional working-class view that his son should start earning as soon as was possible. This outlook was not born of ignorance or malice, but by the necessity of supporting a family of five in the days when welfare meant the hard labour of the workhouse. Consequently, William missed out on a good education that would have nourished his keen scientific mind, and this was a deep well of regret and grievance later in life. He would try to satisfy his hunger for learning by reading voraciously, especially in science, philosophy and politics.

Lack of opportunity was not his only misfortune. When he was 10 years old his family moved south to Blackpool, Lancashire, where William contracted typhoid fever. This bacterial infection is associated with poor sanitary conditions through which the victim ingests contaminated food or water. William's illness was diagnosed late, possibly because the typical skin rash of rose-coloured spots failed to appear. The other common symptoms – abdominal pain, headaches and fatigue – might have been initially mistaken for a more innocuous condition. Without treatment, typhoid often spreads throughout the body, infecting organs. This may well have happened in William's case, because he would be dogged by a serious kidney problem throughout his life. In fact, it would eventually kill him.

When William left school in 1892, aged 14, two major ley-lines of his life – modest education and poor health – had already been established. A third was now added: perpetual menial employment, which gave as little remuneration as it did intellectual stimulation. For the next five years he worked as an apprentice at a local draper's business, with a weekly wage of three shillings. At its completion, he was a lanky, bespectacled 19-year-old, standing over six feet tall, who had the appearance of "an elongated walking stick". His imposing height belied a reserved character: he was solitary, introspective and brooding, with a formal, distant and circumspect manner. In later life, he claimed to be a follower of Stoic philosophy and, in particular, he admired the writings of Marcus Aurelius. When Aurelius wrote, "Let nothing be done rashly, and at random, but all things according to the most exact and perfect rules of art," he could have been describing the fastidious nature of Wallace.

Over the next six years, the young Wallace worked as an assistant in various northern towns, but his drapery career stalled. Perhaps for someone with his background there were fewer opportunities for progression than today, or his insular and punctilious personality meant that he was not an ideal choice for promotion. So Wallace looked overseas for deliverance. He later wrote that this was due to his wanderlust, perhaps stirred by his younger brother, who was working in China, but it is sometimes the excuse given by those wanting to escape the lengthening shadow of failure on their own doorstep. Whatever the reason, William Wallace accepted a posting abroad with his existing employer, taking up an assistant position in the Calcutta outlet of Whiteway Laidlaw and Company, an outfitter to the British Army.

When Wallace reached India in late 1902, he arrived at the heart of the British Empire. His mind might have been filled with romantic scenes of army officers enjoying the high life in an exotic climate. As a young Englishman in India, he would have at least expected to be treated with deference and respect. He might have also anticipated a swift advancement in his career, but he was to be disappointed. He remained a sales assistant, serving the needs of others. Worse, a spectre from his past quickly caught up with him.

Calcutta has a tropical savannah climate. Its average monthly temperature dips below 30° Celsius only in December and January. Sizzling temperatures peak in April and May, with many days often breaching 40° Celsius, before the monsoon season cools the city by dumping nearly three times the average annual precipitation of London in just four months. Many Europeans have difficulty in adjusting to the harsh climate, let alone ones with underlying health problems. The sapping heat appears to have aggravated William's kidney trouble, which had flared up on occasions even in the temperate climate of his homeland. In Calcutta he underwent surgery twice. The solution to his deteriorating health, he later wrote, was a milder climate. Yet he shunned a return to England in favour of following his brother to China.

In 1906, Shanghai was an international city, largely governed by the British, French and Americans. It was already China's largest port, and in the ensuing decades it was to become the world's largest city. The crowded streets, already home to one million people, were often a stage for public punishment and execution, typically cruel and unusual, which Wallace observed with his typical detachment on his excursions in the ancient city.

Wallace remained a Whiteway Laidlaw sales assistant, but his kidney ailment worsened to a point where he could no longer discharge his usual duties. He was found less onerous work, being tasked with dressing the window displays. Decades later, Wallace wrote that in Shanghai he had been "an advertising manager in a general store", a gloss on the truth that the smoothest of politicians could not have bettered. The deterioration in his health was alarming, however. While in Shanghai he underwent further operations on his left kidney, then developed an abscess on his right. He had little option but to return home.

On 19 March 1907, Wallace arrived back in Britain. He was admitted to Guy's Hospital in London, where a radical nephrectomy was performed, removing his entire left kidney. After the operation he was laid low for 18 months, unable to work. He attempted to resume his position at Whiteway Laidlaw in Manchester but, as in the Orient, he once again found the duties too demanding. He was now 30 years old, with no career and suffering poor health. The next three years were a backwater in Wallace's life. It is no surprise that during these wilderness years he became interested in politics, and read voraciously on the subject. Perhaps inspired by his observations abroad, or reflecting on his own experience, he became a Liberal activist in Harrogate, where his father and sister were living.

In 1911, Wallace was appointed the Liberal election agent for the Ripon Division in the West Riding of Yorkshire. Finally he received the attention and respect for which he yearned. For the first time in his life he had an important undertaking, in which he was able to use his talents and make a difference. And in the same year another event occurred that moved his joy to its zenith: he met his future wife.

Enter Julia Dennis.

She had been born in East Harlsey, a hamlet situated thirty miles across the North York Moors from Whitby, in the North Riding of Yorkshire (now North Yorkshire). She was the second child of William Dennis and his wife, Anne.

Even though he was illiterate, William insisted that his children should have the education he forsook as a boy when he learned his trade as a farmer. Julia was taught by a governess at her home, furnishing her with the basics of a good education. Tragedy struck, however, when Julia was 10 years old: her mother died giving birth to her seventh child. The death devastated the family. The security and solace of a loving environment was replaced with uncertainty and constant upheaval. The family moved several times. William Dennis gave up farming to become a tenanted innkeeper, which was a disaster. He had already turned to the bottle to numb his profound grief, and this position was effectively a death sentence. Within two years he had died of liver disease. Julia, aged just 13, and her siblings were orphaned and homeless.

The next period of Julia's life is veiled in obscurity, only lifted when she appears in Harrogate several years before William Wallace's arrival. She lived with her niece, whom she taught music and French, reflecting her own educational accomplishments. Her father had at least bequeathed her that. William and Julia were living two streets apart and, although the exact circumstances of their first encounter are unknown, it would not have taken long for them to meet.

After her death, William wrote of Julia: "She was a lady of good birth and social position, whose tastes were similar to my own. Dark-haired, dark-eyed, full of energy and vivaciousness, she filled in every corner of the picture I had dreamed of 'that one woman in all the world' most men enshrine in their hearts. She was an excellent pianist, no mean artist in watercolour, a fluent French scholar, and of a cultured literary taste. From that first moment we met, we found in each other the friendship, companionship, and love we needed."

Despite filling in every corner, it took several years for the picture to be completed. The couple married on 24 March

1914. The marriage certificate states that William Wallace, a secretary (presumably for the local Liberal Party), was 36 years old. Julia Dennis was 37 years old, no stated occupation, but her father was described as a veterinary surgeon. This was a fabrication. We know her father was a farmer-cum-publican. Significantly, her stated age was also a lie.

It had always been assumed that Julia was a year or so older than her husband. Her headstone in an Anfield cemetery clearly states her age at the time of her death: 52 years. Based on the burial register, this appears to be literally rock solid evidence of her age. In *The Murder of Julia Wallace* (2001), James Murphy reveals that Julia Dennis was actually born on 28 April 1861: she was 17 years older than her husband. It was a tremendous piece of historical research overturning a lazy assumption that had been unchallenged for seven decades. Was William aware of the tremendous age difference? Even if she had not disclosed the truth, the tell-tale signs of middle age – the loser skin, wrinkles and eye-lines – would have been difficult to disguise. One supposes that he harboured suspicions that Julia was older than she claimed. Evidently, he did not mind – at least, not at the time of his marriage.

Irrespective of the age gap, William and Julia now faced life together as man and wife. According to his published writings, William looked back on their time in Harrogate as "the days when all the world and the future seemed rose-coloured, sunlit and steeped in everlasting happiness".

Just when William might have thought his fortunes had changed for the better, the wheel of fate turned again. Those sunlit days ended when the thunder clouds of the First World War rolled across Europe. The conflict, Wallace was to later claim, ended party political activity and forced him not only to resign from his position of political agent but to relocate to Liverpool, where he took a job as an agent for the Prudential

Assurance Company. It appears that this position was secured through the contacts of his father, who was left behind in the workhouse at Knaresborough, a parish of Harrogate, where he shortly died.

In July 1915, the couple moved to 29 Wolverton Street. This modest, rented accommodation was to be their home for the next sixteen years. For William, they were years filled with humdrum routine and drudgery, pounding the dreary streets to collect premiums from his five hundred or so customers. It was a tedious task of form filling and small talk, day after day, year after year.

It might have been fulfilling for someone with an easy charm and gregarious nature, but it must have been difficult for an introvert whose spare time was devoted to quiet, intellectual pursuits. His back bedroom was a laboratory where he lost himself, looking through the eyepiece of his expensive microscope, his only luxury. He was particularly keen on botany and chemistry. He also loved chess, although he conceded that he was a mediocre player. Two nights a week he might be hunched over a board at the Central Liverpool Chess Club, pursing his lips, deep in thought, considering his next move.

For Julia, her days were filled with menial housework. Rarely venturing outside, seldom inviting others in, her life appears to have been demarcated by the drab walls of the cramped house. Her chores revolved around the comings and goings of her husband. Julia's escape was music, playing on the upright piano in the front room, and religion. In contrast to her husband, she regularly attended church, although she made few strong friendships even there. Diffident and inscrutable, Julia does not appear to be the vivacious lady that Wallace described. Or perhaps time and marriage had changed her.

To an outsider, there were few notable events during those 16 years. Two seemingly trivial events at the end of

1928, however, are relevant to the case. At the end of November, William had the first of five violin lessons with his work supervisor, Joseph Crewe, himself a keen musician, acting as tutor. These lessons were held at Crewe's house and, as you will later see, this added to the case against Wallace.

The most significant event occurred the following month. Just before the turn of the year, Wallace was bed-ridden for nearly two weeks with bronchitis. During this time his workload was covered by two young men, who dropped off the collection money at Wallace's house. Two years later, after Julia Wallace was brutally slain, there would be lingering suspicions that one of them was her killer.

*

Having explored the background of William Wallace, and as he is a prime suspect in the murder of his wife, we need further answers to two questions: What was he like? And how was his marriage?

His personality was complex. According to some witnesses, he was courteous and good-natured. His chess-playing friend, James Caird, testified that Wallace was "highly strung" but also placid, studious and without ill temper or any sign of violence. This last point was corroborated by Joseph Crewe, Wallace's superior at the Prudential for a dozen years. He added that Wallace was honest and "an absolute gentleman".

Others saw a different side. Alfred Mather, a retired Prudential agent who had also known Wallace for 12 years, found him morose and nauseatingly conceited. He described him as "the most cool, calculating, despondent and soured man he had ever met". Florence Wilson, who nursed Wallace for three weeks at his home when he suffered an attack of pneumonia, recalled that he appeared to be "a man who had suffered a keen disappointment in life". This might be a euphemism for finding him despondent and tetchy. Of course, this might have had something to do with him being unwell.

Wallace was a meticulous introvert. He thrived on details and getting his accounts exact. Today we might label his social detachment and fondness for detail as 'geeky'. This should be borne in mind later, when you discover how he related to witnesses and reacted to his wife's death.

It is interesting to note that Wallace never progressed in any of his careers – as a draper, political secretary or insurance agent. This seems strange for a studious and diligent man who had been working for nearly 40 years. What had held Wallace back? His poor health played a part, but was he also difficult to work with? And live with?

Wallace wrote of his marriage: "We lived in perfect happiness and harmony for 16 years. Our days and months and years were filled with complete enjoyment, placid perhaps, but with all the happiness of quietude, and mutual interests and affection. Neither of us cared much for entertaining other people, or for being entertained; we were sufficient in ourselves."

This passage is taken from Wallace's 'Life Story', a 55-page memoir that was planned for publication so we need to be cautious of gloss {see Exhibit 9}. He also kept a diary and, although it disappeared after he died, some extracts were copied by the police before the trial. These may provide a more reliable glimpse of the man and his marriage. Two entries in particular are revealing.

Writing about his 16th wedding anniversary (in an entry dated 25 March 1930), he believed that neither he nor Julia regretted their marriage: they had "pulled well together", they derived as much pleasure out of life as most people, and a shortage of money was their only trouble. This appears to be a realistic and authentic assessment, free from the saccharine prose about bliss-filled years. The fact that they had pulled together implies they had faced difficulties, and these might have been monetary. Financial pressures are rarely trivial; even in the strongest of marriages they often reveal fault lines in a relationship.

Later in the year, on Monday 15 December 1930, Wallace expressed anxiety when Julia failed to return home after a trip to Southport. At 1am he went to the local police station to enquire whether there had been any reported accidents. Julia arrived back at the house shortly afterwards, having been seriously delayed by a derailed train. He wrote: "It was a relief to know she was safe and sound, for I was getting apprehensive, feeling she might have been run over by a motor car or something." His fear of a car accident was perhaps understandable: in 1930 two million vehicles were responsible for a staggering 7,000 deaths on British roads.

The entry is notable because William shows genuine concern for his wife's welfare, and it was written only the month before her murder. Even accepting that he would be unlikely to commit to paper any intimate problems in the marriage, there is nothing in his writings to suggest that it was broken. Certainly, James Caird believed that William and Julia made "a very happy couple". Joseph Crewe testified that they had the "best possible relations" and "appeared to be all in one together". John Johnston, who lived next door and has a part to play in our drama, testified that he thought they were "a very loving couple". These may be neighbourly words, because Johnston never stepped foot in the Wallace household until the night of the murder. His wife, Florence, had been invited inside just three times in a decade, and each time she spoke to Julia alone. The Johnstons, who were separated from the Wallaces only by a party wall, testified that they never heard their neighbours quarrelling. Although this is a point in favour of the marriage, both William and Julia were undemonstrative. Sharp tongues do not have to be loud. Indifference is always silent.

It is worthwhile to recall the remarks about murder of James Stephens, an erstwhile High Court Judge: "There is no need to look for motive when the parties are man and wife... what lies under the veil is known only to themselves, and the relation may produce hatred and bitterness." A flower, whatever its bloom, may have a rotten root. Some thought this was true of the Wallace marriage. Nurse Wilson remembered William and Julia as a peculiar couple. She observed during her three-week stay that the relationship appeared strained, and devoid of sympathy and affection. Dr Louis Curwen, who had attended both William and Julia through their many complaints over a period of five years, did not believe they were a happy couple: he thought that harmony was sustained only by indifference. According to Alfred Mather, the retired agent, Julia had always showed contempt for her husband's occupation. Such an attitude often coexists with an underlying contempt for the husband.

A former colleague – a young man named Gordon Parry, who we will meet later in our story –described Julia as untidy and implied she was lazy. The house was untidy, insalubrious and polluted with a dreadful smell. Nurse Wilson confirmed that the house was dirty and that Julia showed no desire to keep it clean; in fact, she showed no enthusiasm for anything. Almost certainly that included her marriage.

There appeared to be a lack of warmth between the couple. This is reflected by the comment of Sarah Draper, who had been cleaning the Wallace house weekly for nine months prior to the murder. She described the couple as being "on pretty friendly terms". This suggests there was nothing obviously wrong with the marriage, at least on the surface, but what lay beneath? And did these stronger undercurrents move Wallace to murder?

2. THE OPENING

Writers on the case all agree on one important point: the identity of the mystery telephone caller is central to understanding who killed Julia Wallace. There has been a persistent belief that the caller made sure his call was logged at the local exchange, to record the fact that it was made just a few hundred yards from Wallace's house {see Exhibit A}. We will come to this later. We now return to the streets of Anfield to witness the events surrounding the call. The following reconstruction, and the others that follow, are based on police reports and the statements of those involved.

The time is approaching 7:15pm on Monday 19 January 1931. The place is 29 Wolverton Street.

*

"Don't forget to post the letter," Julia called out from the cluttered kitchen. "And no loitering on the way home – there's no need to chat about the matches on street corners," she said, referring to his chess evening. In the hall, Wallace took his coat from the stand, his mind focused on the opening that he might deploy in his chess game later. His wife's reminder had to percolate through the moves in his mind until it reached his consciousness.

"Oh, yes," he replied. He stopped to pick up a letter from the small table by the coat stand and slipped it into his inside pocket. Like an incoming tide, Wallace's thoughts immediately returned to the chessboard as he fastened his buttons. He was thinking of opening with a variation on the Queen's Gambit. He grabbed his hat. "I'm off now," he called out automatically. There was no reply. Even if there had been, he would not have noticed. He opened the door and stepped into the night. The sharpness of the cold immediately cleared his head of cosy chess thoughts.

A few minutes later a man, head bowed against the sleet, reached the telephone kiosk at the corner of Lower Breck Road. Without looking up, he pulled open the glass-panelled door and stepped inside, the icy chill following him. Closing the door, he stood motionless in the gloom. He tapped the faulty interior bulb above his head, but to no avail. Rummaging in his pocket, he retrieved two pennies and inserted them into the slot at the top of the coin box. He unhooked the receiver and pressed it to his ear. He heard the change in tone in the receiver before a distant voice asked, "Which number please, caller?"

The man learned towards the mouthpiece. "Operator, connect me to Bank 3581," he instructed assertively. A pause. The line crackled.

"Connecting you now, sir." Another pause. "Go ahead, caller."

He waited, but there was nothing. "Hello?" he said after a while, hoping at least the operator would respond. "Hello? Is anyone there?" He waited again, but nothing. The line sounded dead. Muttering under his breath, he pushed a button on the coin box.

"How can I direct your call?"

"Operator," the caller said, "I have pushed button A, but I have not had my correspondent yet."

"Oh," came the puzzled reply. "Which number did you want?"

"Bank 3581."

At the Anfield Exchange, switchboard operator Lilian Kelly turned to her colleague. "Did you just put a call through to Bank 3581?"

"Yes," replied Louisa Alfreds.

19

"The caller says it never went through." There was a quick discussion about what to do. "Caller, push button B on the coin box to regain your two pennies," Lilian instructed. She then attempted to connect the call, but also received no reply. "Do you think there ought to be a reply from this number?" she asked her caller.

"Yes, it's a restaurant. There ought to be plenty of people there."

"Please hold," Lilian said, motioning to her supervisor to come over. Annie Robertson conferred with her junior before taking the headset and attempting the connection.

7:20pm. In central Liverpool, a phone rang at Cottle's City Café on North John Street. On hearing it, waitress Gladys Harley yanked open the wooden door to the interior telephone kiosk, which had 3581 BANK embossed on its glazed panel. She picked up the trumpet-shaped receiver and pressed it to her ear. "Hello, city kaff-ee," she announced into the mouthpiece.

"Bank 3581?" the operator asked.

"Yes." There was a pause, followed by muffled voices talking on the line. "Do you want this number?" Gladys asked impatiently.

"Yes, Anfield calling you," Annie Robertson replied. "Hold the line." She removed the headset, returning it to her junior. To log the initial complaint, she wrote the two telephone numbers on a slip – Anfield 1627 and Bank 3581. Next to these she scrawled the acronym NR (no reply). Glancing at the clock on the wall, she also noted the time.

Gladys heard the operator talking. "Caller, insert your two pennies now."

Two clicks. The man spoke quickly in a deep voice. "Is that the city kaff-ay?"

"Yes," the waitress replied.

Having established that the call had got through, the operators at the exchange came off the line, although both were struck by how the caller pronounced the word *café*. It was atypical, at least for locals.

"And the Central Chess Club?"

"Well, it meets here tonight."

"Is Mr Wallace there?"

"I'm not sure I know the name."

"Mr Wallace. It's in connection with the chess club."

"Oh, hold on, I'll speak to the club captain." Gladys pushed open the kiosk door and approached Samuel Beattie, who was engrossed in a game and staring intently at the board in front of him.

"Is Mr Wallace here?" she asked.

Beattie looked up and glanced over the tables and chairs scattered around the room, which was streaked with bluish cigarette smoke. "He's not here yet. I'll have to check if he's down to play later." His gaze returned to the board.

"There's someone on the telephone asking for him. Will you take the message? I won't know what he's talking about."

Beattie sighed. He moved his knight, stood up and walked to the match schedule pinned to the Liverpool Central Chess Club noticeboard. He peered at the 2nd Class Championship schedule and quickly found Wallace's name. Running his finger across the columns he found that Wallace was scheduled to play Chandler. Taking a few steps into the kiosk, he picked up the receiver. "I'm Samuel Beattie, club captain. Can I help?"

"Is Mr Wallace there?" The voice sounded deep, almost gruff.

"No."

"But will he be there later?"

"I can't say," Beattie replied, "but he's down to play tonight."

"Can you give me his address?"

"I'm afraid I cannot."

21

"Will you be sure to see him?"

"I don't know. He might turn up for his game, he might not."

"Can you get in touch with him? This is a matter of importance for Mr Wallace."

"I'm not sure. Why don't you ring up later? If he comes in you can speak to him yourself."

"Oh, no," the voice rasped. "I'm busy with my girl's twenty-first, and I want to do something for her in the way of his business. I want to speak to Mr Wallace particularly."

"Well, I could possibly get in touch with him through a friend."

"Will you ask him to call on me tomorrow night at seven-thirty?"

"I suppose I could."

"You'd better take down my address. Can you do that?"

"Hold on, let me get a pen and paper." Beattie delved into his jacket pocket. He pulled out an opened letter and grabbed the stubby pencil by the phone. He upturned the envelope and placed it against the kiosk wall. "All right. What's your name, please?"

"My name is R. M. Qualtrough."

"You'd better spell that." Following the caller's dictation, Beattie wrote out the name on the back of the envelope. "And the address?"

"25 Menlove Gardens East, Mossley Hill."

Beattie scribbled it down. "At seven-thirty? Tomorrow night?"

"That's right," replied the rough voice.

7:24pm. "I'll be sure to pass it on, if I see him. Goodnight." Beattie put down the receiver. He stuffed the envelope back into his jacket pocket and exited the kiosk. Returning to his table, he found his opponent doing his best to hide a smile.

"A good move, then?" Beattie asked.

"I think so." His opponent slid his bishop diagonally across several squares. Beattie winced, as if someone had kicked him under the table: he immediately recognised that his knight was now pinned against his king.

"How did I miss that!" Beattie placed an elbow on the table and sunk his head into his hand. As the game progressed, more members of the chess club arrived. A few gathered around the noticeboard, peering at the latest score sheets and announcements.

7:45pm. William Wallace descended the steps from the damp street into the warm hubbub of conversation, punctuated by the clinking of cup on saucer. He stopped by the stand in the entrance to hang his coat and hat, and cleaned the raindrops from his gold-rimmed spectacles with his handkerchief.

"Care for a game?"

Wallace resettled his spectacles and saw his long-time friend, James Caird, walking towards him. "I'm down to play Chandler tonight, I'm afraid," Wallace replied. "I'm behind with my games as it is."

"Well, perhaps later?"

Wallace nodded, although he knew a game with one of the best players in the club was likely to result in a crushing defeat. Lighting a cigarette, he weaved around the tables, looking out for his opponent. After a few minutes, Wallace decided that Chandler was a no-show. Several games were now underway, and conversations were tailing off into the library-like silence of play. He spied Thomas McCartney, another second-class championship player, talking at a far table. Knowing that their game from the previous November had been postponed, he walked over and suggested they played, to which McCartney readily agreed. Sitting down, they hurried through the preliminaries. The clock started ticking, and the game was underway.

7:55pm. James Caird wandered around the tables, quickly appraising each game and offering advice in the friendlies. He approached the captain's table.

"Hey," Beattie said, looking up. "You know Wallace's address, don't you? I've got a message for him."

"Sure, but why don't you tell him yourself. He's in tonight." Caird pointed to a table.

Beattie excused himself again and walked over to Wallace's table with Caird traipsing behind. "Mr Wallace, I have a message for you."

Wallace frowned, without averting his gaze from the game: "A message?"

"Yes, a telephone message. It was left earlier this evening."

Wallace glanced up. "Oh, who from?"

Beattie removed the envelope from his pocket. "From a man named Qualtrough. He wants you to call on him tomorrow night at seven-thirty. Something to do with your business."

There was silence as Wallace's eyes resumed scanning the board. "Qualtrough?" he queried, pushing forward a pawn. Leaning back in his chair, he looked at Beattie. "Who's Qualtrough?"

"Well, if you don't know, I'm sure I don't! He's not a member here."

"I don't know anyone called Qualtrough. Where did he say he lives?"

Beattie glanced at the envelope. "25 Menlove Gardens East."

Wallace scowled. "Where's that? Menlove Avenue?"

"No, Menlove Gardens," Beattie corrected.

"I don't know where that is."

"Perhaps it's opposite Menlove Gardens West," suggested Caird.

24

"It has to be near Menlove Avenue, doesn't it?" Beattie said. "Deyes might know." He walked back to his table.

McCartney could not help but overhear the conversation. He looked up. "Where do you live?"

"Anfield. Wolverton Street."

His opponent thought for a bit. "You should take the car that runs from Spellow Lane to Smithfield Road."

Beattie returned, shaking his head. "He only knows the area. He says it's not a good place to be knocking about after dark. I think your best way to get there is to go to Penny Lane and enquire."

"Well, I belong to Liverpool, and I have a tongue in my head. I'll find out," Wallace declared confidently.

"You'd better take the details down," Beattie advised. Wallace took out his pocket book and pencil. Beattie spelled out the name, which Wallace wrote down.

"25 Menlove Gardens West," Wallace repeated softly after Beattie, and began to write the address.

"No. It's East, not West," Beattie corrected. He slid the envelope across the table. Wallace peered at it before writing 'Menlove Gardens EAST' for emphasis.

"Tomorrow night?" Wallace asked.

"Yes, at seven-thirty."

Play resumed. The evening moved on.

9:30pm. Sliding his rook to the back rank, Wallace forced checkmate. McCartney outstretched his hand. Wallace shook it and leaned back in his chair with the unmistakable demeanour of victory. He took a cigarette from the packet in his jacket and lit it. He sat there for a while, replaying the game in his mind, savouring his rare moment of triumph. As more games were completed, the hubbub returned. Wallace was a little more gregarious than usual, inquiring of others about their games so he could relay the details of his.

Buoyed by his success, and with some time left before closing, Wallace agreed to play a 'skittle' game with another member. The rapid game, for sharpening chess reflexes rather than encouraging deep thought, lasted barely twenty minutes. He then agreed to take the tram back to Anfield with James Caird.

10:50pm. The two men walked through the wet Anfield streets, on the last stage of the journey home. The sporadic conversation had largely centred on Wallace's chess game but, as they neared Caird's house, Wallace stopped and turned to his companion.

"Have you heard of Qualtrough before? It's a funny name."

"Yeah, it's unusual, but I knew someone called that," replied Caird.

"And what about Menlove Gardens? Do you know how to get there?"

"I would take the bus from Queens Drive."

Wallace paused, considering the proposed route. "I think the most direct route would be to go into town then take the tram out again."

"You're going then?"

Wallace hesitated. "I'm not sure yet." He removed his trilby hat, brushing off a few drops of rain from its rim. "Mind you, it could put a few pounds in my pocket."

"Sounds like a good commission to me."

Wallace nodded and neatly replaced his hat. The conversation morphed into a different topic and fizzled out with small talk. After saying goodnight to his friend, Wallace turned and walked the short distance to his door.

*

Members of the Cold Case Jury, the message delivered to William Wallace might seem unremarkable, but both the name and address of the caller were bogus. There was a Menlove Gardens North, South and West, but no East. There were about a dozen families in Liverpool at the time named

Qualtrough, but no one had the initials R.M. There was never any business for Wallace. It was a ruse.

The call was either a sinister decoy to prise Wallace from his house, or an ingenious alibi created by Wallace that might have come from an Agatha Christie novel. So, who made it? Later we will piece together the available evidence to discover the answer as best we can. At the moment we have more pressing concerns – we need to establish what transpired on the day that Julia Wallace was murdered.

3. THE MIDDLE GAME

Irrespective of who stepped into the kiosk, the telephone call was the opening gambit in a deadly sequence of events that culminated in the brutal killing of Julia Wallace. We now return to Anfield on the morning of the murder. It is Tuesday 20 January 1931, and Liverpool has awoken to leaden skies and persistent rain.

*

Breakfast over, William Herbert Wallace looked at the large clock on the mantelpiece. "It's almost ten thirty," he said, pulling out his pocket watch from his jacket to double-check. Each week, he synchronised his watch to the BBC time signal and then regularly checked his other timepieces against it. His chronomania was so acute that if someone stated the time, he would pull out his pocket watch to verify, believing that everyone appreciated knowing precisely how fast or slow the pronouncement had been.

Julia looked up from her sewing. "It's still raining hard," she observed. Full of catarrh, she spoke as though her nose was pinched.

"Best wear my mackintosh," Wallace retorted, manoeuvring his tall frame out of the chair. He left the warmth of the kitchen for the cold, musty-smelling hall. He matched his surroundings: an unkempt moustache, the edges stained nicotine yellow like his crooked teeth, and a grimy mackintosh made him look most unwholesome. The bowler hat only elongated his gangling frame.

He called out, "Goodbye," but there was no reply. He opened the door and stepped into the downpour. He quickly found his peculiar stride. Slightly hunched forwards, he stomped like a petulant child trudging through shingle. By the time he reached the tram stop, rain was sluicing off his coat and he was pleased to take refuge in the one-penny tram to Clubmoor, even if all the windows were steamed up. It was no loss. He knew all too well the outlook on the way to his round; it was life's tramline to mediocrity.

Back at 29 Wolverton Street, Julia was nursing her cold and doing little. She filled a bucket with water for a window cleaner when he knocked on her door. Later, she went into the front bedroom to see if the cleaner had started on her windows. They had not. Her neighbour's daughter-in-law, who was standing in the same bay window next door, waved. Julia smiled faintly and held up her hand, before disappearing behind the veil of the net curtain. She was like a dreary moth, fluttering around a fading light.

2:10pm. By the time Wallace returned home for lunch, the rain had ceased. It was always a late lunch, the morning round taking almost four hours. After he had finished eating, he lit up a cigarette. His thoughts gently drifted, like the blue plume of smoke dispersing in the air above him. There was little conversation. He commented on the change of weather and returned his mackintosh to the stand in the hall, preferring his overcoat, and an hour later he left for his afternoon round.

3:30pm. Amy Wallace, William's sister-in-law, called at 29 Wolverton Street. Julia ushered her into the kitchen, where a hot kettle was on the range.

"It will have to be a quick cuppa, Julia, I can't stay long," Amy said, taking off her white gloves. "How's your cold?"

"It's a touch of bronchitis, but it's getting a bit better," Julia replied, taking a cloth and grabbing the handle of the whistling kettle. "Although this weather doesn't help." She poured the steaming water into the brown ceramic teapot and brought it to the table. "Everywhere is so damp and cold."

"At least the gales have blown themselves out."

"Yes, it's a relief. I've been so worried about Puss being out in this awful weather. She didn't come home again last night."

"Oh, Julia, you know what cats are like. It'll turn up sooner or later. They always do."

"I don't like it. You know what they say: if a black cat walks away, it takes its good luck with it."

"I'm sure the only thing that alley cat will take with it is its fleas!" Sensing the comment displeased Julia, Amy added, "Perhaps it's gone back to its owner." The tactless attempt at reassurance only made matters worse. Julia had looked after the cat as a favour while a neighbour was on holiday, but the cat became so attached to its temporary owner that the neighbour agreed Julia should continue to care for it. Deeply fond of her feline companion, Julia feared it might abandon her as it had the neighbour.

Amy had enough sense to change the subject. "I was wondering if you had thought some more about *Mother Goose*. Will you be well enough to come on Friday?" As Julia pondered the question, Amy continued, "You can get all dressed up. Wear one of those fancy hats of yours, if you must."

"I don't want to go like this," Julia remonstrated, pointing to her nose.

"It would do you good to get out of the house, Julia," Amy retorted.

"I'll think about it."

"Yes, do. I'll pop round tomorrow to see how you are. We'll make a decision then."

Julia noted that it was not her decision to make alone, a typical assumption of her domineering relation. She brooded on the comment, and the conversation stalled. Amy filled the void: "And how is William?"

"Oh, *his* cold is better. He gave it to me." Julia picked up the jug of milk from the centre of the table. A firm believer that milk should always precede the tea, she poured a little into two china cups, one of which, Amy noticed, had an ugly chipped lip.

"Is he still playing chess at the club?"

"Yes, he went last night, the first time he's been in some while. He came home like the Cheshire cat. The game was practically replayed for my benefit at breakfast this morning." She rolled her eyes, smiling. "He insisted on telling me everything about his evening, from start to finish. There was one odd thing, though. He said that during the game he was given a telephone message."

"How unusual. What was it?"

"Business, what else?"

Amy frowned, puzzled. "Who would know to telephone him there?"

"Someone from Calderstones, apparently."

"These days you take business however you come by it, I suppose."

"So he's out again tonight, painting the town black," Julia commented wryly. They giggled. She placed a strainer on one of the cups, and poured through the hot tea. "No doubt it will result in a few shillings commission," she sighed and passed the cup. "Will you be staying with us for tea?"

"No, I'm in a rush, but thanks just the same."

Relieved, Julia changed the topic of conversation. Just over a mile away, her husband was walking briskly along Maiden Lane, in the heart of Clubmoor, to earn his next few shillings. Head bowed, he did not see Police Constable James Rothwell cycling in the opposite direction. Wallace walked on, to his next appointment.

5:55pm. When Wallace emerged from the final house of his afternoon round, darkness had already squeezed the last gasps of light from the dying day. Julia was preparing tea:

freshly baked scones and hot tea were waiting for him when he arrived home 10 minutes later.

Conversation over the kitchen table was sporadic, but congenial enough. Julia related the events of her afternoon, particularly the visit of Amy. Her husband talked of his: a jolly conversation with Mrs Harrison, the usual cup of tea with the Lawrences, and the forms he left with Mrs Martin to sign, which he would pick up tomorrow. The light meal was over quickly. Wallace took the papers that he thought he might need for his evening appointment from his desk, and headed upstairs to wash and change.

6:30pm. Julia heard the *Liverpool Echo* being thrust through the letterbox. She rose from the kitchen table and walked slowly to the front door. She pulled it free, unfurling it as she made her way back. The first page was given to advertisements, most showing the running order of the many picture houses across the city. One caught her eye, because Julia knew the novel by Remarque. "At last, at last, at last!" it proclaimed. "The picture Liverpool has waited for. *All Quiet on the Western Front.*"

She sat down at the table and turned the page. She read that university students were plastering the city with posters for 'Panto Day', which reminded her to speak to her husband when he came down. The headline on the opposite page was 'A Valuable Life Lost'. It reported on the coroner's inquest into a fatal accident that had claimed the life of a young dock worker the previous week. As she read the article, an eerie silence descended like a cold mist, punctuated only by the soft ticking of the mantelpiece clock.

Moments later, the peace was shattered by a sharp rap on the front door. Julia waited to see if her husband would answer. When it was clear he would not, she rose from the table. On opening the door she found a milk can on the doorstep. Next door, a boy making deliveries was pouring milk from a similar can into a jug that had been left in the vestibule by her neighbour. Julia picked up the can from her step, and went into the kitchen to pour the milk into the table jug. When she returned to the open door, the milk boy was waiting. The light escaping from the kitchen gently illuminated his flushed face and bright eyes. As she handed him the can, Julia noticed his red-raw hands.

"Look at you!" she exclaimed. "You'll catch your death of cold wearing nothing but a shirt in this weather." On cue, the boy coughed. "You see! You need to go home and get warm, otherwise it will go onto your chest." The boy nodded and turned, as if he had been scolded. Julia closed the door, and went back to her paper.

Its sensational headline the following evening would be about her murder.

*

Members of the Cold Case Jury, we must pause to highlight a crucial point: the time at which the milk boy called. Precisely when this mundane event occurred is arguably the most important – and the most controversial – piece of evidence in the entire case. It was the last time Julia Wallace was seen alive by an independent witness.

The boy was 14-year-old Alan Close. After school he delivered fresh milk to houses in the area for a local dairy. The day after the murder he was asked on two separate occasions by school friends whether he had delivered milk to the Wallaces the night before. His answer was the same each time: "Yes, at quarter to seven." One of the friends realised immediately that this was important evidence, as that day's *Liverpool Echo* reported that Wallace had left his house at 6:15pm. If true, Wallace could not be the murderer. In fact, the report was incorrect – Wallace actually left half an hour or so later. In any event, Close was urged by his friends to inform the police about his encounter with Mrs Wallace.

When Alan Close made a written statement to the police four days later, however, his account had changed. He was

33

less definite about the time, stating he had delivered the milk between 6:30pm and 6:45pm. When he later testified in court, he had changed his mind again: the time was 6:30pm. There is little doubt that Close was led by detectives to alter his testimony to fit their case against Wallace. In fact, there is evidence to show that Julia probably shut her front door at 6:40pm {see Exhibit 7}. A difference of only 10 minutes or so might appear a pedantic quibble, but in this case minutes matter.

The time Wallace left his house to keep his appointment is equally important. Based on tests conducted by both the police and Wallace's legal team, it is almost certain he departed before 6:50pm {see Exhibit 3}. There was approximately 10 minutes between Julia closing the front door and her husband leaving by the back. This is critical evidence, as you will soon discover.

For now, we return to the night of the murder, rejoining the story as Wallace departs his house.

*

6:49pm. Wallace ambled briskly down the poorly lit entry (a narrow passage) behind the row of houses on Wolverton Street. He turned right, taking another entry in a series of shortcuts that eventually led to a tram stop a third of a mile away. The mission to keep his appointment with Qualtrough had begun.

6:55pm. Wallace arrived at the tram stop at the end of Belmont Road, overlooked by the imposing St Margaret's Church, its soaring bell tower a dominating presence even in the dark. After a short wait, an unmistakable drone heralded the arrival of a tram car. He stepped into the road as the No. 26 tram slowed to a stop, and boarded. It ferried him nearly two miles south to the corner of Lodge Lane and Smithdown Road, where he got off, joining the back of a small crowd waiting for a connecting tram.

7:06pm. Shortly after, the No. 5 tram arrived and Wallace shuffled forward and boarded. "Does this car go to Menlove Gardens East?" he asked the conductor.

Thomas Phillips shook his head, but after a short pause, corrected himself: "Thinking about it, you might change at Penny Lane to catch the No. 5, 5A, 5W or a No.7 car. If you buy a penny fare now you will need to buy another ticket when you board the next car. Or you can get a transfer ticket."

Wallace nodded and walked to the nearest available seat. "Fares please!" the conductor shouted, as he moved through the bottom deck of the tram. After serving several other passengers, he approached Wallace. Before Phillips could speak, Wallace said, "I'm a stranger in the district and I have urgent business at Menlove Gardens East."

"Change at Penny Lane," the conductor repeated, ripping off a penny ticket and handing it to Wallace.

Wallace placed the fare in the conductor's palm. "You won't forget, mister. I want to get to Menlove Gardens *East*."

The conductor nodded, and moved on: "Fares please!"

A few minutes later Wallace asked again, "Guard, how far is it now? Where do I change?"

"At Penny Lane..." As the conductor spoke the tram squealed to a halt at the junction. Through the front window he saw a waiting No. 7 tram. "We're here. Take the No. 7. Quick!"

"Thank you," Wallace replied, jumping up. He stepped out and ran towards a waiting tram.

"Not that one!" the conductor yelled after him, gesticulating wildly. "The No. 7 over there!" He saw Wallace veer towards it before he lost sight of him in the dark.

7:16pm. A little out of breath, Wallace reached the No. 5A tram. Perhaps he remembered the earlier remarks that the 5A went to Menlove Gardens or he knew the tram routes better than his behaviour suggested. He boarded. Wheezing slightly, he immediately asked the conductor: "Would you drop me at Menlove Gardens East?"

Arthur Thompson nodded. Wallace paid his fare and took his seat. A few minutes later, as the tram halted in Menlove Avenue, Thompson summoned Wallace to the platform. "That's Menlove Gardens West," he said, pointing to the street perpendicular to the tram stop. "Menlove Gardens has at least three roads, like a triangle. You should find it around here somewhere."

"Thank you. I'm a stranger in these parts, you know."

7:19pm. Wallace stepped from the tram; the last part of his quest would be on foot. From what he could observe by the glow of the street lamps, Menlove Gardens was an attractive middle-class area of pebble-dashed, semi-detached houses that surrounded an open, triangular-shaped common. After walking along Menlove Gardens West he turned into Menlove Gardens North.

7:25pm. Seeing a woman leaving a house, Wallace approached her and raised his hat. "Good evening. Do you know where I may find Menlove Gardens East?"

"Never heard of it," she replied, obviously in a hurry. "It might be on the other side of Dudlow Lane, I suppose." She observed Wallace's blank expression and pointed him in the right direction. "I'm sorry, but I really need to go."

Accepting her suggestion, Wallace retraced his steps back to Menlove Gardens West, turned right, and was soon at the junction with Dudlow Lane. He crossed over, but discovered that the opposite street was only a continuation of Menlove Gardens West. He backtracked and asked directions of a fair-haired pedestrian standing at the junction.

"There isn't a Menlove Gardens East," Sydney Green answered. "Why don't you try 25 Menlove Gardens West? Perhaps that's the place you want."

Wallace walked down the road, carefully noting the number of each house, a task he found difficult in the dark. He identified No. 19 but thereafter all the houses had names. He counted off the next three to be sure he had arrived at No. 25, which was called 'Brierley'.

7:35pm. He knocked on the door and a smartly dressed woman answered. "Good evening," he said, raising his trilby. "Is there a Mr Qualtrough at this address?"

"No, no one of that name lives here," replied Katie Mather.

"I am looking for Menlove Gardens East. They tell me there isn't any."

"Well, I've never heard of it, to be honest."

"Are there any other Gardens about here, do you know?"

Mather frowned. "No, I don't think so. Who told you there was an East?"

"I've had a message on the telephone. It's funny, isn't it, that there is no East?"

"Well, I'm sorry I cannot help. I'm listening to the wireless, so if you don't mind..."

Wallace thanked the woman and headed along Menlove Gardens South, a tree-lined street that eventually carried him back into the broad thoroughfare of Menlove Avenue, where a man stood at a tram stop. Again he asked for directions and yet again he drew a blank. Wallace crossed the avenue into Green Lane, a place he recognised instantly, even in the dark. He strode down the street and knocked at the door of No. 34, hoping that his supervisor and erstwhile violin teacher would help. There was no answer. He would later discover that Joseph Crewe and his wife were at the cinema.

7:45pm. When Wallace reached the end of Green Lane, he flagged down a police constable, who had the presumptuous surname of Serjeant. Wallace was again informed there was no Menlove Gardens East. "Why don't you try 25 Menlove Avenue?" the constable suggested.

Ignoring the remark, Wallace asked: "Where m-m-might I find a street directory?" The constable noticed the stammer and thought Wallace appeared nervous.

"You could try the Allerton Road Post Office," he replied, pointing to a street leading away from where they were standing.

"I don't think it is yet eight o'clock," Wallace commented, pulling out his pocket watch. "No, I thought not. It's q-quarter to." The policeman confirmed the time. Knowing that the post office would still be open, Wallace said goodnight, and hurriedly walked the hundred yards along Allerton Road. There was no directory at the post office, however, and he was directed to a newsagent on the opposite side of the road in the expectation that it would have one. It did. As Wallace leafed through its pages at the counter, the manager asked if she could be of any assistance. Again Wallace explained about the phone call and his appointment, and again he received the same answer. Neither was there a directory entry for Mr R. M. Qualtrough. His quest had been a wild goose chase. At last, a little after 8pm, he conceded defeat, and trudged to the nearest tram stop.

*

Members of the Cold Case Jury, I draw your attention to Wallace's surprising behaviour on his quest to trace the elusive Qualtrough, as some authors believe it can only be interpreted as proof of his guilt, most recently Mark Russell in *Checkmate* (2021). He certainly did not appear to be his usual reserved self on the outward journey. From the statements of the conductors, he was peppering them with questions, and repeatedly telling them that he was searching for Menlove Gardens East. Was he trying to be remembered in order to establish an alibi? The sooner he was seen by an independent witness away from his house, the greater the doubt that he had sufficient time to commit the murder.

Wallace's Prudential supervisor Joseph Crewe lived in Green Lane, which is not far from Menlove Gardens North {see Exhibit B}. In his statement to the police, Crewe said that Wallace had been to visit him "many times", but he was more cautious when it came to the trial. He testified that Wallace had visited on only five occasions. Yet, if Wallace had visited Crewe at least five times is it plausible to believe that Wallace had not used this tram route before? Further, from his diaries, we know Wallace and his wife occasionally visited Calderstones Park, which is less than a mile from Menlove Gardens and presumably Wallace used similar trams to travel there. Was he really a stranger in the area, as he had remarked on not one but two occasions to the conductors?

Author James Murphy believes that Wallace was lying. During the tram journey he was badgering conductors on a four-mile tram journey across a city in which he had lived for 16 years. Wallace ignored the advice of Thomas Phillips (the second tram conductor) to transfer to the No. 7 car at Penny Lane and instead boarded the 5A {see Exhibit 8}. Even if he remembered the earlier advice of Thomas, who advised him that he could take the 5A, did his choice reveal that he knew all along which tram he needed to catch?

Murphy argues that Wallace's suspicious behaviour continued when he arrived at Menlove Gardens, where he asked no less than six people for directions, yet was told by the second person he encountered that the address he sought did not exist. According to Katie Mather's police statement, Wallace appeared to realise there was no Menlove Gardens East when he spoke to her at approximately 7:30pm, yet he persisted in his quest. He spoke to a police constable and visited a newsagent to examine a street directory before boarding the tram home about half an hour later.

Is it also significant that Wallace appeared nervous when he spoke to the police officer? The other witnesses did not report any sign of anxiety. Did Wallace plan to visit his supervisor's house as part of his alibi and, unexpectedly finding Crewe out, felt compelled to talk to the police officer as an alternative? Did this improvised conversation with the law unnerve him?

Wallace's behaviour appears suspicious, but can it only be explained in terms of his guilt, as Russell insists? Staying with the last point, it's possible that Wallace was uncomfortable when speaking to someone in authority. Indeed, we should place all of his behaviour in the context of his character before leaping to conclusions. Recall that Wallace was described by his best friend, James Caird, as "highly strung". Further, his chronomania, punctiliousness, preoccupation for detail and need for control suggest someone with a compulsive personality. So we cannot blithely assume that it is a typical person who made the journey that night, but an anxious and obsessive person.

Robert Hussey points out in *Murderer Scot-Free* (1973) that if Wallace really wanted to time-stamp his journey to Menlove Gardens, he should have made a fuss on the first tram, but he does not – at least not sufficiently well to be remembered. Why? Wallace would have been familiar with this ride, which departed close to his house, but possibly less so with the rest of his journey. He claimed to have taken a different route when he visited Joseph Crewe two years previously: "I think I took a car which would branch off in the other direction and come down to what I now know is Allerton Lane. I would get off at the Plaza Cinema and walk to his house." Even if he had used the second and third trams before, he might not have been sure of precisely where he should alight, especially at night when he might not have been able to recognise where he was. In these circumstances, an anxious person would become more agitated, explaining why Wallace asked questions on these trams and not the first.

Another strange behaviour was his persistence in searching for Menlove Gardens East even after being told it did not exist on at least two occasions. His dogged actions might be unusual for a typical person, but it might have been typical for Wallace. They are consistent with a compulsive-finisher who, after embarking on an hour's return trip in the hope of a large commission, was never going to leave a stone unturned before he was *completely* satisfied that his destination did not exist.

But why did he not mention in his police statement that he called at Joseph Crewe's house? Again, it may be explained by his personality. From his trial testimony we know Wallace interpreted questions literally and, in most cases, answered precisely. If he was asked "Who did you *talk to* that night?" then he might not mention knocking on his absent supervisor's door. But, in any case, it is hard to see what Wallace would have gained from including this detail when Crewe was unable to verify it.

There are two interpretations of Wallace's fruitless search. He was either calmly and shrewdly establishing an alibi knowing full well that the address did not exist, or his behaviour was a symptom of his anxious and compulsive personality. If it's the latter, however, we might expect such a person to reduce their angst by simply looking up the address in a street directory and examining a tram timetable before departing. On the other hand, recall what was stated at the chess club. Beattie advised that "the best way to get there is to go to Penny Lane and enquire," and Wallace remarked, "I have a tongue in my head. I'll find out." Isn't that exactly what he did? Or was he already signalling that he would pester the tram conductors the following night? If so, Wallace had carefully planned his response to the phone message being passed on.

Similarly, when he said "Menlove Gardens West" had he simply misheard Beattie or had he intentionally misstated it, knowing that he would be corrected, and thereby subtly draw everyone's attention to the non-existent address? Was Wallace executing a meticulously detailed gambit to rival the best chess openings or was it natural interaction?

I suggest we do not rush to judgement but wait until all the evidence has been presented. There is so much more of the story yet to tell. Next, we will see what happened when Wallace returned home to discover the grisly scene at 29 Wolverton Street.

4. DISCOVERED CHECK

To fully appreciate the events that follow, it is helpful to know the layout of 29 Wolverton Street {see Exhibit D}. Had you been invited inside the house hours before the murder, what would you have seen?

Like the others in Wolverton Street, No. 29 is a thin terraced house, 50 feet long from the front door to the back yard wall, and 16 feet wide. Entering through the drab front door, you find yourself in a cold, cramped vestibule. A door leads from here into a narrow hall, which ends in a flight of stairs ascending to the upper floor. The hall is enclosed, making it dark and dingy. There are two doors situated a little way along the hall on your right. Opening the first, you are in the corner of the front room or parlour. Its striking features are a large bay window and a grand Victorian-style fireplace, located in the middle of the wall opposite the door. It has a tiled hearth bordered by a brass rail.

The fireplace houses a modern gas fire, which plays a part in our drama. Manufactured by Wilson & Mathiesons of Leeds, it is a Sunbeam – "the gas fire like a coal fire". It has the appearance of a coal fire but warms the room by radiant heat. There is no flame effect – the coal-like fireclays radiate the warmth when they become hot; this typically takes a few minutes. The gas is turned on and off by a key-shaped knob on the right-side of the fire.

It is not just the fireplace that has a Victorian feel. The walls, papered with a light-coloured stripe, are covered in framed paintings. Every available surface is crammed with photographs and ornately decorated porcelain. Directly facing you is the side end of a heavy, wooden dresser and beyond this, in the corner to the left of the fireplace, a large armchair. Along the wall to your right is an upright piano, above which hangs W. Hatherell's drawing of *Lord Kitchener's Homecoming from South Africa* in 1902. In front of the bay window, and to the right of the fireplace, is a chaise longue covered with chintz cushions, and in front of this a small table draped with a floral cloth on which stands a potted aspidistra, Orwell's symbol of middle-class pretention. A scattering of chairs and a music stand complete the room, which Julia and William use only to play music or entertain guests.

If you spin on your heels, return to the hall, and turn to your right, you find the second hall door, through which is the kitchen, although this is a misnomer. It is more a living room, where the couple spend most of their time together. The focus of the cluttered room is a large range, crowned by a tasselled mantelpiece. To its right is a walled display cabinet with glass-panelled doors and a desk below, where William conscientiously does his bookkeeping. To its left is a high bookcase, full of old books and folios, above a two-door cupboard. In the centre of the room sits a large, cloth-covered table, around which are several lined wicker chairs. A large window, guarded by heavy drapes, looks out onto the walled back yard. To the left of the window is another bookcase, also messy with piles of books and documents.

On the far side of the kitchen, to the left, a door leads to the back kitchen. This has a small range in the far wall, a copper (a container for boiling laundry), a sink and draining board. This is where almost all the cooking and washing chores are undertaken by Julia. On the right is the back door, opening onto a narrow stretch of cobbled yard. Turning left, and walking towards the back gate, the yard opens out. On the left is an outside lavatory and coal shed, and ahead is a gate that takes you into the 'entry', a narrow, cobblestone passageway that runs behind the row of houses. It connects to other entries and streets, forming a maze of backstreet shortcuts through the neighbourhood.

Heading back through the gate, you see the kitchen window at the end of the yard, and above it a bedroom window. It is the middle bedroom, where the couple sleep, and is one of the four rooms upstairs. The front bedroom, which is above the parlour and overlooks the street, is used primarily for storing Julia's clothes. The back bedroom, which overlooks the yard outbuildings and the entry, is William's laboratory, where he keeps his scientific equipment and specimens. Only the first two bedrooms have fireplaces. With no central heating system, many of the rooms are cold, bitterly so in the early winter mornings.

The final room upstairs, squeezed between the middle and back bedrooms, is a tiny and tired-looking bathroom. A deep bath is heavily stained with dirty limescale underneath the taps and the toilet pan is darkly streaked. Hanging up by string next to the toilet is an empty roll holder and sheets of newspaper. Typical of the bathrooms of the day, a large cistern is attached high on the wall with a pull chain. Looking like a bracket, a single gas fitting protrudes from the wall above the bath, providing a modicum of heat as well as a dim glow. As you will see, this unremarkable room would become a focus of the police investigation.

This is the set for the next act of our drama, when William Wallace returns home from his fruitless search for the mysterious Mr Qualtrough.

*

8:33pm. "Aren't you ready yet?" John Johnston hollered up the stairs at 31 Wolverton Street.

"I'm getting ready now," his wife, Florence, called back, looking into her bedroom mirror. "If you had helped clear away the tea things instead of readin' the paper, I would be ready by now."

45

"How long will yer be?"

"Ten minutes. Why don't you do somethin' useful and make sure dad doesn't want a cuppa before we leave?" Her husband rolled his eyes, and plodded from the foot of the stairs into the front room to speak to his father-in-law.

Several hundred yards away, their neighbour sat silently in a tram, gazing out of the rain-spotted window. The whine of the engine dropped in pitch as it slowed, and a bell signalled its arrival at the stop near St Margaret's Church, where he had boarded less than two hours previously. Wallace followed several other passengers and alighted. He walked briskly along the dimly lit backstreets and dark entries, heading home.

8:40pm. Wallace walked the last few steps along Wolverton Street before he turned through a gap in the low brick wall, and stood on his doorstep. He inserted his key into the lock but it would not turn. He knocked and waited – no answer. He walked to the side entry, the thin passageway that cut between two houses in the street and which led to the back entry. He strode to his back gate, which was closed but not bolted. He entered the yard and walked to the back door. The handle would not turn. He knocked three times and waited. Still no answer.

Returning to the front door, Wallace found this time his key turned in the lock but still the door would not open. He hurried back to the rear of the house.

8:45pm. "Better late than never, I suppose," Johnston remarked tetchily to his wife, as they walked from their back yard into the entry.

"We've got plenty of time. I told Phyllis we would be there at nine." As they closed the back gate, Wallace hurried past them. "Good evening, Mr Wallace," Florence Johnston called out.

"Have you heard an unusual noise in my house during the last hour or so?" Wallace asked anxiously.

"Why, what's happened?"

"I've been out on business and I can't open the front door. It's been bolted against me."

Johnston asked: "Have you tried the back?"

"Yes. I couldn't open that either."

"That's funny," his neighbour remarked. "Try the back door again. If it doesn't open, I'll see if my key fits."

As Wallace walked to his back door, he turned to the couple waiting by the back gate. "She will not be out; she has such a bad cold." When Wallace tried the back door a second time, the handle turned. "It opens now," he called back.

"We'll wait here. You have a look round to see if everything is all right," Johnston said, expecting soon to start the short journey to see his daughter. Wallace scurried through the back kitchen into the kitchen, which was in darkness. He took out his box of matches and struck one to light the gas lamp. The room was much as he left it two hours before. He headed upstairs, twice calling out his wife's name.

He headed straight for their bedroom – the middle bedroom. The gas lamp was still on, as he had left it after he changed earlier in the evening. He checked the bathroom before heading into his laboratory, which was in darkness. He struck a match and looked around. Everything looked as it should. He strode across the landing into the front bedroom. By the light of another match, he could see the room was in a state of disorder: the sheet had been pulled back from the bed exposing the mattress; two handbags and hats were laid out on the bed; and two pillows were on the floor by the fireplace.

He rushed downstairs. There was only one room left: the parlour. He pushed opened the door and struck a match. As he held it up he saw his wife sprawled diagonally across the rug, her feet by the fireplace. Her head was nearest the door and, even in the flickering gloom, Wallace could see that it

47

was brutally battered, her hair congealed with blood. The match burning down, Wallace blew it out and dropped it by the door threshold. He walked around the dead body towards the fireplace and lit the right-hand gas lamp.

As he turned up the light, the horror of the scene was clear to see. Julia was lying on her right side, an arm trapped beneath her body. Her feet were lying flat on their sides, almost touching the fender, her toes pointing towards the bay window. Her left arm was bent at the elbow, her forearm draped across her chest and pointing towards the floor. Her head, surrounded by a halo of blood and brain matter on the carpet, faced the window. Above her left ear was a gaping hole in her skull. By the corner chair, next to the dresser, flecks of blood covered the wall. Curiously, a crumpled and heavily bloodstained mackintosh was stuffed under Julia's right shoulder and along the top of her back.

8:50pm. Wallace held his wife's left hand but found no pulse. Rushing out of the house, in distress and with a raised voice, he called to his neighbours. "Come and look! She has been killed!" They followed Wallace into the parlour, Mr Johnston remaining in the doorway. The dreadful silence was broken by Wallace: "They've finished her! They've finished her!"

Florence Johnston stooped down and held Julia's left hand. "Oh, the poor darling," she said, her voice quivering with emotion.

"Is she cold?" her husband wanted to know.

"No."

"Don't disturb anything," John Johnston advised. "I'd better go for the police."

"And the doctor," Wallace added pitifully. "Although he won't be much use."

"Anyone in particular?"

"The nearest one." Wallace stooped over his wife, examining her hands. He mumbled something about her rings, before adding, "Perhaps, she hadn't them on."

The three returned to the kitchen. "See, they've broken that off." Wallace pointed to the broken door from a photographic equipment box, a piece lying on the floor by the bookcase.

"Is anything missing?" Mr Johnston asked.

Wallace reached up to the top shelf of the bookcase and retrieved his cashbox, where he kept his collection premiums. He opened it and glanced inside. "Yes, about £4 has been taken, I think. I'll have to check my books to be certain." Talking about his collection books, Wallace reverted to his usual dour and unemotional demeanour.

"Is everything all right upstairs before I go to the police?" Mr Johnston delayed his departure while Wallace examined the bedrooms. He returned shortly. "It looks all right. They haven't taken the £5 from the jar in our bedroom."

9pm. Mr Johnston left to fetch the police, while his wife did her best to comfort Wallace. She followed him back into the parlour and affectionately held Julia's hand again. Already it seemed cooler to her.

"Look at her brains!" Wallace exclaimed ghoulishly.

Florence glanced around, the fixtures and fittings of the living room now the ornate decorations of a mausoleum. "I wonder what they have used?" Her gaze fixed on a table squeezed into the recess of the bay window and behind the chaise longue. Next to a pot plant she spotted a box of Bryant and May. "Are those Mrs Wallace's matches?"

Wallace glanced across. "Uh, yes." He stood up and stepped over the body. "Whatever is she doing with her mackintosh and my mackintosh?" he muttered. He knelt down and felt the material lying beside Julia's right shoulder, as if someone had made a pillow for her.

"Is it yours?"

Wallace looked carefully, touching the edge of the bloodstained coat. "Yes, it's mine."

Florence stood up. "Let's wait for the police now," she suggested, walking Wallace into the kitchen. "It's a bit cold in here, let's get the fire on." Opening the door to the range, she noticed that a good fire had almost burned out. She threw in some wood chips, while Wallace stirred the few live embers at the bottom to light it. Once the wood had taken, he threw on some lumps of coal and closed the range door.

9:10pm. "A cup of tea?" she asked. Slumping into one of the chairs, Wallace shook his head. Rocking back and forth in his chair like a chastised child, he sobbed quietly to himself, wiping his tears with the back of his sleeve.

There was a heavy rap at the front door. Florence hurried into the hall, followed by Wallace. She fumbled with the lock. "Oh, you better do it." Wallace unbolted the door before turning the latch above the handle. He pulled open the door.

"Come inside, officer. Something terrible has happened."

Police Constable Fred Williams entered the house and was immediately shown into the parlour. He knelt beside Julia's body. He could not detect a pulse, and thought Julia's skin was slightly warm to the touch. "How did this happen?" he asked. Wallace explained his night, as he lit the left-hand gas lamp in the parlour, illuminating the shocking scene more brightly. Williams observed that Wallace showed no trace of emotion – he looked calm and in control.

"This looks like a mackintosh," the constable stated.

"It's an old one of mine." Wallace pointed to the stand in the hall. "It usually hangs there."

Wallace escorted Williams around his house, first into the kitchen and then upstairs. "Anything taken from here?" the constable asked as they entered the back bedroom. Wallace shook his head and they moved into the bathroom. "Is this how you left it?" Williams asked, pointing to the gas jet burning on low.

"We usually have a light on in here."

They entered the middle bedroom. "This light left on, too?"

"I changed in here before I left, and probably left it burning," replied Wallace.

"What about downstairs? Were any lights on when you entered?"

"No, except for the two lights up here, the house was in darkness." Wallace made his way to the mantelpiece in his bedroom and picked up a jar, which contained a small bundle of folded £1 treasury notes.

"Don't touch anything!" Williams shouted when he saw Wallace unfolding the notes. Shaking a little, Wallace did as instructed, but thought that it was closing the proverbial stable door: he had already touched his wife's bloodied body and many other items around the house.

9:50pm. Barging into the parlour, John MacFall announced his arrival in a loud, confident tone: "Clear the room, please!" Six foot three and massively built, MacFall had a commanding presence, which he used to impose authority. Although he had risen to the top of his profession, and despite impressive credentials, the opium-smoking medical examiner was disliked by his colleagues, who found him careless in discovering the facts and reckless in presenting them. However flimsy the evidence, his pronouncements were categorical. His intellect was riddled by egoism, which at times bordered on megalomania.

He set to work, making no notes. The first step was to establish the cause of death. He noted the cavity in the skull – three inches long by two wide – through which broken bone and brain matter protruded. There was also a depression at the back of the skull, on the left-hand side, with severe wounds. The manner of death was clearly homicide.

He observed the old bundled-up mackintosh beneath Julia's right shoulder. He later examined it and found that it was covered in bloodstains and burnt on one side. He noted a characteristic blood splatter on the left sleeve, which he inferred had been made by a spurting or splashing of blood onto the mackintosh. His conclusion was that the mackintosh had been involved in the attack, presumably by someone wearing it. He also noted that Julia's hands were bloodstained, but there was nothing under her fingernails.

10:05pm. As MacFall finished his cursory sketches of the body position in the parlour, a strong Irish brogue filled the hall. A large, red-headed man with an over-waxed moustache entered the room. Detective Superintendent Hubert 'Rory' Moore, the recently promoted head of Liverpool CID, had arrived. This was his first murder case since his promotion, and solving it was always going to be a personal test.

"What have we got?" Moore asked.

"A dead woman, battered around the left side of the head," MacFall replied, without looking up from his pad of paper. "See for yourself."

Moore peered at the head wound. "Do we have any idea when she was done in?"

"The hands are cold but I can only find rigor in the upper left arm, and even that's not marked. The body is warm. I would say about two hours ago."

Moore nodded and then headed to the kitchen, where Wallace was hunched in his chair sipping brandy. For the third or fourth time, he repeated the night's events. Wallace showed the superintendent the broken cabinet lid by the bookcase. As he crouched down to inspect it, Moore also observed a half-crown and two shillings on the floor. He straightened up and looked at Wallace. "I understand from the constable there's been a robbery."

"Yes. Four pounds has been taken from my collection box." Wallace pointed to the cashbox on top of the bookcase.

After a struggle to reach the top shelf, which was over seven feet from the floor, Moore managed to retrieve it.

"Where did you find the box tonight?" he inquired.

"Where you just got it from."

"You always keep it there?"

"Yes, always."

Moore opened the box and rummaged through its contents. There were a few loose coins, some stamps and a solitary dollar bill. He closed the lid and stared at Wallace. "I wonder how the thief knew where to find it." He then craned his neck to peer at the top of the bookcase. "And for the life of me, I cannot understand why he would go to all that trouble to put the box back, can you? I mean, it's not easy to get to, is it?" To emphasise his point, he closed the lid and, standing on tiptoes, returned the box to its place on the top shelf. "Why did he do that?"

After asking Wallace further questions, Moore also discovered that Julia's handbag was in the kitchen untouched, with over £1 inside. The thief knew about the cashbox, which was almost hidden at the top of the bookcase, but had missed the easy pickings by the kitchen table. The superintendent was already suspicious. When he examined the ordered disarray in the front bedroom, he was sceptical that it had been ransacked by a thief looking for valuables. It looked as though it had been staged. In the middle bedroom he found the folded treasury notes in the jar, and he noted that one was smeared with blood. Would the murderer have kindly returned cash? This was no burglary, he concluded.

10:25pm. Another officer at the door. As Detective Sergeant Harry Bailey entered the premises, Julia's black cat returned. Streaking into the house like a witch's familiar, it added a touch of the sinister to the macabre events.

"Don't let it into the front room!" Florence Johnston shouted.

If a returning cat brings back good luck, it was far too late for Julia. Sensing something was wrong, it arched its back and hissed at Bailey before dashing into the kitchen. The sergeant found Moore, MacFall and Wallace in the parlour, which he noted was not disturbed in any way except for the obvious presence of a dead body sprawled on the floor. The furniture and ornaments appeared to be in their proper places with no sign of a struggle.

10.30pm. After a loud knock, Moore opened the door to Detective Inspector Herbert Gold, who would play a leading role in the police investigation. Already four officers were moving about the small house, sometimes interfering with the crime scene before it had been properly recorded and photographed. The number would soon swell to over a dozen.

The opening of the door prompted Moore to take Gold's torch and inspect the lock that had proved so troublesome to Wallace earlier that night. "This door has not been forced," he announced, "and there is no obvious sign of damage to the lock." He summoned Wallace.

"Can I have your front door key, Mr Wallace?"

Moore inserted Wallace's latchkey and, after some jiggling, the mechanism unlocked. He stepped outside, closing the door behind him. Moments later, the door opened and he walked back in. "I can open it all right," he declared, "but there's something slightly wrong with the lock. If you turn the key more than half way it slips back."

"Well, it wasn't like that this morning," Wallace retorted indignantly.

10:35pm. Moore ushered Wallace into the parlour, where MacFall was sitting on the arm of a chair taking notes. Bailey and Gold followed and stood either side of the body, while Wallace leaned against the dresser and lit a cigarette. After a lingering stare of disapproval, Moore asked tersely, "Is this your mackintosh, Mr Wallace?"

Wallace looked at it blankly. This was at least the fourth time he had been asked about its ownership. The silence dragged on, to the point that Moore became impatient. "Does it belong to you or to Mrs Wallace?" Incredibly, Wallace remained dumbstruck.

"Take it up, and let's have a look at it," Moore instructed Bailey, clearly unperturbed that the police photographer had not yet arrived to take pictures of the crime scene. Held up by the collar, the mackintosh unfolded, clearly revealing that a large section of a lower side had burned away. Two partly spent matches tumbled from a fold of the coat and pieces of burnt material floated to the floor like blackened autumn leaves.

"It's a gent's, by the look of it," Moore commented.

Wallace stepped forward and inspected the garment. "If there are two patches on the inside, it is mine," he mumbled. "It's mine. Of course, it was not burnt like that when I wore it this morning."

"Where did you leave it?"

"Hanging in the hall."

There was silence, as Moore's critical eye evaluated the scene. His instinct told him that something was not right. "The gas lamps," he stated slowly. "Were these on when you first came into the room?"

"No, the room was in darkness. I lit the right-hand jet when I entered."

Moore fell silent. It was considerate of the murderer to turn off the lamps, he thought. The criminal appeared to be a house-trained savage. Moore looked down at the battered and twisted body at his feet and a question sprang to mind: "If it was dark, how did you avoid tripping over the body or stepping in the blood?"

"I lit a match as I always do when I enter a room in the dark. I held it up and saw my wife lying on the floor. I thought she'd had a fit. I stooped down holding the match and saw the blood by her head. I knew something dreadful had happened. I carefully stepped over her and lit the lamp nearest the window."

"Why that one?"

"It's the one we always use."

"Then what did you do?"

"I went to my wife and felt for a pulse but there was no sign of any. I looked into her face and it was clear she was quite dead. I can hardly remember what I did next, but I must have rushed out to my neighbours by the back gate."

The superintendent carefully scrutinised Wallace, who nonchalantly flicked the ash from his cigarette into a plant pot before bending down to examine his wife's head wound as if it were a scientific specimen. Directing a column of smoke high into the room, he withdrew. Moore slowly stroked his moustache. He was already convinced that this was a domestic – it was simply a case of joining the dots.

10:45pm. "I can find no signs of forced entry, sir," Bailey reported to Moore, who was standing in the hall. "I can only assume Mrs Wallace let the burglar into the house."

"Or there never was one," Moore muttered. "Any sign of a weapon?"

"None, sir."

"Keep looking, Sergeant. I'm sure it's here somewhere."

"Yes, sir."

Moore found Fred Williams in the kitchen talking to Wallace, who was sitting in an easy chair stroking the cat. He motioned to the constable. "What did he say when you spoke to him?"

"He said he left his house at 6:45pm to keep an appointment…"

Noticing that Williams was not referring to his notebook, he interjected: "Have you got it down?"

"No, sir."

"Get it in your book now, Constable."

"Yes, sir." Williams leaned against the kitchen dresser and began making notes of the conversation from almost two hours previously. His notes would prove controversial, as he insisted Wallace had told him that Julia had walked a little way down the entry with him, leading the constable to conjecture later that the assailant might have entered the house at that time.

11pm. MacFall's frame almost filled the tiny bathroom. For the previous half hour he had been searching for trace evidence throughout the house. Despite an attack which must have transferred at least some blood to the assailant, he had found no bloodied footprints leading from the parlour, no bloodied fingerprints by the cashbox or broken cabinet in the kitchen, and no smears by the gas lamp jets or doorknobs. Outside of the parlour, the house appeared to be free of bloodstains.

He bent down and examined the bath, which appeared dry and with no visible signs of blood. Resting on the side of the bath was a nailbrush, its bristles wet, but with no trace of blood.

As he was about to leave the bathroom, MacFall's torch highlighted a single globule of blood on the toilet pan, on the front rim. It was small – three sixteenths of an inch in diameter – and conic in shape. It was a clot, rather than a drop. Apart from a blood smear on a banknote in the middle bedroom, it was the only trace of blood transfer in the entire house. It could not be ruled out, however, that these had been made by Wallace or one of the dozen officers traipsing through the house *after* entering the bloodied crime scene.

11:30pm. Wallace left Florence Johnston in the kitchen and headed to the back kitchen. Standing by the sink, he casually sliced up some meat and tossed it on the floor for Julia's cat, as if nothing had happened. Robert Johnston, Florence's 22-year-old son, had popped round to see his mother and watched in amazement. For the rest of his life, this image would be imprinted on his mind.

11:45pm. Accompanied by Inspector Gold and Sergeant Bailey, William Wallace was whisked away by car to the Anfield Road police station for his witness statement to be taken. Despite the lingering suspicions of Superintendent Moore, Wallace was not yet an official suspect in his wife's murder.

"I got a message last night," he said, sitting in the middle of the back seat, staring straight ahead.

Sitting next to him, Gold said, "What message?"

"A telephone message was left at the chess club. It was from somebody called Qualtrough. He wanted me to go to Menlove Gardens tonight. That's why I wasn't at home."

"Make sure you mention it in your statement. We'll be at the offices soon."

1am. Looking tired and nauseous, Wallace signed his statement and reached for his packet of cigarettes. Tobacco was his lifeline right now; not only did it calm his nerves, it was something tangible from his old life, the one that had died with his wife in the parlour.

Inspector Gold scooped up the three typed sheets of paper. "Thank you, Mr Wallace." He sat back in his chair and gulped down the last of his tea from a heavily stained mug. "Now, I've got a few questions before we finish up." Wallace nodded. "Did you see anyone loitering near your house tonight?"

"No."

"Did you speak to anyone when you walked to the tram?"

"No." Wallace struck a match and lit his cigarette.

"And what about walking back to your house later on?"

"Only the Johnstons, as I said."

"No one at all?"

"No."

"And when you arrived home, did you think there was someone in your house?"

"Yes, because when I went to the front door I couldn't open it, and I couldn't open the back door." He wafted the match and dropped it extinguished into a cup improvising as an ashtray.

"What about the yard gate?"

"That was closed but not bolted."

"Did you hear anything?" Gold asked, waving away the pall of match smoke drifting over the table.

"From inside the house, you mean? No, nothing."

Gold wearily rubbed his bloodshot eyes. "What was in the cashbox exactly? Can you remember?"

"Oh, definitely, I am to-the-penny with my accounts, Inspector." Wallace flicked some ash into the cup and, without hesitation, reeled off its contents. "There was a £1 note, three 10 shilling notes, about 30 to 40 shillings in silver, a postal order, a cheque and four penny stamps. The stamps were not taken. There was a dollar bill, too."

"Was that taken?"

"No."

Gold nodded. "Now, turning our attention to yesterday night, when you got this message, the telephone message you mentioned in the car. Do you know anyone called Qualtrough?"

"No, I don't know anyone of that name."

"Did anyone know you were going to the club?"

"No, I hadn't told anyone and I can't think of anyone who knew I was going."

"Is there anyone who would be likely to send a telephone message to your chess club?"

"No, I cannot think of anyone."

"One last thing, Mr Wallace, before we call it a night. Please show me your hands."

Wallace leaned forward and placed his cigarette across the cup. He outstretched both hands, which Gold examined carefully. There were no obvious signs of blood.

*

Members of the Cold Case Jury, we need to understand the crime scene. Julia's feet were positioned at the right-hand corner of the hearth, her body was bent at the hips so that her head was more or less in the middle of the room. Because the chaise longue was tucked in the right-hand corner, behind the line of the chimney breast, anyone rising from this chair would have naturally stood to the right of the hearth, placing their feet almost exactly in the position where Julia's were found.

However, almost the entirety of the blood spatter was confined to the left-hand corner of the room by the armchair, by which there was a noticeable bloodstain on the floor {see Exhibit E}. Julia's head was positioned in the centre of the largest pool of blood. There was one other bloodstain, in between the two, so that the bloodstains formed an arc, as if her head and torso had been moved across the floor from near the armchair to the centre of the room, her feet and legs acting as an anchor point. The crime scene appears to be telling an important story: Julia Wallace was standing to the right of the fireplace when she was first assaulted, her body falling across the hearth, and even partially across the gas fire, towards the armchair. At some point during the attack, her upper body was moved, her head finally coming to rest in a more central position in the room.

This contradicts the opinion of John MacFall, who suggested that Julia Wallace was possibly sitting in the armchair when the first blow was struck. This is also unlikely because there was a violin case resting across the chair's arms, making sitting more difficult. Most importantly, however, if Julia was attacked while on the chair, it would be impossible for her body to become oriented in the opposite direction with her feet and legs two yards further to the right unless someone deliberately lifted the body into the position in which it was found. The body was not dragged – there was no smearing of bloodstains on the floor – so the deadweight would have been lifted to the other side of the room, rotated and staged. There appears no reason for any killer to undertake such an onerous task, let alone Wallace, who wanted to avoid any blood transfer onto himself.

MacFall believed the blood spatter on the walls in the left-hand corner "concentrate or focus on a point just in front of the chair." Of course, this is consistent with Julia falling across the hearth – either by an initial blow or a push – and then attacked when her body was prostrate on the ground. The last point fits with another finding: there appears to be no blood run-off on her upper body or clothes, so Julia was not sitting or standing when wounds were opened on her scalp. These are important points to consider – and in Exhibit 5 you will discover opinions of modern-day forensic scientists which support this interpretation.

An important task during the initial investigation was for the medical examiner to establish a time of death. According to MacFall's original estimate, which he submitted in an early report, Julia Wallace was killed at approximately 8pm. It appears to be consistent with Mrs Johnston's observation that Julia's left hand was not cold when she held it at 8:45pm and PC Williams' report that Julia's right wrist felt "slightly warm" half an hour later. If the estimate was accurate, William Herbert Wallace would be exonerated of bludgeoning his wife because he was four miles away at the time. Yet, nothing is straightforward in this case. MacFall changed his mind, later testifying that the time of death was at least four hours before his arrival at the crime scene, placing the murder before 6pm.

MacFall estimated the time of death solely by assessing the progression of rigor mortis in Julia's body. Although all times of death are estimates, establishing it by this method alone is notoriously inaccurate. Yet, at the trial, MacFall was unshakable in his conviction about his revised opinion. Clearly, it was impossible for Julia to have died before 6pm if Alan Close spoke to her later in the evening. Rather than admit he was in error, MacFall denied that the milk boy spoke to Julia Wallace. He conjectured that Close actually talked to William Wallace who, dressed in his wife's clothes, had impersonated her. This must rank as one of the most extraordinary and ludicrous claims ever made by a medical examiner. We will briefly discuss it later.

At 1:15am on the Wednesday morning, Julia's body was taken to the mortuary. During preparations for the post-mortem, the condition of Julia's skirt was noted by the city analyst: "At the bottom of the Placquet [a flap hiding buttons or a zip] there were three recent horizontal burns, which could have been caused by contact with the hot fireclay of a gas fire."

The placquet was normally worn on the left hip, suggesting that these burn marks were parallel to the hem on the left-hand side of the skirt. This suggests that Julia's skirt had probably lain across the the hearth and adjacent to the vertical bars at the bottom of the Sunbeam fire. In conjunction with the burnt mackintosh, it also implies the gas fire was on when the attack occurred, which is significant. As the parlour was rarely used by the Wallaces, it suggests that the room was being readied for a musical evening or that Julia was entertaining a visitor. This inference is confirmed by the fact that there were no signs of a struggle anywhere in the house.

The post-mortem preparations also revealed an oddity. Julia's undergarments included a corset with a pocket that contained over £1. It was an odd place for Julia to keep money, as she would have needed to lift her skirt to retrieve it, something she was unlikely to do in public. The last undergarment was the most extraordinary: a roughly cut square of white flannel, folded into a triangle and pinned like a nappy. Do these facts have any bearing on the murder? We will examine them again in Chapter 9.

The post-mortem, conducted by MacFall, found that the victim was a female who stood a fraction of an inch over five-feet tall. Her age was estimated at about 55 years. If her genealogical information is correct, Julia looked 15 years younger than she actually was. There were no signs of rape, nor any marks of violence apart from the obvious head wounds. Her hair, matted with blood and brain tissue, was shaved off to reveal a large, open wound above her left ear, from which fragments of her skull had been forced into the front of her brain. At the back of the head were 10 diagonal incised wounds, several of which were lacerations of the scalp. In his original post-mortem report {see Exhibit 4}, MacFall states the lacerations were "in parallel lines", which suggests that several were inflicted per blow. This is consistent with the report's conclusion: "I am of the opinion that death was due to fracture of the skull by someone striking the deceased three or four times with terrific force with a hard, large-headed instrument."

But once again MacFall changed his mind. By the time he testified in court, there was no reference to a large-headed instrument and, astonishingly, now there had been 11 blows to the head. There are suspicions that MacFall amended his conclusions to fit the police case. Sarah Draper, the Wallaces' charwoman who helped to clean and tidy the house every Wednesday, later inspected the premises with the police. She had last cleaned it on 7 January (she had missed a week due to the death of her husband) and the police were interested in establishing which items, if any, might have been removed. She identified two items that were missing: from the kitchen, a nine-inch-long steel poker with a knob on one end; and from the parlour, a thin twelve-inch iron bar that was used to retrieve debris from under the gas fire. Wallace believed the former had been thrown out with the ashes, but denied knowledge of the latter.

Despite intensive searches in and around Wolverton Street, neither item was ever found. The murder weapon was never identified, although the police believed it to be the thin iron bar. A thin iron bar, however, is not a large-headed instrument, and for it to account for all the wounds it would need to have been wielded 11 times, not three or four.

Before we move on, we must say something about Wallace's demeanour. The police believed that he was unusually calm, even cold-hearted, for someone who had just discovered his wife battered to death in their front room, yet his neighbours saw a different side. Florence Johnston said: "Mr Wallace sat in the chair, and was very, very distressed, half collapsed... His shoulders heaved, and he was sobbing. Whenever the Police came into the kitchen, Mr Wallace pulled himself together, but when they were out, and he was alone with me and my husband, he broke down several times and sobbed" {see Exhibit 13}. If Wallace was feigning grief for his neighbours, he could have faked it for the police to greater purpose.

Perhaps Wallace's most unusual behaviour concerned the mackintosh, which has been described as one of the most bizarre and puzzling clues outside crime fiction. Given its tightly crumpled condition tucked against the body, it is surprising that Wallace managed to identify it as a mackintosh at all – it could have been a cycling cape, a piece of material or a ground sheet. He had already disclosed several times that it was his mackintosh, but became strangely evasive when confronted by Superintendent Moore. Was it at this point that Wallace realised he might be asked how he had recognised it earlier? Or had the repeated police questioning simply made Wallace anxious, and he became more circumspect. When the different theories of Julia's murder are re-enacted, you will be better placed to make your judgement about which is correct.

One final point. Wallace entered his house and was inside alone for two or three minutes. He lit the gas lamp in the kitchen and walked past the parlour door to head upstairs. If you are worried someone might be in the house, would you not check each room in turn? Wallace stated that if his wife was not in the kitchen she would have gone to bed, so he checked their bedroom next. If he saw no line of light issuing from underneath the closed parlour door, he might have reasonably assumed his wife was not in there. Do you accept there was an innocent explanation or is this yet more suspicious behaviour?

What happened at 29 Wolverton Street between 6pm and 8pm? Why was the crime scene lacking a murder weapon and blood transfer? Why was a partially burnt mackintosh tucked under the victim? Why was the cashbox returned to its shelf? And who made the Qualtrough call? The coming chapters will reconstruct and analyse the theories that have been advanced to explain Julia Wallace's baffling murder. The first is that William Wallace was a lone wolf in sheep's clothing.

5. BATTERY

In chess, a battery is an arrangement of two pieces in line with the opposition king, so that if one of the pieces moves the other delivers check. If Wallace acted alone, this seems an apt metaphor for his devious plan, which cleverly aligned two pieces: the Qualtrough call and the killing.

The following reconstruction assumes that Wallace made the telephone call to the chess club on the Monday night before arriving there himself to receive the message, ensuring his alibi appeared genuine and was witnessed by many people. This aspect of the case is discussed in Chapter 6. For now, we concentrate on how Wallace might have battered his wife to death and disposed of the murder weapon. In the first edition of *Move to Murder*, my reconstruction was largely based on the prosecution's case at the trial in April 1931 and *The Murder of Julia Wallace* (2001) by James Murphy. However, as I explain later, I believe this account is flawed in one critical respect, and the following is a totally different interpretation. It is based on many sources, particularly discussions that have appeared online over the last few years.

Let us rewind time to the evening of Tuesday 20 January 1931 to see how William Wallace might have murdered his wife. He has returned home from his afternoon round. Julia Wallace has half an hour to live.

*

6:05pm. Wallace walked the few yards from the gate to the back door. It was always the same, everything the same. After hours of pounding the same streets, filling in the same forms with the same faces, it was back to the same prison walls. As he stepped inside, he knew all too well that tea would be the same gruel, served with the same look of disappointment and resentment.

Julia sat at the kitchen table, head bowed, sewing. On the table were some clothes she was mending, a sewing kit, scissors and a roll of linen.

"It's getting cold out," Wallace said, stepping into the kitchen.

Julia did not look up. "There are some scones on the range. I thought you might like your tea now."

Wallace walked to the range and warmed his hands. There was a pause. "I've decided not to go out tonight," he said with his back to Julia.

"Oh?" she muttered. "Turning down a chance to grasp a few shillings? I am surprised."

Wallace ignored the comment and picked up a plate. He looked disdainfully at the two buttered scones. She had not even bothered to make a sandwich. He took his plate to the table. "I thought we could have a music evening…"

"I'm in the middle of darning," she shot back, almost before Wallace had finished speaking. "And I still feel under the weather."

"You said how much my playing had improved last time."

Julia stopped sewing, and looked up with a withering look of pained resignation and condescension, as if she was saying, "Do I have to put up with *that* again?"

Wallace clenched his teeth. "No, I insist," he said. He looked at her, trying to dredge up the last drops of respect and affection from a well that had dried up long ago. In his eyes, she was like a nameless, lonely old street woman squatting in his life. He was the living proof of Oscar Wilde's dictum that "each man kills the thing he loves".

67

She had been such a bright thing, once. In Harrogate, there had been a vivacious sparkle in her eye, and she seemed to radiate a warmth that enriched the lives of those around her. God knows, he had loved her then. But the marriage had fathered only problems. Ever since he had been forced to leave Harrogate, little by little, day by day, her sparkle faded. She hated what she had lost: her independence, her friends, her self-respect. He hated what she had become: sullen, apathetic, bitter. It was not her silent resentment that he could no longer abide. Rather, her face was a mirror reflecting his mediocrity and failure, and he despised her for it. His conceit had mutated his self-loathing into a murderous revulsion for her.

As Wallace bit into a scone, crumbs fell down his front, which he brushed onto the floor. Julia got up to bring the kettle to the table. Wallace grabbed the milk and poured a little into the two empty tea cups. He peered into the jug.

"It's not off," Julia said, returning to the table.

"It's getting rather low."

"The milk boy hasn't been yet."

That was the bit of information he had been fishing for. He would not implement his plan until the milk had been delivered: he could not risk being interrupted. Wallace returned the jug to the centre of the table. Julia set aside her sewing, poured the hot tea, and sat down for her last supper.

6:15pm. Wallace lit a cigarette. His thoughts gently drifted. He recalled the words of his hero, Marcus Aurelius: "Whatever doth happen in the world is, in the course of nature, as natural as a rose in the spring." Wallace found solace in the fatalism: it relieved him of worrying about consequences. The good and the bad, he would face them as if they were the same. His mind was set.

He stubbed out the cigarette and peeled back a corner of the bedsheet that Julia was working on. Julia watched him, frowning, as he placed a tin of shoe polish and brush on the table. "I thought you were staying in?"

"I thought I would get my shoes shined for tomorrow, that's all. Aren't you supposed to be readying the parlour?" Julia blew her nose like a trumpet into her handkerchief. Having made her point, she picked up her needle and returned to her sewing.

6:20pm. Wallace placed his cleaned shoes by the kitchen door. "I'll quickly freshen up and then get the parlour ready." He stooped, kissing his wife on the top of her head. It was perfunctory, the affection eviscerated from the act after 17 dreary years. Unknown to anyone but him, it was a final goodbye. The thought intoxicated him; he savoured the power. Julia did not respond. Wallace left and headed upstairs to the bathroom, where he splashed his face with water. In the bedroom he changed his shirt before he descended and entered the parlour.

Using the borrowed light from the kitchen, he walked over to the bay window and drew the heavy blinds. The streets were rarely empty at this hour – children delivering to doorsteps and adults returning home – so he could not risk the parlour light being seen, showing it was used before he left for his appointment. He struck a match and, protecting the fragile flame with a cupped hand, walked over to the fireplace. On the wall, to the right, he lit the gas lamp. He wafted the match to extinguish it and casually dropped it on the floor, as was his habit to leave it to the charwoman to pick up when she next cleaned. He bent down to the Sunbeam fire and, turning the knob on its right-hand side, ignited the gas with another match, which he again wafted and dropped.

He glanced at his watch as he returned to the hall. He checked his mackintosh was hanging on the coat stand in plain sight and nearest the parlour door. Like a trapdoor spider waiting to pounce, he retreated back inside and closed the door behind him. Nerves gnawing at his insides, he began to pace.

6:30pm. There was a rap at the front door. Wallace froze and a surge of anxiety welled up in the pit of his stomach. What if someone was calling for him or his wife? There were so many loose ends to a murder plan, unexpected events that he could not control. He listened intently. After a long pause, he heard Julia walk to the door, pull the paper from the letterbox and return to the kitchen. When was the milk boy coming? He was not normally so late. Wallace told himself to calm down and think about what he had to do. He moved the chair in front of the piano to the sideboard facing the chaise longue to make it look like a visitor had been ushered into the seat by Julia. He placed a box of matches on the table by the bay window – if he was asked he would say they belonged to his wife. Again, this would make it appear that Julia had prepared the parlour for a visitor while he was out. All was set; there was nothing more for him to do but wait. Wallace resumed his pacing. He could not risk being in the hall or the kitchen when the milk was delivered – *Julia had to answer the door*.

6:35pm. In the kitchen, Julia finished a cursory glance of the newspaper and placed it to one side, sighing. She had dishes to clean and clothes to darn; she certainly had no intention of having a musical evening any time soon.

6:37pm. There was another knock at the door; this had to be the milk boy. For Wallace, an agonising silence followed. Was Julia going to answer it? Had she not heard? Wallace's heart pounded. His senses were so strained that the gentle hiss of the gas fire sounded like a roaring waterfall. Moments later, his wife traipsed from the kitchen. Wallace listened keenly as the latch was turned and the front door opened. More footsteps were followed by another unnerving silence.

6:38pm. He strained to hear the conversation by the front door. "Look at you!" he heard Julia exclaim. "You'll catch your death of cold, wearing nothing but a shirt in this weather." Someone coughed. "You see! You need to go home and get warm. Otherwise it will go onto your chest."

He grabbed the iron bar from the hearth, and manoeuvred himself in front of the fire, looking towards the sideboard. In his right hand, hidden against his right leg, he held the weapon. This was it. He was approaching the point of no return.

6:39pm. Wallace heard retreating footsteps on the pavement, and the door closed. "Julia!" he called out, his voice tremulous. "Bring me my mackintosh."

She opened the parlour door, scowling. "What?"

"I've decided to go out after all. A musical evening will be too tiresome in your condition – you can relax in here with the paper until I come back." He smiled. "My mackintosh, please?"

6:40pm. Julia rolled her eyes and grabbed the old coat from the stand and slouched into the parlour. "Oh, and no doubt you want me to help you put it on?"

"Yes please, dear. Thank you."

Julia walked to the right-edge of the fireplace, facing her husband's turned back. In the sideboard mirror Wallace watched like a motionless cobra eyeing its prey before striking. Holding each shoulder of the coat, his wife held it up to drape it around his frame as Wallace pirouetted round, moving to his wife's left. There was no time to scream, no time to raise an arm in defence. He struck the back of her head with controlled force; there was a sickening crack and blood sprayed onto the mackintosh. In an instant, Julia lost consciousness and her body buckled. Her head landed on the floor in front of the armchair, her body sprawled across the hearth with her skirt pressing against the gas fire. Caught underneath her torso, the lower part of the mackintosh fell across the red hot fireclays.

He stepped back, stunned that he had actually struck his wife… the mackintosh! It had fallen under Julia's body and across the fire. It started to smoulder with small flames licking upwards. He quickly lifted Julia's torso, her body twisting as if her legs and feet were a fulcrum, and moved it into the middle of the room. He pulled the mackintosh free and stamped out the flames. Tiny pieces of fabric fell across the hearth rug like shards of blackened glass. Julia groaned. Although in the twilight of consciousness, she managed to stir, blood running down the side of her face, her eyes mercifully closed to what was to come next.

6:41pm. Wallace gathered the mackintosh, grasping it with his left hand and let it drape over his arm like a matador's cape. He knelt down beside Julia, lifting his left arm as high as he could to place as much of his body and head behind the improvised shield. Snarling, Wallace wielded the iron bar in his right hand and brought it down onto Julia's head, but not as hard as he hoped. He did it again. Blood flicked onto the mackintosh as more blows rained down on Julia. He had to make sure she was dead; there could be no chance of a miraculous survival. Lowering his cape slightly, he repositioned the bar in his hand so it pointed downwards. Like a swordfighter, he lifted it vertically and then drove it down with all his weight behind it. It cleaved open Julia's skull above her left ear with a sickening crack, blood spurting onto the mackintosh. He knew he had delivered the killer blow.

6:43pm. There was no emotion. No feeling of elation or revulsion. No feelings at all – just thoughts of what had to be done next. Exhaling deeply, he stared at the blood and brain matter oozing from the gaping head wound onto the rug. Dispassionately, he wiped the blood from the bar onto the already bloodied mackintosh, placing the coat alongside his wife's body. Standing up, he nudged it against her body with his foot – the blood oozing from her wounds would account for its condition and no one would know how it had been used in the attack. After he caught his breath, he examined his clothes carefully for any flecks of blood. He took his time – any bloodstain could send him to the gallows. Finally, he used the sideboard mirror to check for blood on his face and hair; there was none. The mackintosh had done its job.

6:46pm. Wallace carefully positioned the iron bar on the hearth before rolling it through the short gap between the bottom of the fire and the tiled hearth. He knew it would fit; it was used to scoop up debris from underneath the fire. There was a rumbling noise, followed by a clunk. The bar had caught on something or fallen somewhere. He waited for a moment to ensure that it would not roll back out, then turned off the gas fire and stood up.

6:47pm. He twisted the brass knob under the glowing lamp on the right-hand side of the fireplace, killing the flame. A yellow glow from the kitchen lamp dimly illuminated the hall but struggled to enter the gloomy parlour. He struck a match and, bending down to highlight the twisted body at his feet, skirted around it. He straightened up by the parlour door and, as if extinguishing his old life, blew out the match. He dropped it to the floor and stepped into the vestibule. He flicked the front door bolt; some houses in the street had the same locks, so a few neighbours could actually use their keys to enter his house. Although it was extremely unlikely this would happen tonight, he had to be sure – his life depended on the body not being found until he returned.

6:48pm. In the kitchen, he dropped three coins from his pocket onto the floor, then pulled off the top half of the photographic cabinet door and placed it beside them. Having already emptied his cashbox apart from a dollar bill and some stamps during lunch, he had no need to dispose of its contents, and he was thankful for that preparation now. He looked at his watch – he was behind schedule. Turning down the kitchen gas lamp, he put on his overcoat and left the house, locking the back door. He walked down his yard and paused by the back gate. He listened intently for footsteps in the entry beyond – he preferred not to bump into anyone at this critical time – but only heard a wireless playing in a nearby house and the voices of children in a distant street. He slowly opened the gate, closing it behind him.

6:49pm. Wallace ambled briskly down the poorly lit entry behind the row of houses on Wolverton Street. He turned right, taking another entry in a series of shortcuts that eventually led to a tram stop a third of a mile away. The mission to keep his appointment with Qualtrough had begun.

8:33pm. "Aren't you ready yet?" John Johnston hollered up the stairs at 31 Wolverton Street.

"I'm getting ready now," his wife called back, looking into her bedroom mirror. "If you had helped clear away the tea things instead of readin' the paper, I would be ready by now."

"How long will yer be?"

"Ten minutes. Why don't you do somethin' useful and make sure Dad doesn't want a cuppa before we leave?" Her husband rolled his eyes, and plodded from the foot of the stairs into the front room to speak to his father-in-law.

Several hundred yards away, William Wallace sat silently in a tramcar, deep in thought. On his journey home, he had replayed all of the evening's events in his mind. Had he missed anything? He did not think so. Was he ready for the final phase of his plan? He had to be. The whine of the tram engine dropped in pitch as it slowed, and a bell signalled its arrival at the stop. Wallace followed several other passengers and alighted. He walked briskly along the dimly lit backstreets and dark entries.

8:40pm. Wallace walked the last few steps along Wolverton Street. It was quiet, deserted. This was not what he had hoped. He turned through a gap in the low brick wall, and stood on his doorstep. He knocked and waited, but no neighbour stirred. He inserted his key into the lock, and then withdrew it. He retreated and ambled through the entries to his back gate, which he knew was closed but not locked. He entered the yard and walked to the back door. He knocked three times and waited, wondering what he should do if no neighbour appeared. He decided to return to the front door, but was again disappointed to find no sign of life on the quiet street. He inserted the key into the lock and waited anxiously. Time was passing – he could not wait indefinitely for a witness to come by. He hurried back to the rear of the house.

8:45pm. "Better late than never, I suppose," Johnston said to his wife, as they walked from their back yard into the entry.

"We've got plenty of time. I told Phyllis we would be there at nine." As they closed the back gate, Wallace hurried towards them. "Good evening, Mr Wallace," Florence Johnston called out.

"Have you heard an unusual noise in my house during the last hour or so?" Wallace asked anxiously.

"Why, what's happened?"

"I've been out on business and I can't open the front door. It's been bolted against me."

Johnston asked: "Have you tried the back?"

"Yes. I couldn't open that either."

"That's funny," his neighbour remarked. "Try the back door again. If it doesn't open, I'll see if my key fits."

As Wallace walked to his back door, he turned to the couple waiting by the back gate: "She will not be out; she has such a bad cold." Wallace turned the handle of the back door. "It opens now," he called back. He hesitated – he did not want his neighbours to leave but he did not want to ask them to stay.

"We'll wait here. You have a look round to see if everything is all right," Johnston said. Relieved, Wallace nodded and calmly entered his house. Once inside, he strode through the back kitchen into the kitchen, which was in darkness. He took out his box of matches and struck one to light the gas lamp. The room was as it was when he left two hours before: the table strewn with cups, plates, newspapers, a sheet and a sewing kit, and on the floor the broken lid from the photographic box. Moving upstairs he twice called out his wife's name, and entered the bathroom. A quick check: everything looked fine. He entered the back room, lit a match, which he knew would be seen by his neighbours waiting in the yard. Downstairs, striking another match, he carefully stepped over his wife's dead body, and lit the gas lamp to the right of the fireplace. He was all set for the biggest game of his life.

8:48pm. Rushing out of the house, Wallace called to the waiting Johnstons: "Come and look! She has been killed!"

*

Members of the Cold Case Jury, the analyst William Roberts forensically examined Wallace's clothes from the night of the murder, and others from his house. He applied the extremely sensitive Benzidine Test, which is primarily used to detect blood traces invisible to the naked eye, typically in urine or faeces, and is capable of revealing the presence of blood in dilutions of one per 100,000 parts of water. There were no traces of fresh blood on any of his clothes. If Wallace committed this murder, he did so without getting blood spatter on himself.

Of course, Wallace might have been fortunate and actually avoided any blood transfer during the attack. Indeed, one modern forensic opinion suggests this is possible {see Exhibit 5}. But Wallace could not have known that beforehand. He must have taken precautions before being seen in public immediately afterwards, otherwise we can dismiss the idea of him carefully planning his wife's murder. So how did he prevent getting bloodstained? This is a pivotal question in the case, and it centres on the mackintosh.

The reconstruction showed Wallace using it as a shield, but this theory was not advanced by the prosecution at Wallace's trial, who claimed the raincoat had been used like a protective overall. Wallace stripped to his underwear to avoid the possibility of any blood transfer to his clothes and wore the mackintosh to minimise the amount of blood transfer to his body. This would make for an easier and quicker clean-up. This echoes the famous case of valet François Courvoisier, who murdered Lord William Russell in 1840. Courvoisier was naked when he cut Russell's throat, and then calmly washed away the bloodstains from his body after the attack. Yseult Bridges compared the murders in her book *Two Studies in Crime* (1959).

The prosecution's hypothesis leaves – literally – a burning question: how did the mackintosh catch fire? One explanation favoured by the police was that Wallace attempted to destroy the evidence by burning the mackintosh after he killed his wife. If this was the case, however, the room would have filled with smoke and tiny pieces of charred fabric, which would have settled in his hair and clothing – forensically, it would have been as damning as the blood spatter he was desperate to avoid. Even if he were unaware of this, Wallace would never have risked setting fire to his front room and drawing attention to the dead body inside. This idea can be set aside.

To have burned his fastened mackintosh while wearing it, Wallace must have stood in the hearth and against the red-hot fire, which would have also burned his trousers or bare skin; an action that was as unnecessary as it is ridiculous. In fact, it was hardly possible. The forensic evidence {see Exhibit 5} indicates that Julia was first hit, or pushed, while she stood to the right of the fireplace and fell against the fire – this is when her skirt was most likely scorched. With Julia's body sprawled across it, there was no room for Wallace to have stood directly against the fire. If he wanted to move the body, he would have simply pulled or rolled it towards him. We can conclude beyond a reasonable doubt that Wallace was not wearing the mackintosh – certainly not for the first blow. And if it was not worn for the important initial strike, it is difficult to believe that it was worn at any time by the assailant.

If it was not the killer who wore the mackintosh, perhaps it was the victim. In *The Murder of Julia Wallace*, James Murphy suggests just that. He argues that Julia placed the coat around her shoulders before entering the cold parlour. When she bent down to turn on the gas fire, Wallace launched his frenzied attacked – naked. As Julia crumpled to the floor, the raincoat fell into the fire, which Wallace retrieved and extinguished the flames. After the murder, Wallace washed in an already-run bath upstairs, dried, dressed, cleaned and dried the bathroom, washed and dried the iron bar, placed a wet towel in front of the range to dry, turned off the gas fire and lamps and staged a robbery before leaving the house. All of this was done in about 15 minutes from the moment Julia closed her front door for the last time.

This account is intrinsically plausible but, like many beautiful theories, it can be ruined by ugly facts. And there is a most unsightly problem here. Murphy argues that the milk was delivered at 6:33pm, yet the evidence suggests the milk boy left at about 6:40pm {see Exhibit 7}. By his own estimate of how long Wallace needed, this rules out the naked killer scenario: there is too much for Wallace to do in too short a time to make the tram when he did. And there are two other problems. It is unlikely Julia would have wrapped a coat around her shoulders if she was preparing the parlour for a musical evening with her husband or was expecting guests – she would have most likely lit the gas fire and then retreated back to the snug kitchen to continue sewing or reading the newspaper, rather than needlessly waiting in a cold room while it warmed up. Also, if Wallace struck as

Julia bent down to light the fire, it clearly would not have been hot enough to scorch her skirt.

Wallace may be the prime suspect in the killing of his wife, but it is most unlikely that he committed the murder naked or wearing the mackintosh. I believe the reconstruction shows the most plausible scenario: he did it fully clothed, kneeling and using the coat as a shield. Remarkably, this idea originally came from Wallace himself. In the final series of articles published in *John Bull* magazine in 1932, he believed his wife had admitted her killer, intent on burglary, into the parlour. "Two strides took him into the lobby, where he had observed my mackintosh hanging and he held it as a shield between him and her body while he belaboured her to death." Was he audaciously telling the world how *he* committed the crime?

The murder weapon was never found, the police suspecting it was the iron bar and that Wallace had carefully disposed of it. But could Wallace have hidden it in his house as depicted in the reconstruction? As an ending to the case, it would rival the denouement of any Hollywood thriller. Jonathan Goodman in *The Killing of Julia Wallace* (1969) relates that the Sunbeam fireplace at 29 Wolverton Street was removed by the landlord in the mid-1930s to fit an electric fire, and one of the workmen cleaned out a narrow channel between the hearth and back wall. The gap was about two inches deep, and a screwdriver was needed to prise out the debris, which included an iron bar. Knowing the history of the house, the police were informed and the bar was handed over. Unfortunately, it appears that it was not tested and subsequently discarded.

Was the recovered iron bar the same one that went missing from the Wallace household? James Murphy argues not, because the police removed the fireplace during the investigation and discovered nothing. He conjectures that Wallace dumped the weapon on waste ground near the

Liverpool Water Works pumping station on Menlove Gardens West. As there was no suggestion that Wallace carried a brief case with him that night, he would have needed to carry the weapon, and possibly bloodstained gloves, in his overcoat. This would have been awkward to conceal, especially riding on three tram journeys, and risked blood contamination onto his clothes. Surely, he would have found a place much closer to home? One thing is for certain: the murder weapon and where it was discarded remain mysteries to this day.

The reconstruction overcomes one of the biggest obstacles to Wallace's guilt: how he avoided blood spatter and left the house in short order. If you accept the account as plausible, Wallace remains firmly in the frame for the murder of his wife. There is other evidence to support his guilt. Was the trouble with the locks a charade designed to draw the attention of his neighbours and suggest that something was wrong? Wallace needed an independent witness to establish when he returned home and that he was locked out. He wasted no time in doing this – as soon as he saw the Johnstons he asked, "Have you heard anything unusual?"

Locksmith James Sarginson established that the front door latch would slip back when the key was turned just after half-way round, as Superintent Moore had observed. The lock mechanism was extremely dirty, rusty and worn, and had been for some considerable time. Yet Wallace told Moore that the lock "was not like that this morning". Surely, if the lock had been faulty for some time, he would have known this? Furthermore, in his written statement, Wallace described the lock failing in exactly the way Moore had discovered. So why did he not tell Moore that?

At his trial, Wallace testified that the key did not turn in the front door lock on the first attempt, something that had never happened before. On the second attempt he claimed the lock slipped back, as Moore found; also the first time this had occurred. Had the lock really failed in two different ways, each for the first time, just when his wife was lying dead on the parlour floor? It's improbably suspicious.

The back door lock was also examined by the locksmith. It was rusty and stiff, making it difficult to turn the knob. Sarah Draper confirmed the lock was troublesome. In his written statement, Wallace thought it might have been bolted against him, although he was uncertain. By contrast, he was adamant that the front door was bolted, claiming he discovered this fact when he opened the door to PC Williams. Florence Johnston, who was standing near the door at the time, could not remember whether he unbolted it or not. Did Wallace want to give the impression that, on his arrival, both doors were bolted and the killer was still inside? At his trial, he could not remember telling Inspector Gold that he believed someone was in the house when he returned, and agreed that the killer was not inside. But had Wallace over-engineered this part of his plan and simply abandoned it when it failed to convince?

Not all break-ins leave ransacked rooms in the burglar's wake. Some look as though no one has been in the house until expensive items are found missing. Were the coins and cabinet door on the floor by the bookcase a convenient and all-too-obvious sign saying "This is a burglary – look inside the cashbox"? The top half of the cabinet door had already been broken and repaired. It would have been easy for Wallace to remove it and place it on the floor as part of a naively-staged burglary.

The kitchen gas lamp and the parlour gas fire and lamp were all turned off. Although this took little time, the killer went out of his way to do this. Why? Wallace would have wanted the house in darkness to eliminate the possibility the body might be discovered while he was away. He could not risk a curious caller looking through a gap in the parlour curtains or blinds, or a neighbour coming to the back door and, seeing the kitchen light on, entering the property. There was no such imperative for a murderous thief, who curiously had time to turn off the gas lamp in the kitchen but not to pick up the three coins lying on the floor a few feet away.

John MacFall testified that 11 blows rained down on Julia's head in a "frenzied" attack. Such assaults are typically driven by huge emotive force and are highly personal. Although the murder of Julia Wallace appears motiveless, it is easy to assume Wallace above all others was moved to act with such savagery; there are jagged rocks that lie beneath the most serene waters of a marriage. Of those who think Wallace was guilty, the view of writer F. Tennyson Jesse is typical. She believed that Wallace regarded his wife as inferior in every respect, and had found her presence unbearable.

Another intriguing possibility for a motive comes from a former colleague – a young man named Gordon Parry, who we will meet later in our story. "Mrs Wallace was a good and pure woman who had suffered disappointment," he remarked, "and appeared to lose heart as the years went by." He described Julia as untidy and implied she was lazy. Could Wallace no longer tolerate his slovenly wife? Had a poisonous pride turned to murderous hate?

Whatever the motive, if he was guilty, Wallace devised a meticulous plan so he could get away with murder. He made the Qualtrough call to suggest a mysterious person had lured him from his house. He committed the murder in the parlour to make it appear that a visitor had called, and used the mackintosh to prevent blood transfer to himself. He staged the robbery of the insurance money in the kitchen to make it look like burglary was the motive. He embarked on a laboured search for an address he knew to be non-existent to provide an alibi and, when he returned home, contrived to be locked out of his house, indicating the killer was still inside.

The case against Wallace appears damning, but is he as guilty as it seems? Let's first consider the putative plan. As the husband, Wallace would automatically be a suspect, so he would need to cast suspicion away from himself. The easiest way to do this would be to imply that virtually anyone could have been the burglar, yet Wallace was adamant that Julia would not let strangers into the house while he was away and, therefore, she must have known her killer. At a stroke, the suspect pool was limited to 15 named colleagues and friends.

Rather than personal cash or possessions, it was the insurance company's money from the cashbox that was stolen. If Wallace was culpable, this is surprising. It appears he paid back the losses to his company {see Exhibit 16}, a cost the penny-counting agent could have easily avoided. More importantly, of the 15 named people, Wallace identified only two former colleagues who also knew where the cashbox was located. So, by involving the cashbox, Wallace limited the suspect pool to just two former colleagues – and himself.

If Wallace planned this crime, he targeted the cashbox for a reason. An obvious explanation is that he was attempting to frame a specific person for the murder of his wife – one of the two individuals who would have been admitted to the house and knew about the cashbox. But if you believe Wallace meticulously staged the crime scene to *make it appear* that a visitor had called and stolen from the cashbox, it is equally plausible that a visitor *actually* did just that. Or put another way, if it quacks like a duck and waddles like a duck, why assume it is an illusion and not the real thing? Isn't the simplest explanation that one of these two individuals *was* the killer and not that Wallace tried to frame them in an intricate set-up that left him out of pocket and carried a high risk of making him the only prime suspect?

Wallace's murder schedule appears to pivot around the departure of the milk boy. It provided the last known sighting of Julia – if Wallace acted immediately and rapidly it would sow further doubts as to whether he had time to commit the murder. But he did not know precisely when Alan Close would call that night. What if Julia was indisposed when the milk was delivered? What if the milk boy called earlier than usual, say around 6pm, before Wallace returned home? In each case, he would have had to abort his plan and lose the careful set-up of the Qualtrough call. The milk boy's arrival was a crucial factor that Wallace could not control; he could have arrived any time from 6:10pm to 7pm, a large window of uncertainty. Would Wallace have felt comfortable with such a plan? Does a chess player roll the dice for murder?

Mark Russell in *Checkmate* (2021) believes the timing of the milk delivery was merely fortuitous for Wallace; it simply coincided with his schedule to kill his wife. This is an extraordinary claim. It implies that Wallace, in planning his crime, was relaxed about the possibility of someone knocking on his front door while he bludgeoned his wife just yards away in the front room. Further, as Wallace would not have been able to come to the door, Alan Close might have commented about the Wallaces not answering to Florence Johnston, who might have called round. Can you think of a worse possible scenario for Wallace?

Due to the number of blows inflicted on Julia Wallace's skull, MacFall inferred that she was killed in a "frenzied" attack {see Exhibit 4}. He appears not to have realised that a frenzied attack points away from an organized and unemotional assassin anxious to avoid blood spatter. Russell queries whether the attack was frenzied, suggesting such a vicious assault would have been heard by the neighbours. He conjectures that Wallace placed the armchair cushion underneath Julia's head to dampen the sound of the blows against the floorboards. Although it was found to have small blood stains on one side, the cushion cannot have been used in this way. Julia's head was cleaved open, creating three pools of blood on the floor, so the cushion would have been blood-soaked and spattered with hair and brain matter. A better candidate would be the scrunched-up mackintosh, although it was not found under Julia's head. But if the mackintosh was used in this way, how was Wallace preventing blood spatter onto his clothes?

Indeed, the mackintosh is the most puzzling aspect of the crime scene. If it was used by the killer to avoid blood spatter – an imperative for Wallace as he would soon be seen in public – the most obvious and effective way was to throw the raincoat over Julia's head. Yet the cast-off on the wall, the lack of hair and brain tissue on the mackintosh and the absence of rips and tears in its fabric tell us that it was never used in such a manner.

Turning to the pattern of blood left in the parlour, two modern forensic scientists judge that the spatter on the wall *and* the bloodstain on the floor by the armchair were most likely produced as a result of at least two blows, probably more, delivered in this corner of the room {see Exhibit 5}. This is at odds both with the reconstruction and Mark Russell's account (given in the last chapter of his book) in which Wallace had to first move the body to retrieve the mackintosh and then, with the raincoat protecting him, unleashed all but the first blow while in the centre of the room. So can the Wallace theory plausibly account for the blood found almost exclusively in the left-hand corner of the parlour? This is something we will return to when we discuss other theories.

Wallace's "suspicious" behaviour with the front door lock makes little sense. All he had to claim was that the door was bolted from the inside. In fact, according to John Johnston {see Exhibit 13}, Wallace said exactly that when he bumped into his neighbours, a position he steadfastly maintained throughout. What did he gain by inventing two additional problems with the front door? Did he suppose that a killer would bolt it *and* break the lock?

Back to the murder weapon – or lack of one. A killer other than Wallace had the time to dump it virtually anywhere, possibly days after the killing. If it was pre-mediated murder, he would have most likely brought it to the house and taken it away with him. If the killing was heat of the moment, he might have feared leaving his fingerprints on an improvised weapon and removed it. Does this better explain the mystery of why the weapon was never found? That someone other than Wallace was the killer?

In summary, Wallace's supposedly well-organised "assassination" of his wife jars with some of the facts: a frenzied and bloody attack, reliance on events he could not control, such as the milk delivery, and a peculiar robbery that kept him squarely in the frame for murder.

Finally, before we move on, you might be wondering about the blood clot that MacFall found on the toilet seat. Isn't this evidence that the killer washed upstairs? No, it is a red herring. Two experts later testified that the blood was not fresh when it was dropped there because it would have splashed. It was almost certainly cross-contamination, and we can ignore it.

You have witnessed how Wallace might have acted alone in brutally slaying his wife, and have explored some of the evidence against him and some counter-arguments for his innocence. But not all the evidence is yet before you. In particular, we need to revisit the phone call from the night before and, in doing so, we will examine another theory of how Julia Wallace was murdered.

6. TRANSPOSITION

In chess, when the same position is achieved using a different sequence of moves it is called a transposition. It neatly summarises the theory adduced by the crime novelist P. D. James. She suggested that a former colleague made the Qualtrough call as a practical joke, yet the result was the same: Wallace killed his wife, fiendishly exploiting the call to create an alibi.

Writing in a *Sunday Times* article in October 2013, James claimed the former colleague lost his position at the Prudential after Wallace allegedly reported financial irregularities. The colleague's revenge was to send Wallace on a wild goose chase on a winter's night. But the prank turned deadly because Wallace, who had been planning to murder his wife, realised the telephone message left at his chess club provided him with the perfect alibi. He decided to kill his wife and keep the appointment.

The former colleague was 22-year-old Richard Gordon Parry. His father, William Parry, was a man of some stature in the community. He was a senior circuit steward for the Liverpool Methodist Church and the Assistant City Treasurer for Liverpool. Gordon Parry was a handsome young man with penetrating blue eyes. Charming, suave and snappily dressed, he was a ladies' man, never short of attention from the opposite sex. He was a member of the Mersey Amateur Dramatic Society, which also met regularly at the City Café, where Wallace played chess. His dramatic ability and sharp wits meant he could spin a yarn and talk his way out of almost any situation. These talents were the positive aspect of a dual personality. There was a darker side. He had a reputation for being an unscrupulous and incorrigible liar, conning customers and even friends to part with their money.

In 1926 Parry joined the Prudential, working as an insurance agent. The wants of his lifestyle eclipsed his limited financial means. When interviewed by author Jonathan Goodman in the mid-Sixties, Parry agreed that he had stolen various sums of money and freely admitted that he was "a young man with tastes that exceeded his unaided financial capacity to indulge them". There were at least two occasions when Parry was suspected of skimming takings from his collection round. One was while he was working for Wallace in January 1929, during Wallace's bout of bronchitis, although Parry claimed it was a genuine mistake. His father made good the difference, and Parry left the company several months later. For a city treasurer, the financial irresponsibility of his son must have been a source of embarrassment and disappointment, even anger. This can only have increased when, in the years after the murder, his son pleaded guilty to five counts of theft from telephone boxes, stealing motor cars and embezzlement.

If this petty criminal believed that Wallace was responsible for getting him fired from his Prudential career, a four-minute telephone call might have been an easy way of obtaining a measure of revenge. Is there any evidence to support the Prank theory? The circumstances surrounding the call need to be examined more carefully. Indeed, Wallace's solicitor, Hector Munro, considered the behaviour of the caller to be the most important point in the entire case.

Although it is possible that the call was made by someone unknown, there can only be an extremely small pool of candidates. The caller knew Wallace was an insurance agent, attended the chess club at the café and knew his match schedule. Apart from Wallace, there is only one canonical suspect: Gordon Parry.

Which one of the two more likely made the call? Clearly, it needs to be Parry if the Prank theory is to be sustained. Are there any characteristics of the call that point more to one than the other? To answer this we need to ask three questions:

- Why did the call initially fail to connect?
- What was said on the call?
- Why was it made from the kiosk nearest to Wallace's house?

The call was made from a public telephone connected to a manual exchange. It was a pre-payment system, the cashbox having two buttons labelled 'A' and 'B'. Lifting the receiver, the caller would insert two pennies into a slot at the top of the coin box and speak to the operator, who would connect the call to the desired number. When the call was answered, the caller pressed 'A', depositing the coins into the coin box, allowing the call to proceed. If the line was busy or there was no reply, the caller pressed 'B'. The line was disconnected and the coins retrieved from a return chute.

As you will recall, Qualtrough connected to the operator a second time and said, "Operator, I have pushed button 'A' but I have not had my correspondent yet." For decades, writers and criminologists have tried to explain what happened, most concluding there was a fault with the telephone system. The fact that the operators had difficulty in making the connection supports this supposition but this does not explain what was said. As writer Dorothy Sayers noted as long ago as 1936, a caller only pushed 'A' *after* the call had been answered. If there was no reply, even due to a fault, the caller should have pushed 'B' and re-inserted his two pennies to start over. Why did the caller apparently push 'A' prematurely, losing his money, and insert another two pence to reconnect with the operator?

Sayers suggested that either the caller was unfamiliar with a public call box or was agitated and made a mistake. The first suggestion points away from both our suspects. Wallace used pay telephones and Parry certainly knew his way around a kiosk a year later when he was convicted of stealing cash from them. The second idea appears more plausible, especially as both telephone operators believed the caller to be "a person accustomed to using telephones". Perhaps the caller became anxious when his call was not answered. If this was the case, however, one would expect the caller to say, "Operator, I've made a mistake and I pushed button 'A' before I had my correspondent."

Perhaps, in the dark of the unlit kiosk, a nervous caller might have hit button 'B' instead of 'A', although they were in different locations on the coin box. However, the caller would have immediately realised his error when the coins were returned, and probably would have re-inserted them and simply requested the number again on the second call.

Maybe there was a problem with the coin box, so when 'A' was pushed the two pennies were not deposited. However, in this case the caller would hear his correspondent answer, although he could not be heard. After a while, the correspondent would hang up. Presumably the caller would say, "Operator, I pushed button 'A' when I had my correspondent but they could not hear me."

There is another explanation. It was possible to scam a free call with an A/B box connected to a manual exchange. After being put through to the desired number by the operator, the caller replaced the receiver on its hook, keeping the money in the slot. After reconnecting to the operator, the caller would claim the line went dead and he had lost two pennies. Knowing, or verifying, that a call had just been made from the same telephone box, and believing that the caller had inserted another two pennies to reconnect, the operator would instruct the caller to push 'B' and the second call was connected without charge. Of course, the scammer had not paid for the first call and so received a free one.

If it was an attempted free-call scam, it would strongly indicate that the conman Parry, rather than the financially scrupulous Wallace, was standing in the kiosk. If it was not, the caller fumbled with the wrong button and, in speaking to the operator, said something that does not make sense.

Let us move to our second question. Does the content of the call give us any clue to the identity of the caller? We know that the caller asked to speak to Wallace and wanted his address. If the caller was Parry, the last thing he would have wanted was to speak to Wallace, who might have recognised his voice and, no doubt, quizzed him on the nature of the business and asked for directions. So, if Parry was the caller, he must have watched Wallace leave his house and assume he was in transit to the chess club at the time of the call – quite an effort for a mere prank. However, Parry might have been motivated for other reasons, which we will explore in later chapters.

Why would the caller ask for Wallace's address? Both suspects would have wanted to leave a message that required Wallace to visit Qualtrough, not the other way round. The last thing either would have wanted was for chess club captain Samuel Beattie to reply, "Hold on, let me get it for you." Perhaps the caller was trying to imply that they did not know the insurance agent that well. Wallace would have known that Beattie did not have his address, and could safely ask the question. Parry might have known, or guessed, that addresses would not be given out, or had a line of conversation worked out if it was. Nevertheless, this detail points marginally more towards Wallace.

The caller said he was busy with his daughter's 21st birthday. Why use this particular excuse as the reason that he was not able to call back later? It appears Parry was involved with a 21st birthday at the time because he discussed it with a friend the following night. Is this a mere coincidence or a subtle clue to the identity of the caller?

One aspect of the call was remembered by the operators: the unusual way the caller pronounced the word *café*. He most likely said "kaff-ay" when the typical pronunciation would have been "kaff-ee" or "kaff". If so, would this point more to the chess player or the amateur actor? Both Wallace and Parry referred to the City Café at least twice in their police statements, so detectives heard how both men articulated the word, yet its significance was not appreciated. It was a little clue – circumstantial evidence – yet it might have helped reveal the caller.

By examining what was said during the call, there is little to differentiate between the two suspects, but what about the sound of the caller's voice? Beattie said it sounded "rather gruff" and confident, answering questions without hesitation. The telephone operators agreed that the voice sounded confident, inferring that the caller was accustomed to using telephones, but also claimed that it was ordinary, not gruff. The waitress who answered the call at the City Café thought that the caller spoke quickly in a deep voice, and sounded more like an older gentleman.

Did the caller use his normal voice when speaking to the operators, but a disguised one when speaking to the two people at the café? Certainly, Wallace's voice was well known to the chess club captain but not the telephone operators. However, Parry frequented the same café for drama rehearsals, and his voice might have also been known to those that worked there; he too would want to disguise his voice. Perhaps the actor in Parry could not resist a performance, and stepping into character. He was certainly capable of doing so. He was known to pick up a telephone, dial a number randomly and, using an assumed voice, speak to whoever answered his prank call. We know this from an acquaintance called John Parkes, who we will meet again in the next chapter.

Many writers and criminologists have debated how easy or difficult it is to disguise your voice to someone you know. This misses the point. Would Wallace have taken the risk that his voice might be identified on the call? Would you? If his disguised voice sounded similar to his natural one, or he used idiosyncratic expressions or figures of speech, the noose would be dangling over his head.

After hearing Wallace speak at the trial, telephone operator Kelly was not sure that his voice was the same as the caller's. The final word on this point should rest with Beattie, who had known Wallace for eight years and actually spoke to the elusive Qualtrough for several minutes. He testified that the voice did not sound like Wallace. There is one conclusion that we can safely draw: if it was Wallace, he disguised his voice well.

Now we turn to the location of the telephone box. Why did Qualtrough make his infamous call from a telephone kiosk only 400 yards from Wallace's home? If Wallace was the caller, it was an obvious choice, but one with a substantial risk. The other kiosks in the area were inside libraries or shops, well-lit and often unenclosed, so they were unsuitable to make a clandestine call. Yet, using a kiosk so close to his home, there was a chance he would meet someone he knew, thereby placing him near the kiosk at the critical time. Why not use a kiosk somewhere in central Liverpool? It could not be one near the City Café, where there was a similar risk that he might be observed by a fellow chess player. Other than this restriction, Wallace could take his pick.

We only know the location of the kiosk because the call was logged by the telephone exchange. It was logged only because the caller reconnected to the operator. Either the caller was unaware that reconnecting might result in the call being logged or did not mind. Wallace certainly would have cared because it would place the caller suspiciously near his house. In fact, Superintendent Moore revealed later that its proximity to 29 Wolverton Street was pivotal in the decision to arrest Wallace for the murder of his wife. If the call had been logged in central Liverpool, it is difficult to see how the police could have suggested he made it. Instead, at the trial, some of the prosecution's most devastating attacks centred on the nature of the call: "Assuming Wallace left the house on this three-minute journey at 7:15pm, he could have easily been in that telephone box at 7:18pm. By a singular coincidence the man who wanted him – Qualtrough – was in that telephone box at the identical time at which Mr Wallace might have been there and, by another singular coincidence, at that moment he was trying to ring up Mr Wallace."

The prosecution implied that the timing of the call from the nearby kiosk and Wallace's leaving were causally related, but this does not imply that Wallace was the caller. If it was a three-minute walk to the telephone kiosk, it is possible that Parry waited near 29 Wolverton Street and, knowing that Wallace played chess on Mondays, made his way to the kiosk after he had seen Wallace leave. The walk would actually take four minutes at average walking pace, but it would have been even quicker if Parry used a car. He might have parked it in one of the side streets and loitered in Richmond Park, a confusingly named road adjacent to Wolverton Street {see Exhibit A}. From here he could discreetly observe Wallace – tall, trilby hat and distinctive gait – emerge from the entry, and then drive to somewhere near the kiosk. Parry would have been there in a minute or so.

Crucially, the kiosk was also only a two-minute drive from 7 Missouri Road, where Parry's girlfriend lived with her parents. It would have been a convenient call box for

Parry to use on the way to visit her. Expedience is as great a motivation as necessity, especially for car drivers.

Parry's girlfriend was Lily Lloyd, a cinema pianist. She said in her police statement that Parry called for her at about 7:35pm on 19 January. If Lily was correct, Parry arrived in his car just minutes after the call had ended. However, in his police statement, Parry said that he was with Lily from 5:30pm to 11:30pm. Of all the evidence in the case this is one of the few unassailable facts: Parry misled the police concerning his whereabouts at the time of the Qualtrough call. Unforgivably, Superintendent Moore did not pursue the blatant inconsistency.

It has been argued that Parry simply forgot what he was doing on the Monday night. We know from his statement {see Exhibit 11} that he provided great detail for his whereabouts on the Tuesday night and even for the days he visited Wallace two years previously. Clearly, this was a young man with a sharp memory, and it is highly unlikely he became confused about the Monday evening. Could he have lied for another reason? One suggestion is that he was with another woman. Then why did Parry not say so when he was interviewed by author Jonathan Goodman in the 1960s? With the passing of so many decades, what could have been more important than explaining everything and finally clearing his name? Yet, he pointedly refused to do so {see Exhibit 12}. It suggests he still had something to hide, and suspicion that he was in the call box clings to Parry's statement like a putrid smell.

Parry is certainly in the frame for making the call. Can Wallace be ruled out? No. After questioning his members, Beattie told the police he was confident that Wallace had not arrived at the club before 7:45pm. Based on timing tests conducted by both the police and Wallace's defence team, it was possible for Wallace to make the call at the telephone kiosk, immediately board the tram at the nearest stop, just 25 yards away, and arrive at the chess club by 7:44pm {see Exhibit 3}.

Wallace claimed he boarded the tram at a stop several hundred yards from the telephone kiosk {see Exhibit A}. If he instead boarded the tram by the kiosk, he knew there would be at least one witness who could confirm he was lying – the tram conductor. This was an obvious Achilles' heel in his plan and a surprising risk for him to take. This leads to one of the most disappointing aspects of the police investigation. In stark contrast to the questioning of the tram conductors on the night of the murder, there is no record of the police questioning conductors from the night before.

The upshot is that Wallace could have made the call and arrived at the chess club by 7:45pm or shortly after. In which case, he *might* have lied about his whereabouts at the time of the call. On the other hand, we *know* Parry did.

Members of the Cold Case Jury, who do you think is more likely to have made the mysterious telephone call? We have combed the call for clues to establish the real identity of Mr Qualtrough. There is no convincing evidence it was either man, but certain aspects point to Parry, others to Wallace.

Parry as the caller:

- He misled the police as to his whereabouts at the time of the call
- He was an amateur actor who allegedly made nuisance calls
- He would be the most likely candidate for a free-call scam
- Beattie did not recognise the caller as Wallace
- He could have made the call and arrived at Lily Lloyd's minutes later.

Wallace as the caller:

- Only he knew he would be at the club that night to receive the message
- He could safely ask for his own address, knowing Beattie did not have it
- He could have made the call and arrived at the club by about 7:45pm
- The café waitress described the caller's voice as "older".

Which pointers carry more weight? Your opinion regarding the real identity of Qualtrough will have an important bearing on your eventual verdict. P. D. James believed that Parry made the call and that Julia was killed nearer 6pm the following night, shortly after Wallace returned home from his collection round. In her view, this gave Wallace adequate time – over half an hour – to complete everything he is alleged to have done by the police, including washing upstairs. But how does she reconcile this supposition with the evidence of the milk boy, Alan Close? She accepts MacFall's conjecture that the milk boy never saw Julia Wallace on the night of the murder. Rather, Wallace forgot that he was due to call and, when he heard the knock at the front door, rushed upstairs to change into some of his wife's clothes, explaining the disarray in the front bedroom. He then spoke to Close, impersonating his wife. James admitted she initially found this scenario ludicrous but, on reflection, believed it was possible because the hall would have been very poorly lit at night and Wallace could have cowered behind the front door, showing only his arm.

Alan Close was no naïve fool, however. Even if it was dark and the gas lamps were low, a 14-year-old boy would be able to tell the difference between the frame of a six-foot-two man and a five-foot woman. He had known Julia for two years. At no point did he state that she was cowering suspiciously behind the door with an outstretched arm, as James imagines. Such details would have been seized upon by the prosecution had Alan Close ever uttered them.

Also, the Wallace-in-drag scenario does not adequately explain the disorder in the front bedroom as James proposes. Why would Wallace tidy away the clothes but leave several hats and handbags on the bed? There is a more prosaic explanation. The cleaner, Sarah Draper, explained that Julia often kept hats and other items on the bed. It also appears that Julia was mending a bedsheet in the kitchen that day, which explains why the bedcover was pulled back. There is no need to look for anyone other than Julia Wallace to find who was responsible for the disorder in the front bedroom.

If we set aside the wildly implausible Wallace-in-drag scenario, the kernel of the Prank theory is that Parry made the call as a practical joke and Wallace exploited it to kill his wife. What can we say of this simpler version? We know Parry liked to make prank calls for his own amusement. He had form, and this fact must be given due weight. The coincidence of a hoax call to someone already planning a murder explains why Wallace appeared to behave innocently on the night of the call but suspiciously on the night of the murder. It also explains why Parry misled the police as to his whereabouts at the time of the call: he did not want to implicate himself in a murder. He would have become a prime suspect and perhaps believed the police would pin the crime on him.

On the other hand, if you harbour doubts that Wallace battered his wife, you will hardly find the Prank theory any more persuasive. In fact, it adds some additional problems. Why did Parry wait at least 18 months before playing his practical joke? It is often said that revenge is best served cold but such an inexplicable delay is to prefer it frozen. And this assumes Wallace reported Parry to the Prudential and that led to his departure from the company. There is no evidence for either. Further, commentators who marvel at the intricate details of the plan would surely scoff if they were told that Wallace conjured it up in one working day. Perhaps he already had a scheme worked out. In which case, is it likely that the telephone message would dovetail so neatly with it?

Bear in mind Wallace would not have known the call was a prank, so he was not in a position to use it as cover by making it appear that some other murderer lured him away using a fake address. This nuanced subterfuge is consistent only with the Wallace theory (that he acted alone in killing Julia) or one in which he planned the telephone call as part of his wife's murder. As far as he was concerned, the Qualtrough meeting and the address were genuine. In which case, he could have used any work meeting or a scheduled match at the chess club for his defence. The plan would have been the same: kill his wife, leave the house quickly and turn up for the appointment. So why would he act so impulsively on receiving this appointment request via a telephone message?

If, after assessing all the evidence, you believe Parry made the call but Wallace killed his wife, this might be your verdict. Do not rush to judgement yet – there are more theories to examine. And there is a pressing question that needs an answer: if Parry made the call to the chess club, could he not have murdered Julia Wallace as well? It is to this theory we now turn.

7. FOOL'S MATE

Fool's mate is the least number of moves from the start of a chess game to checkmate. It requires a naïve player to make two wrong moves against a superior opponent. In the following scenario, William Wallace's gullibility, when he failed to check the address he was given via the telephone message, played straight into the hands of Gordon Parry, who had sent him on a fool's errand.

At just before midnight on the night of the murder, Wallace made a statement to the police accounting for his movements. Two days later, on Thursday 22 January, he provided a second, which listed the names of 15 people who Julia would have invited into the house had they knocked on the door {see Exhibit 8}. Of these names, six were people associated with his business, including his supervisor Joseph Crewe, eight were friends, and one was a member of the chess club. Wallace provided details of only two, and one of them was Gordon Parry.

These details included Wallace's assertions that he had known Parry for about three years; Parry had visited the house frequently when he helped Wallace and knew the location of the cashbox; Parry was "well acquainted" with his domestic arrangements; and Julia "would have had no hesitation in admitting him" had he called by. Wallace also stated that Parry was an amateur actor engaged to Lily Lloyd.

Not surprisingly, Richard Gordon Parry became a suspect and was immediately quizzed by the police. The following day, in his formal statement, Parry said he had known Wallace since joining the Prudential in September 1926, and he had been to Wallace's house on many occasions, the last being a little over a year before the murder.

In his interview with author Jonathan Goodman in the mid-Sixties, Parry said that he had often had tea at the Wallace house and would sing while Julia accompanied him on the piano. If true, the relationship between Gordon and Julia was more involved than the police were led to believe. We know that Julia kept money on her person, and had her own bank account – on her death it contained £90 (over £5,000 in today's money). Goodman suggested that robbery was a likely motive for the murder, the target being the collection box in the kitchen. The fact that the spoils were so slim is no rebuttal: Parry might have anticipated a greater reward. Another author, Roger Wilkes, claims that the theft was revenge for Wallace reporting Parry's accounting discrepancies, but it was bungled and Julia was mercilessly silenced. Both writers believed that Gordon Parry was the killer, although he was only named as the suspect in January 1981 when Radio City broadcast a series of programmes about the case on the 50th anniversary of Julia Wallace's murder, hosted by Wilkes.

Both authors appear to reject the possibility that Parry entered the house with the intention of killing Julia before helping himself to the takings, and with good reason. Although he was described by one acquaintance as having "a dual personality" and "a vicious character", and by another as "dangerous", Parry had no criminal record of brutal violence – before or after. If he struck down Julia soon after entering her house, it appears he was psychopathically violent for one night only, which is highly improbable.

Neither author sketched how Parry might have committed the crime. In *Murderer Scot-Free* (1972), Robert Hussey gave a more detailed account. Although he never named his suspect, he describes the killer as a petty crook who was intimate with the domestic arrangement of the Wallaces, a clear reference to Parry. He believed the perpetrator never planned to kill but was a sneak-thief who came to steal the money in the kitchen while Julia was left sitting in the parlour. His plan was to deny the theft when it was discovered later, simply brazening it out. After all, if the police failed to find the stolen cash, the evidence against him would be circumstantial.

Before reconstructing the murder according to this theory, we return first to Anfield on Monday 19 January 1931 – the night of the Qualtrough call – to see how Parry might have telephoned the chess club and left that infamous message.

*

7:10pm. The small Swift motor car moved along Richmond Park, heading towards the imposing spire of Holy Trinity Church, a shadowy presence even in the dark. It came to a stop halfway between the parish hall and the turning into Hanwell Street. The rasping engine cut, the bright headlights faded. The car door opened, and out stepped Gordon Parry, reaching inside for his hat. He slammed the door shut and ambled to a high wall, adjacent to a patch of waste ground, where he stood outside the umbra of a nearby gas lamp. Rain fell, turning to sleet.

Looking around, Parry nonchalantly took the light-coloured packet of Players No. 3 from his inside jacket pocket and placed a cigarette between his lips. He patted the pockets of his striped trousers and retrieved a box of Anchor matches. The cigarette lit, he leaned back, placing a foot against the wall. In the shadows, the only sign of his presence was a glowing cigarette tip and the occasional wisp of smoke drifting towards the street lamp.

Parry looked down Richmond Park to the row of red-brick terraced houses on the opposite side of the road, in particular to the small gap between numbers 79 and 81. He checked his watch. He knew that if Wallace was heading into town he would have to leave his house soon. He had checked the noticeboard of the Liverpool Central Chess Club when he was last at the City Café, and had seen that Wallace was down to play tonight, with games starting by 7:45pm. He knew Wallace rarely ventured out after dark, and if he headed out on a Monday night it was a sound bet that his destination was the chess club.

7:16pm. It was only a short wait. Lumbering through the entry was a tall, straight-backed man, wearing a dark overcoat and trilby hat. The distinctive gait was Wallace's. Parry watched him turn, heading towards Breck Road. Parry took a final drag before dropping the cigarette through the grille of a drain. He walked to his car and, moments later, the Swift pulled away, almost immediately turning into Hanwell Street. At the end of the road he parked and got out.

Walking briskly, his head bowed against the sleet, he soon reached the telephone kiosk at the corner of Lower Breck Road. Without looking up, he pulled open the glass-panelled door and stepped inside, the icy chill following him. Closing the door, he stood motionless in the gloom. He tapped the interior bulb above his head, but to no avail. Rummaging in his pocket, he retrieved two pennies and inserted them into the slot at the top of the coin box. He unhooked the receiver and pressed it to his ear.

7:18pm. There was a crackle as the operator came on the line. "How can I direct your call?"

Parry learned towards the mouthpiece. "Operator, connect me to Bank 3581…"

7.24pm. Parry replaced the receiver on its hook, pushed open the kiosk door and stepped into the sleet. He had no doubt that his patter about a 21st birthday would reel in Wallace, who had told him that some of his best-ever commissions were from fathers buying policies for a daughter's coming-of-age. He was sure the old man would take the bait and leave to keep the appointment. The coast would then be clear for him to see Julia. Although this time the conversation and musical evening would be a front. A risky "investment" had become an even worse debt, and he needed to get his hands on a lot of cash quickly. And he knew just where to help himself to about £30 and settle an old score with his previous employer. He reached his car and, after lighting another cigarette, drove to see his girlfriend.

*

Members of the Cold Case Jury, I wish to pause briefly and highlight an important point. If Parry watched Wallace leave, why bother with a phone call? Why not visit Julia immediately? After all, if Wallace was going to the chess club, he would not be returning to his house for several hours and the coast was clear for Parry's plan of sneak-thievery. There is a simple answer. As Prudential agents paid in their weekly takings every Wednesday afternoon, the potential gains were greatest on a Tuesday night. Having worked for the Prudential, Parry was aware of this. He also knew that Wallace rarely left his wife alone in the house after dark – the occasional visit to his chess club on a Monday night being an exception. If the couple left the house together, they always took the money with them. So, if Parry wanted to strike when the cashbox contained more money, he had to lure Wallace away on a Tuesday night.

Wallace was no typical agent, however. He usually paid in his weekly takings on a Thursday, so Wednesday night would have been the optimum time for a burglary. Having worked for Wallace two years previously, Parry would have been aware of this too. However, if Wallace settled his accounts on time, on the Wednesday afternoon, the cashbox would be virtually empty that night. A Tuesday night offered the best opportunity of maximising returns without any risk of drawing a blank.

Parry would have also known that, regular as clockwork, every four weeks monthly premiums were collected, and this doubled the takings on average. For these weeks, Wallace paid a day later – on the Friday afternoon. In January 1931, the monthly collection was the week before the murder, meaning that the night of Thursday 15 January would have been the ideal time to scoop the jackpot {see Exhibit 16}. I suggest we do not fall for the fallacy of the armchair detective in thinking that because Parry did not strike at the optimum time then burglary was not the motive. There might have been reasons, even mundane ones, why he did not strike on the ideal night or week. As it happens, that week Wallace paid in his monthly premiums earlier than usual – on Thursday 15 January – so if Parry had waited for the perfect moment, ironically he would have ended up with an empty cashbox.

Planning to steal the takings on the Tuesday explains the need for the call, but makes a huge assumption: Parry disregarded the option of an immediate but smaller gain on the Monday evening. To make the call and delay the theft to the following night was riskier. If Wallace did not receive, or act upon, the telephone message, the opportunity was lost, and Parry would end up with nothing for his efforts. Indeed, many commentators believe the uncertainty inherent in such a plan decisively counts against Parry making the call. These claims will be examined in the next chapter.

Let us now fast-forward a day to the evening of Tuesday 20 January 1931. Using Hussey's theory as its foundation, the following reconstruction shows how Parry might have committed the murder. Wallace has returned home from his afternoon collections and is having tea with Julia in the kitchen.

*

6:05pm. Wallace brought the cold with him into the kitchen. He glanced at the clock on the mantelpiece: there was enough time, he thought.

"I've prepared tea in case you wanted to go out," Julia said.

"I think I might," Wallace said, walking into the hall to remove his coat.

"If you think it's worth the trouble of going to Calderstones," she remarked casually as her husband returned. "Do you know the customer?"

"He said his name was Qualtrough," Wallace replied as he sat at the table, picking up a scone from his plate. "It's about his daughter's coming of age or something. That's all I know."

"Good commission?"

"Could be as much as a few pounds, I would wager. But it might be a waste of time, of course. I'm still in two minds." He took another bite.

"When *aren't* you?" she smiled.

Her husband said nothing, but pursed his lips; a sure sign that he was deliberating. Julia sighed. "You're like Buridan's ass – you don't know whether to turn left or right half the time!" They both laughed. "If you don't go, your mind won't be on the music, that's for sure. You'll be mulling it over all night." She smiled at her husband; she could tell he was still pondering his options as he ate.

6:15pm. Wallace had moved on from his light tea to a cigarette. "I suppose it's only a half-hour journey."

"A penny fare for a few pounds commission?"

"Well, with the return, it's a few pence."

His wife ignored his usual pedantry and realised she would have to settle the decision while making it appear to be his. "Look, to be honest, I don't feel up to much this evening." Without any subtlety, she blew her nose like a trumpet into her handkerchief.

Wallace glanced at the clock. "Well, I need to get ready if I'm going out. You should get an early night, dear." He stubbed out his cigarette on his dinner plate and gently kissed his wife on the top of her head. Unknown to anyone but the fates, it was a final goodbye.

6:35pm. Fifty yards away, Gordon Parry walked in the shadows of Richmond Park. The occasional street lamp cast a yellow spotlight on the grey pavement, but failed to banish the misty gloom. A dog barked, punctuating distant shouts from children playing in the street. Without looking up, he turned into the narrow entry between two houses. As he walked, the urban echoes faded and a rolling wave of darkness engulfed him.

It was a moonless night, and the only light was the diffused yellow from the gas lamps glimmering from the back rooms of several of the houses. When his eyes had acclimatised to the gloom, Parry looked left, counting off the back gates. He focused on the fifth: the one that led to the back yard of No. 29. If Wallace left by his back door, he would see him. Looking ahead, through the narrow opening at the end of the passage, Parry saw a slither of Wolverton Street illuminated dimly by a street lamp. A few boys ran past the opening. If Wallace left by his front door, he would also pass by.

6:38pm. In the dingy and dirty bathroom, Wallace splashed his face with cold water and dabbed it dry with the towel. He leaned over and picked up the nailbrush from the far side of the bath. He dipped it in the shallow pool of water in the oversized basin before gently scrubbing his nails clean. He replaced the nailbrush where he had found it – he was particular that everything should be kept in its proper place. He pulled the plug and gravity slurped down the water like a hungry demon. He thought about lowering the gaslight but decided against it; it was a cold night and Julia would be up soon.

Wallace did not register the knock downstairs or his wife's soft voice as she spoke to the milk boy. In his mind he was replaying last night's game. With more practice, he thought, he might even become a good club player. He walked into his bedroom to change his shirt and gather up some papers for his meeting.

6:40pm. For Parry, time expanded, with each minute seeming like ten. He was concerned that he had arrived too late and Wallace had already departed. There was another worry: what if Wallace had not received the message the night before? He would wait until 7 o'clock, after which time the punctual Wallace would not be able to make his appointment. Only then would he assume that his quarry was not going on his fool's errand.

Parry heard footsteps from behind. He stepped back as a boy walked past the intersection. It was Douglas Metcalf, making his way to Wolverton Street. He had not noticed Parry standing several yards to his right in the pitch black.

6:45pm. A door opened. Parry stopped whistling and listened intently. Some steps. Another door opened, followed by the sound of a shovel in coal. Parry relaxed. "Come on, you old fool," he muttered under his breath. "Where are you?"

6:49pm. A boy on a bike whizzed down the entry. "Come on!" Parry whispered impatiently, stamping his feet to fend off the cold. Another door opened, followed by shuffling footsteps, perhaps of more than one person. Then a man's voice, distant but just discernible on the night air: "…back by nine. Bolt the gate after." Parry held his breath, his heart pounded. A back gate swung open – the fifth one.

Parry strode forwards into the entry that led towards Wolverton Street and stopped after a few steps. He looked over his shoulder to see a figure turn and amble down the entry towards Richmond Park. The stomping gait was unmistakable: it was Wallace. The silly sod had fallen for it! He knew the punctilious old man would swallow the bait about the 21st birthday. It was too tempting for him to turn down.

Parry walked into Wolverton Street, which had fallen silent after the activity of delivery boys and adults returning home from work. He approached the front door of No. 29, knocking gently. There was no answer; this was expected. He knocked again in exactly the same way. She would not answer the front door at night unless she was expecting a visitor or believed the call was important. Gentle persistence indicated the latter. He heard footsteps in the vestibule and then the door opened cautiously, Julia peering out from behind it.

6:51pm. "Gordon," she gushed, her face lighting up in a rare moment of surprise and delight. "What are you doing here?"

"Can I come in?"

"Of course." Julia flung open the door. As Parry was ushered into the vestibule, he breathed through his mouth. The house always had a whiff of musty urine: the scent of old people. "If I knew you were coming, I would have prepared the front room." Julia removed her box of matches from her cardigan pocket and grabbed a raincoat from the coat stand, placing it around her shoulders like a shawl. "You'll need to keep your coat on until it warms up. It's as cold as a church nave in there this time of year."

He stopped by the door. "I'll wait here until you're ready," he said to Julia who disappeared into the dark room. He immediately took the few steps into the kitchen, his eyes immediately fastening on the cashbox on the top shelf of the bookcase. Moving as stealthily as a cat, he lifted a chair and placed it near the bookcase. He was not worried about fingerprints – he had touched the tin box several times when he worked for Wallace two years ago. Leaping up, he grabbed the cashbox and removed the loose-fitting lid.

In the parlour, Julia had lit the right-hand gas lamp and the fire. She placed her box of matches on the table in front of the bay window and began to pull down the heavy blinds –

these kept the warmth in more than the drapes. In the kitchen, Parry was rummaging through the cashbox in growing disbelief and anger. Where was all the money? There should be at least £30 but he found only a few notes, a cheque and coins. He pulled open his lower coat pocket and brushed the contents into it. A few of the coins missed, and fell to the floor like shattering glass. As he hurriedly replaced the tin box, his lower leg hit a homemade cabinet. Part of a broken door came away and crashed to the floor like a clap of thunder.

"Gordon? Is that you?" came Julia's concerned voice from the parlour. Now panicking, Parry stepped down from the chair, which he dragged back to the table. With no time to pickup the cabinet door and coins, he hurried back. Julia was standing to the right of the hearth, having just regulated the gas flow to the glowing fire. "Was that you in the kitchen?"

Parry glanced at the music stand by the piano. "Why don't we play?" When his eyes returned to Julia's he could see his attempted distraction had failed. His eyes followed her gaze, focusing on his jacket. To his horror, Parry realised that the cheque from the cashbox was sticking out of his coat pocket. As he shoved it back inside, he rattled the bulge of stolen coins. "I've got some money I need to bank." With growing alarm, he could see Julia's expression had changed; her eyes were accusing and full of suspicion.

"That noise came from the kitchen," she said, stepping forward. Parry's alarm now turned to panic. If Julia went to the kitchen, she would discover the cabinet door and the coins on the floor – he would be caught red-handed. His plan was in tatters – there was no way he could brazen it out, claiming he had nothing to do with the burglary when Wallace discovered the missing money. Even if he avoided doing some time he would be disowned by his father – his life as he knew it would be over.

Parry was now a maelstrom of anxiety and rage. She had to be stopped: no one would believe his word against hers. He surged forward and, before she knew what had hit her, he threw her to the ground. She fell across the hearth, her head thumping on the floor in front of the armchair. The mackintosh slipped from her shoulders and its bottom edge caught on the corner of the hot fireclays.

Now sheer panic took hold. She had to be silenced – he had no other option now. Seizing an iron bar standing on the hearth, he stood by the sideboard in front of the armchair and brought the improvised weapon down on her head with a sickening crack. After all the musical afternoons he had given her, the hours he had spent in her stinking house, the trouble her husband had caused him at the company... He vented his rage on her, bringing the bar down several more times, blood flicking onto the seat and the violin case resting on it, and onto the walls behind.

Suddenly, he smelled burning and realised the bottom of the mackintosh was alight – the coat had twisted under Julia as he fell and was trapped under her body. Grabbing the shoulders, her head lolling backwards like a rag doll, he lifted her torso towards him, leaving another bloodstain on the floor. With most of the raincoat now exposed, he pulled it free, scrunched it into a hard ball to starve the flames of oxygen. Charred pieces of coat fell over the hearth rug like soot.

Julia's head was a bloody mess but, however unlikely it seemed, what if she was still alive? Like an executioner, Parry bent forward, and rested the iron bar against her left temple. He raised it up slowly and then brought it down with tremendous force, opening Julia's skull above her left ear. Another blow smashed the back of her head, distorting it grotesquely out of shape, and forcing brain matter through the wound.

6:55pm. There was no chance of life now. He let the bar slip from his right hand onto the rug. Exhaling deeply, he stared at the blood and matter oozing from the gaping head wound onto the mackintosh and the rug. His hands were heavily bloodstained and there was blood on his trousers and shoes. He told himself to calm down and think. He wiped his hands and the soles of his shoes on the hearth rug.

Conscious that the bloodied bar would almost certainly betray him with a fingerprint, he realised that he had to take it with him – but not in its current state. He took out a beige mitten from his left coat pocket and used it to wipe the bar, removing obvious bloodstains, before slipping it into his inside jacket pocket along with the bloodied mitten. He would get his jacket and trousers cleaned, or even disposed of, later.

7pm. Wanting to shut the horrific scene out of his mind, and to avoid the possibility that a nosey passer-by would peer through a chink in the blinds and see the dead body on the parlour floor, he needed the room in darkness. He took out his handkerchief from his top pocket and approached the lamp to the right of the fireplace. He turned the brass knob under the gas jet. With the vanquishing of the light, he felt calmer.

Using the dim glow issuing from the kitchen, he skirted around the body and headed to the back door. Keeping to the shadows and making sure he was not seen, he made his way back to his parked car.

7:10pm. Parry sat in his car, his mouth dry and his stomach nauseous with the adrenalin surge. What was he to do now? From his inside jacket pocket, he removed the stained mitten and stuffed it inside a small box resting on the passenger seat. He had to get cleaned up, but there was a more pressing problem: disposing of the weapon. If anything was to link him to the murder, it was this. But where to dump it?

Seeing that the street was deserted, he climbed out of his car and walked to the other side of the road. Calmly, he strolled down the pavement until he found what he had been looking for. He stood over the drain grate whistling nonchalantly, as if waiting for a tram. A car drove past. He waited, taking another look around to see if anyone was nearby. The coast was clear. He slipped the iron bar from his inside jacket pocket and dropped it through the grille. There was a loud crash as it entered a subterranean world, out of sight and beyond the reach of the police. He walked back along the pavement, before crossing the road and making his way to his car.

7:25pm. The Swift came to a halt outside 7 Woburn Hill, about a mile northeast of 29 Wolverton Street. Parry stepped out, locked it, and let himself into the house with his key.

"Is that you, love?" shouted his mother from the kitchen. "You're back early."

"Yeah, ma," he replied, "I need to change. I've got oil on my trousers. The car broke down in Breck Road."

"You'd better tell you father."

Parry quickly headed upstairs and closed his bedroom door. He slipped off his striped trousers, which were skirted with flecks of dried blood, and his shirt and jacket. He washed his hands and face in the bathroom, the faintly crimsoned water circling down the plughole, and swilled the sink thoroughly afterwards. He put on his blue suit and sat in his room to calm himself and think. He decided his best course of action was to act normally and, about an hour later, headed out in his car to buy a badly needed pack of cigarettes. He would do a few tasks he had put off from the weekend, such as collecting his accumulator battery from a local store, and then go to his girlfriend's house. This would give him some cover.

11:45pm. At Atkinson's Garage, just around the corner from Parry's house, a 24-year-old man was busy washing

113

down a Morris Major Six Saloon with a high-pressure hose. Suddenly, two burning headlights came towards him, the car screeching to a stop. The driver squeezed the horn and a piercing shriek echoed around the workshop. The engine was cut and the angry headlights dimmed. John "Pukka" Parkes immediately recognised the small, two-door Swift Ten. Parry opened the driver's door and stood on the running board. "Pukka, can you give this a wash?"

Parkes did not trust his erstwhile schoolmate and was always wary of him. Seeing that Parry was agitated, he called out, "Won't be long, mate. I'll just finish up here." Parry stepped off the running board, leaving the door open. He leaned against the garage wall, nervously drumming his fingers. When he had finished his job, Parkes pulled the hose towards the Swift. "It looks as clean as a whistle, Parry. Are you sure…"

"Just wash it, will yer!"

Parkes sent the water jet over the two-seater vehicle. "And underneath," Parry directed. Parkes frowned, but did as he was instructed, and went to turn off the hose. "And inside," Parry barked.

"Inside?"

"You heard me!"

Parkes leaned inside the open door. "You don't want this wringin', do yer?" Parkes pulled out a leather mitten from the car. To his consternation, as he held it, he realised it was bloodstained.

Parry lunged forward and snatched it from him. "If the police found that, it would hang me!"

*

Members of the Cold Case Jury, in this reconstruction the mackintosh was used in the parlour by Julia and not by a murderous Wallace. It fell into the fire because Julia had it draped around her shoulders. This was highly unusual, according to Wallace, who stated in his memoirs that he had never known his wife to do this {see Exhibit 9}. This suggests that for a musical evening with her husband she would light the lamp and fire, draw the blinds and leave the cold parlour, returning to play music only when it had warmed up. However, had an unexpected visitor called, there would be no time to prepare the room in advance. She never invited guests into the inner sanctum of the kitchen, and she was unlikely to wait awkwardly in the cramped and cold vestibule until the parlour warmed up. In this situation, did she take a mackintosh from the stand and place it around her shoulders for extra warmth? Her husband had hung his raincoat in the hall that afternoon and, presumably, it was uppermost. Is the presence of the burnt mackintosh in the parlour best explained by this scenario or the one in which Wallace used it as a protective shield? It is a crucial decision, one that will help determine your eventual verdict.

In the reconstruction several blows rained down while Julia's head was in front of the armchair, generating the blood spatter in this corner of the room {see Exhibit E}. The attack was interrupted when Parry noticed the smouldering mackintosh trapped under Julia's prone body. To retrieve it, he moved her torso, producing an arc of three stains from the chair to the centre of the room, where the body was left. In your view, is the pattern of blood in the room better explained by this scenario or not?

This reconstruction reveals a violent individual who would ruthlessly kill to silence a witness. Does this square with Parry's character and behaviour? We know Gordon Parry was a thief – he admitted five counts of stealing money from telephone boxes and "taking away motor cars" in 1932. He was convicted of stealing motor cars in 1934 and embezzlement a year later. These offences, which appear unplanned and even inept, involved no violence. In 1936, however, he was accused of assaulting a young woman in his car, in which he lost his temper, seized her by the hair and hit her in the face. He was acquitted. There appears to be no further criminal charges against him.

A friend of Parry's from the 1930s later talked to author Roger Wilkes. Parry was described as someone who would have run away from a fight and fainted at the sight of blood. Of course, this might have been a distortion or downright lie, but it needs to be seen in context with his criminal record. If Parry was the killer, it appears his extremely violent attack was an isolated incident.

Is there any evidence he was involved in the killing of Julia Wallace? The most significant was introduced in the reconstruction: Parry's late-night dash to a garage to wash his car. This information entered the public domain only in 1981 during the Radio City broadcasts. After the original show, a caller claimed Parry's car was washed down at a local garage hours after the murder. The name of the garage and the attendant were withheld by the caller but both were tracked down. Then in his 70s, John Parkes had never forgotten his shift at Atkinson's Garage that night. During an interview, which was recorded and subsequently broadcast by Wilkes, he said that Parry arrived a little before midnight on the night of the murder: "Parry came in with his car... he wanted me to wash it. It was clean, as far as I could see, but I got the high-pressure hose and went all over the car: underneath, inside, on top, everywhere... He stood over me telling me what to do."

Parkes knew it was extremely unusual for a customer to request the inside of a car be washed in this way, yet he was adamant this is what Parry demanded. Parkes continued, "As I was doing this I saw a glove jutting out... it was a thumb and all fingers... I think it had a little tear in it. I pulled it out to stop it getting wet. Parry snatched it off me. It was covered in blood. He said to me: 'If the police found that it would hang me!'... The only suspicious thing I saw was that glove when he admitted it had blood on it and it would hang him.

He started rambling again… He said that he hid the bar in a doctor's house. He said he'd dropped it down a grid outside the doctor's house in Priory Road."

Parkes realised he was washing away evidence but was intimidated by Parry, especially after he found the mitten. He also recalled Parry's mood that night: "He was agitated… in a state of insanity. He had to tell somebody what he had done. He was that way gone. And he told me everything. Now had I been a bit more wide awake I would have got more out of him. He would have probably told me more. All he was concerned about was me washing that car down."

The next morning, Parkes confided in his boss, William Atkinson, and his two sons, who helped run the garage. He was told to keep the five shillings that he was paid by Parry and to say nothing more about it. When pressed by his employee, his boss agreed that if Wallace was convicted they would be morally obliged to tell the police. When Wallace was duly found guilty, Atkinson and Parkes spoke to Superintendent Moore, who allegedly refused to believe their story. Certainly, there is no extant record of any interview. Either Moore dismissed it out of hand, as claimed, or it never took place.

If true, this statement would implicate Parry in the murder. Parkes told Wilkes that he was relieved to get it off his mind after so many years, but how reliable is testimony that has been withheld for 50 years? During that time, the details of the murder had entered the public domain and the only people who could corroborate the story – Atkinson, his sons, Moore and Parry – were all dead.

Author James Murphy is highly sceptical. In particular, he wonders how Parkes could have noticed hours-old dried blood, especially on a dark mitten in the gloom of a garage at night. This assumes, of course, it was a dark mitten and the garage was not well lit. In the reconstruction, I conjecture otherwise. Murphy also wonders what had happened to the second mitten. It is a puzzle, but not one that reflects on the veracity of Parkes. Indeed, the fact that Parkes mentions a mitten at all is surprising. Criminals are not renowned for wearing mittens, and certainly not just one. Would it not have been more natural to fabricate a story by saying he found a pair of normal gloves covered in blood?

Murphy's most pointed attack is directed at the other claims made by the garage attendant. In particular, Parkes said, "He was dressed as he was usually dressed and that's why I couldn't understand why there was no blood on him. When I was told about him borrowing these thigh boots and oilskin coat I then realised why... there was no blood on Parry's clothes. He had these rubbers and they never found them." It is ludicrous to believe Parry went to Wallace's house wearing thigh-high waders and a heavy overcoat to keep blood spatter off his clothes. However, Parkes had been told by friends that Parry had borrowed these items and never returned them. He then put two and two together, and arrived at an improbably high number, but we should only be interested in what Parkes claims to have remembered, not his theories. Murphy is attacking a straw man.

Similarly, Mark Russell dismisses the idea of Parry's midnight dash to the garage as "idiotic", pointing out that Parry would not have left a bloodstained car outside his girlfriend's house for several hours before driving to a garage when the city police were actively conducting a murder investigation. However, the police were not looking for a culprit in a car but pursuing leads for known burglars and surely Parry would have wanted to visit the garage when it was likely to be deserted?

I am more suspicious about the disposal of "the bar". It seems too obvious to be true. Did the garage attendant misremember this conversational detail or even embellish his story to impress a journalist? Anyone familiar with the case knows it was the suspected murder weapon, but a kitchen poker was also missing from the house, an equally good candidate. In fact, the weapon might have been any "large-headed instrument". Yet, all too conveniently, it is the bar that clinches Parry's guilt. Had Parkes immediately told the police about Parry's claim to have disposed of an iron bar, it would have been critical to the case. Unfortunately, as confirming evidence of the murder weapon, it was five decades too late.

Sensational claims made years later rightly arouse suspicion about their veracity, yet there are two factors that provide some credibility to Parkes' statement. First, its central assertion was corroborated. Roger Wilkes interviewed Dolly Atkinson, the garage owner's daughter-in-law, who told him, "I remember Pukka [John Parkes] told me and my husband [Wilfred Atkinson] that he had to wash the car... It was the morning, yes, the morning after... before he went home from his work. I saw Pukka every morning – he was just like a friend to us all. We'd known him for years. He would not make up such a story as that."

According to Dolly Atkinson, Parkes told her hours after the murder that he had washed Parry's car. As she failed to provide specific details, it is only a partial corroboration, but one that supports the statement's authenticity. Second, Parkes and Atkinson did not push themselves forward to appear on the radio broadcasts to gain attention or financial reward. In fact, the opposite was true: they were tracked down separately and then agreed to give interviews. This is not surprising because the story does not reflect well on those who withheld information at the time of Wallace's arrest and trial.

Is there any other evidence Parry might have been involved? In *The Killing of Julia Wallace (2012)*, John Gannon writes that, two days after the murder, Parry's parents visited Sidney Pritchard, who was not only a family friend but a fellow trustee of their Methodist church. Ada, his

16-year-old daughter, listened in at the sitting room door. She reported that Parry's parents wanted to smuggle Gordon out of Liverpool by boat. A blazing row ensued, and Ada's father refused to help.

This statement was told to a researcher – again, years after the event. If true, it reveals that Parry's parents believed that their son was in serious trouble. Occurring just days after the murder, it is surely too much of a coincidence to believe that Parry's situation was unconnected to the killing. Had they discovered incriminating evidence in Parry's bedroom? Did their son confess? One thing we do know: Parry adamantly refused to publicly discuss the Julia Wallace case, his father having made him promise that he would never do so {see Exhibit 12}. Was Gordon Parry's father concerned that his son might incriminate himself otherwise?

But what would have moved Parry to murder? Being caught red-handed by Julia might have been the trigger; a witness to his thievery would land him in serious trouble and almost certainly cost him his job. Did a brutal side to his character show itself when he realised that Julia had to be silenced to save himself? William Wallace thought so, writing in his unpublished memoir, "If the killer was indeed known to my wife and he allowed her to live, his robbery would have been a wasted effort since she would have witnessed against him. From his point of view, he had to kill her."

But is Wallace assuming too much? If Parry was literally caught with his mittens in the cashbox, was killing Julia the only option for the smooth talker? He could have replaced the cash, pleaded for forgiveness and left with the hope that Julia would take no further action. Would he resort to bashing the brains out of a woman with whom he supposedly sang? An individual with such a propensity for aggression would surely commit further crimes of violence. Yet, it appears that Parry, for all his misdemeanours, did not.

After the murder, Wallace became apprehensive about Parry. "I am convinced Parry killed her," he wrote in his diary, "yet it is difficult to get proof. It would be a great relief if he could only be caught, and the foul murder brought home to him." He told *John Bull* magazine that he had fitted an electric switch and lamps to his bungalow because he was "dreadfully nervous about entering the house after dark" and was "on alert for attack" from Parry (although he did not name him for obvious reasons).

Wallace also mentioned an awkward encounter with Parry in his diary: "Just as I was going to dinner, Parry stopped me, and said he wanted to talk to me for a few minutes. It was a desperately awkward position. Eventually, I decided not to hear what he had to say. I told him I would talk to him some day and give him something to think about. He must realize that I suspect him of the terrible crime. I fear I let him see clearly what I thought, and it may unfortunately put him on his guard."

Wallace's private diaries were only for posterity but the *John Bull* articles were for contemporaneous public opinion, and they left little doubt: his description of the killer matched only Parry {see Exhibit 10}. If Wallace was guilty then he was determined to blame someone who he knew was certainly innocent. Under the laws of double jeopardy, Wallace could not be charged with any crime related to the murder of his wife – he had won – so why was he accusing Parry? Was the killing of his wife not the end but a means to entrap the young man? Indeed, I suggest there is one conclusion to draw if Wallace was the killer: his post-acquittal behaviour confirms that his plan was to frame Parry and he was doggedly trying to finish the job.

Of course, there is another interpretation. Wallace returned home that night to find his wife brutally murdered and, after the initial shock lessened, he was convinced that the evidence pointed to Parry as the killer. After all, who else but his former colleague knew about his cashbox *and* his chess schedule *and* would be admitted by Julia in his absence? This interpretation gains further traction when you consider that Wallace only volunteered Parry's name in his second statement when he was asked by police to provide a list of people Julia would let into her house in his absence. For someone framing his former colleague, he was not proactive with the police.

Like much in this case, you have a choice: either chalk up Wallace's post-acquittal behaviour as another devious ploy in his malicious scheme or jot it down as evidence of his innocence. Others have subsequently concurred with Wallace's view that Parry was the killer, including true-crime authors Jonathan Goodman, Robert F. Hussey and Roger Wilkes. Indeed, the unearthing of the garage attendant's story appeared to secure the case against him. Yet whatever this case gives with one hand, it takes away with the other. Unknown to Wallace and these authors, astonishing evidence secreted away in the police archive blows the case wide open.

8. EN PASSANT

Years after the Radio City broadcasts, the full prosecution file was released, which included signed statements from two witnesses providing Parry with an alibi for the night of the murder. At 5:30pm, Parry arrived at the house of Olivia Brine, a 39-year-old married woman. Mrs Brine's 15-year-old nephew, Harold Denison, called at about 6pm while Parry was there. Both stated Parry left at about 8:30pm {see Exhibit 11}.

At a stroke, it explained why the police had not pursued Parry. If he was at Olivia Brine's house for three hours until 8:30pm on the night of the murder, then Parry did not kill Julia Wallace. Yet, as with much in this case, nothing is what it first seems. It will be no surprise for you to learn the alibi was not thoroughly cross-checked. Olivia's daughter was present and a friend named Phyllis Plant also dropped by at an undetermined time, but neither gave statements to the police.

Curiously, Parry refused to expound his armour-plated alibi when interviewed by Jonathan Goodman in the 1960s, decades before the police file was released. He merely said that he was "with friends arranging a birthday party" {see Exhibit 12}. Revealing that he was at Olivia Brine's should have cleared Parry and lifted the veil of suspicion once and for all. Was he dutifully keeping his promise to his father, or did he wish to avoid a journalist poking into his story? Both Mrs Brine and her nephew were alive at the time. It was only when the police case file was released that their identities were publicly revealed, and by then everyone connected to the alibi was dead.

What was the relationship between Olivia Brine and Parry? All we glean is that they had known each other for two years. With a husband away at sea and a young, good-looking man calling at her house, she must have been aware of the appearance it presented to tongue-wagging neighbours. There is nothing to indicate she was covering for Parry, yet doubt slithers across your mind when you read the police statements. They are so short on detail, by far the briefest statements of any witness in the entire file.

All those involved – including the daughter and the visiting friend – should have been questioned about the accuracy of Parry's arrival and departure times. Parry simply stated he stayed until about 8:30pm. Olivia Brine and her nephew gave statements only after Parry had provided his. The times in all three dovetail neatly, perhaps too neatly. The statements of Lily Lloyd and her mother did not provide identical times for when Parry arrived at their house on the night of the call {see Exhibit 11}. Yet, for the night of the murder there is agreement, although none state how they knew the times were accurate. Clearly, they were not asked. It leaves the impression that the police were merely going through the motions for suspects other than Wallace.

If Parry's alibi is accepted, what follows? Obviously, the theory that he was the killer would have to be rejected. Could we eliminate Parry as the caller too? No, because this presumes that the caller and the killer were one and the same person. As we have seen with the Prank theory, this might not be the case. Does it follow that Parkes' story is false? Again, no. Even if Parry did not kill Julia Wallace, it is possible that he gave a lift to the actual killer and subsequently drove to the garage to clean his car of any incriminating trace evidence. In other words, Parry might have had an accomplice.

In chess, when a pawn advances two squares from its starting position it can be taken 'en passant' by an opposing pawn, and is the only move in chess when the attacking piece does not end up on the square of the captured one. This seems an apt metaphor for the next theory, in which Parry never enters the Wallace household on the night of the murder because he has enlisted the help of an accomplice to steal the collection money.

The Accomplice theory is the work of Rod Stringer, a former systems analyst and local historian, who lives near Liverpool. He has studied the Wallace case for many years, visiting the places associated with the murder and reconstructing events with maps, the original witness statements and his own timings. Stringer went public with his theory in 2008, posting his solution on internet forums dedicated to the case.

If Parry worked alone, he could keep all the loot for himself, so why would he want to involve an accomplice? He would have realised that, being known to the Wallaces, he could not simply turn up at the house and help himself to the cashbox while Julia was distracted, perhaps seated in the parlour. As soon as the theft was discovered, the identity of the thief would be known. With his reputation, Parry would have known such a theft was likely to land him in serious trouble, not least with his strict father.

If Parry wanted a low-risk method for him to get his hands on the cash he needed someone to steal it for him, someone unknown to the Wallaces. Timid Julia would not generally let a stranger into her house but, Parry knew from experience that she might if the visit was about her husband's business, a point confirmed by Wallace at his trial. He needed a Trojan horse – and he found it in the form of a telephone call.

The call was essential to the plot, serving three purposes. First, it was the bait that lured Wallace into thinking there was a big-money commission for him. Private telephones were rare in Liverpool at the time and were typically owned by the middle class, so a telephone message implied the caller was wealthy. Second, it gave the accomplice, pretending to be Qualtrough, a pretext to enter the house. It also explains why 'Qualtrough' was used – it is a distinctive name, one that would be recognised on the doorstep. Third, as Julia did not accompany her husband on business trips, it ensured she would be at home when the accomplice called. Wallace testified at his trial that the couple never left any money inside the house if they were both out; they always took it with them, including the insurance takings. If he knew their domestic arrangements as well as Wallace claimed, Parry would have known this.

But who would have agreed to such a plan? It is not difficult to believe that someone with criminal inclinations, perhaps someone who had burgled before, would have been easily persuaded by Parry. It should be remembered that economic times were tough, with high unemployment in Liverpool.

To make the call and set the plan in motion, Parry had only to observe Wallace leaving for the chess club. By 8pm on Monday night, the trap had been set. Let us return to Wolverton Street to see how Parry's plan for some easy money ended in a brutal killing. Responding to the modern forensic interpretation of the crime scene {see Exhibit 5}, the following scenario below differs in key respects to the one published in the first edition.

*

6:48pm. "Right, I'm all set for Mr Qualtrough." Wallace glanced at the mantelpiece clock. "I think the tram should get me there in half an hour. Fifteen minutes should leave enough time to find the address."

"I'm sure it will," Julia replied, her nose blocked with a cold.

Wallace placed his hat on his head. "I should be back by nine. Don't answer the door while I'm out." Julia nodded. He turned, walked into the back kitchen and was gone.

7:10pm. Sighing, Julia closed the *Liverpool Echo* and placed it to one side of the table. As much as she enjoyed catching up with the news – she was an incorrigible newspaper buyer, much to the annoyance of her penny-pinching husband – she had to clear away the tea things and finish her sewing. Deciding the dishes could wait, she gathered her sewing equipment and laid it out on the table. She increased the flow to the gas lamp; it was never a good light to sew by but at least it was directly above the table. In silence, she set about her task of darning some socks and a dress.

7:30pm. After lurking in the darkness of the entry, the smartly dressed man emerged into the yellow-lit gloom of Wolverton Street. Anxious he was running late, he walked quickly to the step of No. 29 and made three gentle raps on the door. As he waited for his knock to be answered, he went through everything Parry had told him. The hardest part was getting into the house, which would require nerve and patience in equal measure. Inside, Julia paused when she heard the door knock. Heeding her husband's instruction, she continued sewing.

7:31pm. When it was obvious there was no answer, the man knocked again in exactly the same way, nothing too hard or brusque to alarm Julia or alert the neighbours. Parry knew that Julia would not answer the front door at night unless she was expecting a visitor or believed the call was important. Gentle persistence indicated the latter. Although she had ignored it the first time, there was something about the knock that told Julia it might be Gordon. He had not visited for some time and she had missed their musical afternoons. But why would he call at this hour? She put down the dress, stuck the needle in a pin-cushion and pushed back her chair.

The visitor heard the movement inside and noticed a diffuse light stream through the fan light. He braced himself for Wallace answering, but he had a failsafe: he would say that he was lost, asking directions for Twyford Street. If Julia answered the door, however, it meant Wallace was out and they were in business. The front door was cautiously pulled ajar. Timidly, Julia peered around it.

7:32pm. "Good evening. Mrs Wallace, I presume?" the man asked, faithfully following Parry's script. "I'm here to see Mr Wallace. I have an appointment." Julia frowned, and was about to respond when the visitor spoke again. "My name is Qualtrough." As Parry had foreseen, the name was like the combination to a safe. Julia's expression instantly changed to one of surprise.

"Oh my!" she said, placing her hand to her face. "Mr Wallace left not an hour ago to meet you at your house." Julia spoke so softly her voice was barely discernible. "Isn't that what you said when you telephoned the chess club last night?"

"I only gave my address so Mr Wallace would have my details in advance. I actually said I would call *here* tonight at 7:30pm. There appears to have been some mix-up."

"Oh dear, there must have been," Julia said, her face showing concern. "Do you think you could come back later, Mr Qualtrough, when my husband has returned? I'm sure he won't be long once he realises the mistake."

"But I have come all the way from... uh... come especially to see Mr Wallace," the man mumbled, misremembering his lines. "It's about my daughter's 18th birthday, you see." Julia noticed that the daughter's age was different to the one her husband had been told, but she thought nothing of it. It only confirmed, she believed, that

128

the telephone message had been scribbled down in error the night before.

"About a policy, you mean?"

"Yes, it's about... uh... business for Mr Wallace. That's right."

Julia hesitated. There was something about the visitor she did not trust. For a start, he did not seem old enough to have an adult daughter, but she reminded herself that she was no longer an accurate judge of a young person's age. He also appeared a little vague as to what he wanted. On the other hand, she knew her husband was keen on the commission, and would be bitterly disappointed travelling back empty-handed. Perhaps it need not be a fruitless evening for him after all.

"In that case, Mr Qualtrough, why don't you come inside and wait until he returns?" Like the gates of Troy, the door swung open. As he crossed the threshold, the visitor smiled, revealing a missing tooth in his upper jaw. Julia closed the door. "Wait here while I see to the parlour. It's as cold as stone until the fire gets going." Taking the top-most coat from the stand, which happened to be her husband's mackintosh that he had hung there at lunchtime, she wrapped it around her shoulders.

As she entered the darkened room, Julia struck a match to see her way to the gas lamp, which she lit. As she bent down to light the gas fire, the visitor turned and bolted the door: if Wallace returned while he was in the house this would buy him precious seconds to flee out the back. The gas fire lit, Julia placed her box of matches by the bay window table, and drew the heavy blinds, as much to keep the warmth in as for privacy. She dragged the piano chair to the sideboard so it was opposite the chaise longue and then invited her guest into the room, directing him to his seat. She plumped up the cushions on the couch and reclined, the mackintosh acting as an improvised shawl.

7:40pm. After some small talk, a deathly silence smothered the conversation. Julia glanced at the man and noticed his large, coarse hands and the cheap signet ring on the ring finger of his right hand. It showed no aesthetic taste, she judged. She also noticed the five o'clock shadow on his chin. On closer examination in the better light, he did not look like someone who typically bought an expensive endowment. Julia began to feel uneasy and suspicious. The situation did not feel right. Something had been troubling her thoughts about the telephone call, but until now she had been unable to give it a definite form or conscious expression.

"Mr Qualtrough, do you know my husband?"

"No, I don't."

"Then why did you ask for him, particularly?"

The visitor had none of Parry's manipulative charm and the question unsettled him. "Um… he was recommended."

"By a friend, I suppose?"

"That's right, yeah."

"I see." Julia frowned and traced a circle with her finger on the fabric of the chaise longue, something she always did when she was thinking carefully. "How did you know to call my husband at his chess club? He only made up his mind to go there not half an hour before he left yesterday night."

The visitor was dumbstruck and decided he had to make his move. His words were exactly as Parry had instructed. "I'm sorry to impose, Mrs Wallace, but can I use the lavatory?" As he expected, Julia directed him to the outside toilet. The man insisted that Julia remain seated by the warmth of the fire. He walked through the cramped kitchen into the musty back room, where he opened and closed the door to give the impression that he had gone outside, and retraced his steps into the kitchen.

The plan was simple: steal the cash, replace the cashbox and return to the parlour so as not to arouse suspicion. After a couple of minutes, he would make his excuses and leave a written note for Mr Wallace. But even the simplest plans often overlook trivial details with important consequences, and this one was no exception. Parry had stressed the need to wear gloves to avoid leaving fingerprints. The accomplice owned none but said he would borrow a pair for the evening, and ended up scrounging the most unsuitable kind imaginable for a burglary.

Once in the kitchen the man took out an old pair of leather mittens from his jacket pocket and quickly moved to the left of the range. With his tall frame, he was able to reach the cashbox on the top shelf, just where Parry said it would be, but handling it with mittens was a different proposition. He lifted the loose lid from the box and was dismayed to find so little inside – a cheque, a postal order, some notes and coins. For a moment he stood stunned, but the shock was soon replaced by a surge of unadulterated anger. Where was the easy ton he had been promised? He desperately needed the money – he had not done all this for a couple of quid.

Still angry, his attempt to scoop out the money wearing mittens was clumsy, bordering on farcical, resulting in a small shower of coins tumbling to the ground. Trying to catch the falling debris, an instinctively outstretched hand accidentally thumped the homemade cabinet that sat above the cupboards. An unhinged door came away and clattered to the floor. Stuffing the miserable haul of notes and coins into one pocket, he replaced the cashbox and hurried back, removing his gloves as he did so.

7.45pm. When he reached the parlour, Julia was sat on the edge of the couch and her demeanour had changed. "What were you doing in my kitchen, Mr Qualtrough?" she demanded. Immediately, the visitor knew Parry's little game was over and he was in trouble. Trying to hide her fear, Julia rose from the couch, adjusted the mackintosh around shoulders, and spoke as assertively as she could. "You will leave now." To make her point, she turned her back, stooping down, and turned off the gas fire.

Parry had unwittingly enlisted the services of a man with a short fuse whose reaction to confrontation invariably involved violence, especially towards women. He wasn't going to be told what to do by her! As Julia straightened up, he lunged forward, his right fist striking the back of her head. The was a small cry, almost a whimper, as she fell across the hearth hitting the floor with a thump. Dazed and partially conscious, she groaned. "Where's the rest of it?" he snarled, his anger at being short-changed erupting like a volcano. As Julia blacked out, her last flicker of consciousness was the smell of alcohol on his breath. In pure rage, he punched her repeatedly, his ring opening scalp wounds. He spied the iron bar lying on the hearth and picked it up. Several blows rained down, blood flicking off the tip of the weapon on the upswing, causing blood spatter on the armchair and wall behind.

7:46pm. He stopped when he smelt the unmistakable tang of acrid burning. Turning to his right he saw smoke billowing from the mackintosh on the fireclays. Instinctively, he moved to extinguish the burning but realised it was trapped under Julia's body. He grabbed her torso, pulling it towards the centre of the room in two lifts, her bloodied head leaving stains on the floor each time. Now accessible, he pulled the mackintosh from the fire and onto the hearth rug where he stamped out the glowing embers in the material. Holding it up to make sure the burning had stopped, a scattering of blackened pieces of fabric were left on the rug by the fire.

He dropped the mackintosh next to Julia and pushed it against her side with his foot. He was unsure whether he had delivered the killer blow, but he could not risk the chance of leaving her alive. Kneeling down, he held the end of the weapon with both hands above her head like a dagger, and then thrust it downward. A gaping wound opened above her left temple and brain matter oozed out like a yolk from a broken egg. It was done.

7:48pm. He wiped the excess blood from the bar with his glove and placed it in his inside jacket pocket; it might prove useful if his exit was blocked by Wallace returning. He wiped his hands on the rug and, placing the gas lamp lever between the knuckles of his index and second finger, turned off the light. The darkness calmed him a little – he was less worried about being seen.

8:30pm. Unnoticed, the small car slowed in Lower Breck Road and turned sharply into the recreation ground, ponderously traversing the gravel to the agreed rendezvous, a mature tree stripped bare by winter. With the engine and headlights cut, the Swift Ten was blanketed by the dark. Parry lowered the window and, in urgent, hushed tones, called for his accomplice. No reply. He casually leaned back and lit a Player No. 3 cigarette, its glowing tip the only sign of his presence in the blackness.

8:35pm. A figure emerged from nowhere, threw open the passenger door and hurriedly slipped into the seat. "At last," Parry growled, flicking his lighted cigarette from the open window.

"Let's get out of here!" There was tension but no alarm in the companion's voice.

"How did it go?"

"You don't wanna know."

"I damn well do! How much did we bag?"

"A few quid. And a cheque for five or something."

"Rubbish!"

"That's all there was in that bloody cashbox. It was just small notes and silver, all right? I left a Yankee bill and some stamps." The man stared at Parry. "Unless you want to go back for them!"

"What are you trying to pull?"

"I'm tellin' yer, that's all there was! Now bloody drive!" Parry anxiously wound up the window and started the engine. Lights on, he turned the car around and headed out the way he entered. As the car bumped over a verge and into Lower Breck Road, he failed to hear the faint thud as the accomplice let the iron bar slip from his sleeve and onto the floor.

As the car sped through the streets of Anfield, Parry smirked at his passenger. "You look awful. Did the doddery old dear frighten you?"

"You could say that."

The reply was stony cold. Parry felt a knot twisting in the pit of his stomach. Something was wrong. He noticed a mark, possibly blood, on his accomplice's right cheek. "Is that a cut on your face?"

His passenger ignored the question, pulling a mitten from his pocket. "There's a couple of things you need to get rid of," he mumbled, placing the mitten in a box on the floor by his feet.

"What things?"

"Just get rid of them. Later tonight, when it's quiet."

"What's going on?" Alarm cut through Parry's voice.

By contrast, his accomplice appeared brutally calm. "We're thieves. We stick together, don't we?"

Parry frowned. "What have you…?"

The man raised his large hand dismissively. "Just drive!"

8:40pm. The solitary car pulled into an anonymous street full of unremarkable terraced houses and parked in the shadows between the diffused halos of two gas lamps. The man flung open the door and heaved his large frame from the seat. Bending over, he peered back inside. "Now get off to your gal's. Stick to the plan." He moved to close the passenger door.

"Hey!" Parry shouted. "Aren't you forgetting something? Where's my cut?"

"You havin' a laugh? Five bloody quid! Just get rid of the stuff like I told yer."

"What do you take me for?" The answer was a slammed door. Parry cursed under his breath. Glancing down at the floor by the passenger seat, he could see a portion of a glove sticking out of the box and, lying next to it, another object which looked like a bar. He surmised that his mate might have taken it with him as a precaution, although he was puzzled why he would be so heavy-handed. It was such a simple job. He was more concerned that he was no richer than at the start of the evening. It had been his plan, yet he had nothing to show for it. After checking his watch, he accelerated away in the car. He would be at Lily's by 9 o'clock, as he had promised.

11:15pm. "Have you heard the news?" Mr Lloyd asked, popping his head round the living room door.

"What?" his daughter asked, looking up.

"There's been some trouble in Anfield. Mrs Wallace has been found dead. You know her, don't you, Gordon?" Parry's insides dissolved. Stunned, he was unable to reply.

"That's dreadful!" Lily exclaimed.

Mr Lloyd continued. "They say Mr Wallace has been arrested for it. Can you believe that? Well, what do they say? Still waters run deep." He grunted. "You can never tell. Well, I'm turning in."

After the door closed, Lily turned to her boyfriend. "Isn't that awful news? Poor Mrs Wallace."

"Yes, really shocking," Parry replied anxiously. He glanced at his watch. "I really must be going," Trying to keep his composure, he stood up. "I'll see myself out." Lily insisted on accompanying him to the door. As usual, there was an affectionate kiss and then a wave when Parry reached his car. As soon as the front door closed, Parry threw open the Swift's passenger door and hurriedly examined the objects his accomplice had left behind. With shaking hands, he lifted the box lid and saw a single mitten stained with a dark substance that Parry feared was blood. He placed it close to his nose. There was a faint, metallic whiff. He picked up the iron bar, and nearly retched. At one end, among the rough grooves lined with rust, there was dried blood stippled with human hair.

11:30pm. His eyes bulging like a man insane with terror, Parry tore down Priory Road and screeched to a halt near to the grille of a drain. With the engine still running, he leaned over and flung open the passenger door. Using it as a shield, he rolled the iron bar down the drain. It was a tight squeeze, but if fell out of sight, far from history's knowing gaze. The glare of headlights of an approaching car made him slam the door shut and drive on. He realised his car had to be cleaned to rid it of any damning evidence, especially blood left on the floor by the bar and even from his accomplice. He cursed, rebuking himself for involving someone else. He sped to Moscow Drive, knowing he could intimidate the fool Pukka into cleaning his Swift. But in his adrenalin-fuelled panic, he forgot about the mitten stuffed in the box.

*

Members of the Cold Case Jury, the Accomplice theory accepts that Gordon Parry was at Olivia Brine's at the time of the murder and was not the killer. It explains why no blood was observed on Parry when he visited his girlfriend's house and Atkinson's Garage, if Parkes is to be believed. Nevertheless, he was very much involved in the crime.

Whether Parry worked alone or with an accomplice, it has been suggested that the phone call was such a flawed plan for a burglary that neither theory is plausible. In particular, how could Parry be certain that Wallace would receive the message, or act on it, or tell Julia about it? It is true there were many ways the scheme could fail, but this argument ignores the possibility that the planner did not care about potential problems so long as there was a chance of success.

All that was required was a failsafe: if Wallace answered the door, the accomplice would make an excuse and leave; if Julia refused to let him in, the plan had failed but at no risk and little cost. This was a scam, not a professional heist, something that could have been devised over a pint in a pub. They were focused on the prize: the easy money in the cashbox. In depression-hit Liverpool it is not difficult to imagine two young men, both desperate for money, concocting this sort of scheme. And for Parry, working with an accomplice eliminated any risk for him.

As the reconstruction showed, this was a distraction burglary that turned deadly. Such thefts are typically perpetrated by two criminals – one to distract the victim, usually preoccupying an elderly person in one room, while another scours the house for valuables under some pretence, such as checking the gas. However, they can also be committed by one individual, and remain a modern scourge. In 2003, a Distraction Burglary Task Force reported on this crime. By talking to convicted felons, it established that the key to a successful distraction burglary is to leave the property without the victim suspecting anything so that the theft is not discovered until hours or even days later. However, such crimes may turn violent (or "naughty" in criminal jargon) if the perpetrators are thwarted by the homeowner, become impatient or are under the influence of drugs or alcohol. In one case, it was found that the criminal had a hatred of old people, which sometimes led to violence.

The reconstruction assumed a simple plan. After gaining entry, the visitor would leave Julia in the parlour, raid the cashbox, return to the front room and, after a few minutes, make an excuse and leave. The crime would only be discovered by Wallace, probably the next day. However, as soon as a noise was made in the kitchen and the cabinet door fell to the floor, everything changed. The accomplice hurried to the parlour hoping that Julia had not heard anything but, when it was obvious she had, a lethal confrontation ensued. Although not necessary for the theory to be true, it was conjectured that the accomplice was misogynistic and under the influence of alcohol.

The reconstruction provides a reason for the bolted front door, which Wallace claimed he found when he admitted PC Williams: the accomplice locked it because he did not want to be disturbed by an early-returning Wallace. There was a substantial risk that Wallace might be on the doorstep as early as 7:25pm if a tram conductor had told him that the Qualtrough address did not exist.

It is a long-held view in the case that Julia was struck when she *turned on* the fire but, if this were the case, the bars of the gas fire would not have reached a sufficient temperature to scorch her skirt. But what if she was attacked as she *turned off* the gas after it had been on for several minutes? The fireclays and the iron surround would have been hot enough to scorch her skirt and smoulder the mackintosh. But wouldn't the visitor have fled rather than pulling the mackintosh free and extinguishing the burning material? The whole point of a distraction burglary is to leave inconspicuously and the thief was unlikely to risk a house fire that would have quickly attracted the attention of alarmed neighbours.

If the theory is correct, Parry met his accomplice between 8:30pm and 9pm, after leaving Olivia Brine's house. In examining Parry's statement for the night of the murder {see Exhibit 11}, it is surprising that he takes a circuitous route to drive from there to his girlfriend's house. A journey of no more than two minutes actually took him half an hour {see Exhibit C}. He claimed he had visited a post office, remembered to collect his accumulator battery for his radio from a store and called on a friend to "chat about a 21st birthday party for about 10 minutes". Unfortunately, there was no police corroboration of any of this with the parties involved. Again, we are left wondering whether this was due to the police's failure to cross-check or a desire to overlook inconvenient truths.

A careful examination of Parry's statement reveals an abrupt change in its style when he discusses this period on the night of the murder – it is far more detailed. We are told nothing about what happened during the three hours he spent at Olivia Brine's, for instance, but for this half-hour period we are given details of no less than three places he claimed to have visited and why he did so. We are even told the brand of cigarettes and the newspaper he bought at the post office. Why was Parry so concerned to account for his movements in such detail during this period?

According to psychologist Richard Wiseman, liars often overcompensate for the truth by providing minutiae on trivial points in their stories. It is far from conclusive, but is Parry's statement an example of this? Stringer believes so, claiming that Parry provided the details to make it appear he was fully accounting for this time period when he was actually meeting up with an accomplice. Parry might have taken a route that took him past the recreation ground {see Exhibit C}. Stringer believes this to be significant because, even today, if you visit there at night, it is unlit and pitch black. Ideal conditions, one would imagine, for a clandestine rendezvous with someone walking the 300 yards from Wolverton Street.

An interesting fact of the burglary is that not a penny of the Wallaces' personal cash was taken, even though Julia had over £1 in her handbag sitting on the kitchen chair. Does this suggest that the intention was always to steal only from the Prudential? It is alleged Parry was in financial difficulties and was asking former colleagues for a loan of money {see Exhibit 10}. Could it be that Parry, in desperate need and possibly bearing a grudge against his former employer, knew where he could get his hands on some company cash? Did he convince himself that, as he was not stealing directly from the Wallaces, it was somehow all right?

Like every theory we have examined, this one is not perfect. One source of doubt is that Parry's plan would have allowed Julia to describe the thief to the police. But in an era before identikits, which would not be used in Britain until decades later, suspect descriptions were rarely effective. Perhaps Parry surmised that, so long as the accomplice was not known to the Wallaces, the chances of the police questioning him would be slim. It should also be pointed out that distraction burglaries occur even today with far better surveillance and communication methods – it is an inherent risk of the job.

When noise was made in the kitchen, why did the accomplice not flee through the back door? It would have been an instinctive reaction, yet he returned to the parlour to see if Julia had heard anything. The plan was to leave without Julia knowing she had been robbed, allowing plenty of time before the crime was discovered, possibly as late as the following afternoon. This is an important factor in distraction burglaries, and it also provided the accomplice with a defence if he was ever apprehended: there was no evidence that the money was stolen while he was actually there. However, with the cabinet door and coins lying on the kitchen floor, this defence was destroyed and perhaps the best course of action was to get out quickly.

Florence Johnston heard a knock on the Wallaces' back door at 8:45pm – this was Wallace returning from his futile task. Walter Holme, the other next-door neighbour, believed he heard the Wallaces' front door closing at about 6:35pm. Yet, no one heard a knock or a door closing between these two times when Mr Qualtrough is alleged to have called. Is the lack of aural evidence suggestive that there was no visitor that night? On the other hand, neither neighbour heard Wallace leave by his back door or gate at 6:45pm. Also, neither heard a thump or vibration on the floorboards between 6:45pm and 7:45pm, the most likely time of the attack.

There is yet another puzzle. Why did the accomplice turn off the gas lamp in the parlour? Surely, the instinct of a killer would be to leave the scene of the crime as soon as possible. He might have wanted to ensure it was impossible to see the body from the street, only a few feet from the parlour window, yet the heavy blinds were already drawn. The gas lamp in the kitchen was also extinguished, which is even harder to explain, especially as the cabinet door and coins were left on the floor. Not only did the killer have the presence of mind to turn off the gas lamps in two rooms, he did so without leaving behind fingerprints or bloodstains.

The Accomplice theory explains the phone call, the bolted door and Parry's state of "insanity" at the garage, if Parkes' account is to be believed. However, it fails to answer the biggest question of all: who was the killer? Stringer believes his identity will never be known, but has strong suspicions of a friend of Parry's who lived near his claimed driving route on the night of the murder, but without further evidence it would be inappropriate to publish the name. However, it could have been any acquaintance of his, especially one easily moved to violence.

Although Wallace accepted that Julia might have admitted Qualtrough because she was aware of the message, he believed she knew her killer. When he visited a customer a week after the murder he remarked that Julia was killed by a friend because "she never allowed a stranger over the doorstep". "It was a friend of yours?" the customer queried, shocked. "No," replied Wallace firmly, "a friend of my wife."

If the young, dashing Gordon Parry was Julia's friend, just how friendly were they? And did she have other young male friends? According to the next theory, she did. And it led to her murder.

9. CONNECTED PAWNS

In chess, a diagonal line of adjacent pawns is a strong defence; they protect each other, and often other pieces as well. In our fifth scenario, based on the claims of John Gannon in *The Killing of Julia Wallace*, the murder is the result of a conspiracy orchestrated by William Wallace. It introduces a fourth suspect.

When Wallace gave his second statement to the police, the only other person he detailed was Joseph Marsden, a friend of Gordon Parry. Marsden had worked for the Prudential for several years until 1928, when he left due to alleged financial irregularities. He worked Wallace's round for a couple of days during his bout of illness in early 1929, after a recommendation from Parry. According to Wallace, Marsden knew the location of his collection box and Julia would have asked him inside had he called at his house while Wallace was out. Marsden's time at the Prudential might be significant: one of his clients was a joiner named Mr R J Qualtrough. Although this is the only known connection between the name used by the caller and a suspect in the case, it appears no official statement was taken from him.

According to John Gannon, at the time of the Wallace murder Joseph Marsden was working as a bookmakers' clerk in Birkenhead, a shipbuilding town on the west bank of the Mersey, and he was engaged to Sylvia Taylor. The two were connected: on marrying Sylvia, his employer would become his brother-in-law. Working as part of a family business, he expected to do well. During the engagement, therefore, Marsden had a strong but breakable connection to an influential and wealthy family. It is safe to assume that he would have been keen to avoid severing this tie, especially as a break-up might have also affected his career.

The core of Gannon's theory is that Wallace wanted to rid himself of Julia. In the 1930s, a contested divorce was difficult, protracted and expensive. Knowing his kidney illness was terminal, having been informed as such by doctors only six months previously, murder was Wallace's only option if he wanted to live his final years free from the prison of marriage. He coerced Parry and Marsden into executing his plan: Parry to make the call, giving Wallace his alibi, and Marsden to kill his wife. How he blackmailed the young men will be explained a little later.

On Monday 19 January 1931, after making the telephone call to the chess club, Parry told Julia that her friend Marsden – with whom she was illicitly involved – would be visiting her the following night. The plan was all set. We move on to 8pm on Tuesday 20 January 1931.

*

As the overhead train halted at Breck Road Station, the ear-piercing scream of its brakes did nothing to calm the nerves of the solemn man wearing a dark overcoat. Passengers busily exited and entered the carriage, but Joseph Marsden remained fixed in his seat, fidgeting with his cap. He just wanted to go home, but could not risk losing his beloved fiancée to the filthy rumours that Wallace had threatened to unleash. The last thing he wanted was for the bitter old man to start divorce proceedings, citing him and Parry as the grounds for the irretrievable breakdown of his marriage. A sickeningly smug Wallace had told them that a Liverpool solicitor possessed documents that revealed everything. So, if anything should happen to him, it would all come out anyway. Marsden was cornered, like a rat.

There was another scream, this time from a guard's whistle. Jolted from his brooding, the young man put on his cap and left the carriage. He crossed the platform and slowly moved down the steps from the overhead railway to the road below, which was etched with tramlines. He paused by the iron-clad bridge that carried the railway above Townsend Lane. Like spotlights, the beams of passing cars illuminated the large advert for Walker's Falstaff Ale on the side of the bridge. Doubts and anxieties pecked at his conscience like a murder of crows. He knew he could still turn back, but instead he forced himself on, walking slowly down busy Townsend Lane. If he did something, and thought less, he could cope.

After 15 minutes he passed the telephone kiosk at the end of Lower Breck Road, where he knew Parry had made his call the previous night. Five more minutes and he had reached Richmond Park and the entry that connected the road to Wolverton Street. In the blackness, he hesitated again. It was not too late to abort the venture, but he thought of Sylvia. He would do anything for her. Anything. His doubts finally dispelled, Marsden strode to the back gate of No. 29. As he had expected, it was unbolted. He boldly walked through the yard to the back door. He paused. Breathing in deeply, he summoned all his resolve. This was it.

8:25pm. Julia answered his knock, the door opening cautiously. "Joseph," she gushed, her face lighting up in rare a moment of surprise and delight. "I was expecting you a little earlier."

"Sorry, the train was a bit late," he replied, his mouth dry.

"Never mind, we still have time." Julia flung open the door and Marsden was ushered into the back kitchen, where the crockery from tea was stacked, unwashed. "I haven't washed up. I've been busy making other preparations." Her eyes scanned the features of the young man. "Is everything all right? You look tense, dear."

"I'm fine," Marsden replied.

"Let's go into the parlour." She led her visitor through the kitchen and into the dimly lit hall. "Take off your coat and gloves, won't you?" Entering the parlour, which was illuminated by the amber glow of a single gas lamp, Julia stood before the fireplace. As planned, Marsden removed the mackintosh from the coat stand, spreading it out like a net.

Like a *retiarius* entering the Coliseum, he strode into the parlour. He lunged at her, forcing the coat over her head. Her frail body buckled, cowering like a trapped animal. He picked up the iron bar standing on the hearth – exactly in the position he was told it would be – and brought it down on her head with a sickening crack. Julia's body crumpled into a twisted heap, her left side slumped across the red-hot fireclays. He tugged at the body, pulling it free of the fire, her head resting near the armchair. During her fall the raincoat had slipped from her head. As he hit her several times, blood flicked onto the violin case resting on the armchair and on the walls behind.

He noticed an acrid smell, the unmistakable stench of burning. The bottom of the mackintosh had draped into the fire and was alight. He threw it onto the hearth rug and stamped out the flames. Next door, Florence Johnston heard two thuds. Thinking it was her father clumsily removing his boots in her parlour, she finished cleaning the kitchen table.

There was a soft, almost imperceptible, sigh. Was that Julia's last breath, or was she still alive? Marsden rolled Julia's body further into the centre of the room. He hesitated. The floor had vibrated loudly with each stamp of his boot. Seeing the mackintosh, he rolled it up and tried to stuff it under Julia's bloodied head to muffle any further sounds. Lifting the bar high above his head, he brought it down with such force that it cleaved open Julia's skull above her left ear. Two more blows, forcing blood and brain matter to ooze onto the floor. The job was done. It had taken less than a minute to end her life.

He wiped his hands and the soles of his boots on the rug. He patted his back pocket, expecting to find a heavy rag that he had stuffed there, but it was gone. Had it fallen from his pocket as he walked from the station? He was in a panic – it was supposed to wrap up the bar and his gloves, so as not to stain his clothes with blood. He had to improvise. He frantically looked around the room. Seeing a pair of Julia's mittens on the dresser, he picked up one and wiped the blood from the bar, which he then placed in the inside pocket of his jacket. He folded the bloodied mitten and stuffed it inside his coat pocket. He would dispose of it later. He skirted around the body and headed to the kitchen.

8:30pm. Marsden continued to follow the plan, but had to improvise without the rag. He took a sheet of old newspaper lying on the bookcase and wrapped his bloodied gloves in it, stuffing the package into his coat pocket. He had to make it look like a robbery, but nothing too obvious. He calmly walked over to the homemade cabinet that sat on the bottom shelf of the bookcase. One of its doors was damaged, Wallace had informed him. He gently hit the door with his fist and a piece fell away onto the floor.

He removed the cashbox from the top shelf, and brought it to the table. There were only a few notes and coins inside. He had been promised a far larger bonus for doing all the dirty work. Cursing, he now forgot the plan. Rather than discarding the cashbox on the floor, he put it back.

A few hundred yards away, a car slowed and came to a halt in Lower Breck Road. The engine idled noisily for a few seconds before it was cut, the headlights fading. A man stepped out of the car and walked a few yards before turning into Hanwell Street.

8:35pm. Marsden reached the end of the entry, where it emptied into Richmond Park, and stopped. As expected, a tall man wearing an overcoat and bowler hat was standing in the shadows on the other side of the road. Marsden approached the motionless figure.

"She's finished," he whispered.

"Did you take the money?" Wallace asked softly.

"What, the measly four quid?" Marsden spat with utter contempt. "Is that my bonus? Four bloody quid? I've gotta good mind..."

"I was laid up ill," Wallace interjected. "That's why the takings are not as much as usual."

"I want the money I was promised," Marsden said venomously.

"I only promised what was left in the box. What Parry told you is between you and him."

"I want..."

"You're in no position to bargain," Wallace said with a resolve of tempered steel. "How did you leave the parlour?"

Marsden looked at the older man with angry incredulity. "It's a bit of a bloody mess, to be honest!" he hissed. "What do you expect? A spring clean as well?"

"I didn't mean that," Wallace said firmly. "Did you leave anything on?"

"I turned off the fire, but had to leave the parlour lamp on to see my way out."

"All right, I'll see to that."

"And I might have..." The conversation halted as the sound of clicking heels grew louder. On the other side of the pavement a woman walked by. After passing the two men, she crossed the road and continued on her way.

"Do you know that woman?" Marsden asked with almost inaudible softness.

"I don't think so."

"She's just looked over her shoulder at us. Why would she do that?"

"I don't know," Wallace replied. "Keep your nerve, Marsden."

"That's it. I'm out of here," Marsden said. "And I never want to hear from you again. *Never*."

Wallace watched impassively as his wife's killer turned and headed down Richmond Park. Unnerved by the presence of the pedestrian, Wallace darted across the road and disappeared into the entry opposite. He walked calmly and slowly into Wolverton Street and headed for his front door.

8:40pm. As Marsden turned into Hanwell Street, a man emerged from the shadows. "All done?"

Marsden nearly collapsed with terror. "Bloody Norah, you gave me a fright, Parry!"

Parry pulled Marsden back into the shadows. "You're trembling like a leaf," he said.

"I can't think why," Marsden replied sarcastically.

"So?"

Marsden nodded. "She's sung her last duet, but the tight old bastard only left four quid in the box."

"Four readies!" Parry exclaimed loudly.

"You said there would be at least a ton."

"The monthly collection is always sixty to…"

"A hundred-quid bonus for getting wet, you said. You've both been playing me for a bloody fool."

There were some voices nearby. Then a shout. "God, they haven't found her already, have they?" Marsden asked in panic. "Let's get out of here!" He bolted down the street. Parry sped after him. Panting, the two accomplices reached the car, flung open the doors and bundled themselves inside.

After their breathing calmed, Parry asked: "Where's the iron bar? Did you remember to take it with you?" Marsden pulled open his lapel and showed the top of the blood-streaked tool poking out of his inside coat pocket.

"It's supposed to be clean!"

"I did my best," Marsden served back defensively. "I couldn't find my rag – it must have fallen out of my back pocket on the train. I checked the house – it definitely wasn't there." Marsden pulled out the bloodied mitten. "I wiped it with this instead."

Parry nearly fainted in utter disbelief. "Jesus! That'll send us to the bloody gallows! What were you thinking?"

"But the plan was to clean…"

"So as not to stain your clothes, you idiot! What do you think that mitten has done to your coat pocket, huh? And it connects you to the scene."

"Connects *us*, don't you mean?" Marsden angrily reminded him.

"Well, we've got to get rid of everything, right now!"

Parry climbed out of the car and crossed the road. Marsden sheepishly traipsed behind his younger but more able friend. They both walked along the pavement as nonchalantly as they could. "Down there!" Parry whispered, nodding to the ground. Marsden stepped over the grate while Parry shielded him from the curious gaze of anyone afar. "Wait," Parry instructed, as a car drove past. "The coast's clear." Marsden slid the bar from his inside pocket and, his arm dropping to his side, it dangled above the grille. He let go. There was a reverberating clunk as gravity pulled the iron bar out of history's sight.

"What about the mitt?" Marsden asked quietly. "Shall I sling it too?"

Parry hesitated. "No, wait! I think someone's coming." A pedestrian emerged from one of the side streets that spilled into the main road. "I'll get rid of it later. Let's get outta here now!"

*

Members of the Cold Case Jury, when François Courvoisier slashed Lord Russell's throat with a knife, he placed a towel over the aristocrat's head to minimise the quantity of blood that sprayed onto his naked body. This reconstruction follows John Gannon's account in proposing that the mackintosh was used by the murderer of Julia Wallace in a similar way, placing it over her head when the first blow was struck. This would also have the benefit of smothering any of Julia's cries. It would have been an extremely effective method of avoiding blood transfer to the attacker but no hair or brain matter was found on the mackintosh as would be expected had it been used like this. Further, the blood spatter on the walls shows us that, if it was used at all, it was for only the first blow, suggesting that the killer was unconcerned about his clothes becoming bloodstained.

This theory has echoes of the Accomplice theory. It explains why Parry lied as to his whereabouts at the time of the telephone call to the chess club but had an alibi for the night of the murder: he was the caller, not the killer. It conjectures that Marsden was picked up during the half-hour period after Parry left Olivia Brine's. The similarities end there, however. Gannon's Conspiracy theory interprets Wallace's suspicious behaviour on the night of the murder as an attempt to establish an alibi because he was a blackmailer who organised his wife's execution.

Two new pieces of evidence were introduced in this reconstruction, and each also lends some support to Gannon's theory. Lily Hall, a young typist who claimed to have known Wallace by sight for three years, came forward a few days after the murder. She told the police that she had been walking down Richmond Park at about 8:35pm when she saw Wallace in conversation with another man, who she described as about five feet eight inches tall, stocky, wearing a cap and dark overcoat. When she first saw the two men they were 30 yards away on the opposite pavement, Wallace facing her, the other man with his back to her. She passed them, crossed the road, and then saw the men part company. Significantly, Lily Hall claimed she recognised Wallace, which is typically far more reliable than identifying a stranger. However, it was a dark, moonless night and the men were not standing directly under a gas lamp, which only provided good lighting in its immediate vicinity.

Hall said she saw the two men part after she passed them, so she must have looked over her shoulder. It was never ascertained why she took such an interest in the men as she hurried home to ready herself for a trip to the cinema later that night. She also stated that, as they parted, one headed down Richmond Park. If the other man was Wallace we would expect Hall to see him cross the road and disappear into the entry leading to Wolverton Street {see Exhibit A}. Although there was confusion concerning Hall's testimony at the trial on this matter, it appears Hall observed both men walking away from Wolverton Street, suggesting neither was Wallace {see Exhibit 15}.

At his trial, Wallace denied speaking to anyone on his walk home. Clearly, either Lily Hall was mistaken or Wallace was lying. One reason for Wallace to lie was to protect the identity of a conspirator. Yet, surely it would have been reckless for Wallace and his hitman to meet immediately after the murder in a public place so close to the scene. It is hard to understand the advantage in this rendezvous when it had to outweigh considerable risks – such as being observed. And if no such meeting occurred, and Lily Hall was mistaken, it removes a significant piece of evidence supporting the Conspiracy theory.

There was another sighting of a stocky man just minutes after Hall's and almost at the same place. Harry Greenlees stated that about 8:40pm he was stopped near his house in Richmond Park by a man asking for directions. Curiously, the stranger was searching for a non-existent address, just like Wallace. Greenlees knew both Hall and Wallace by sight and saw neither of them {see Exhibit 15}.

Florence Johnston told the police, "I did not hear any sound from the Wallaces' house until about 8:25pm to 8:30pm. I was then in my kitchen and I heard two thumps, which I thought was my father in my front parlour taking off his boots." She had clearly heard some sounds from the front (recall that the kitchen is situated behind the front parlour). The sounds were loud enough for her to believe they had emanated from her house and they were the only unusual noises she heard that night {see Exhibit 13}. This raises an important question. Could Julia have been bludgeoned to death in her parlour without any sound being heard by a next-door neighbour? If you think not, then this aural evidence might suggest that the time of death was far later than the police thought, which would clear Wallace of the actual act of murder but not his involvement in it. Indeed, it seems implausible to suggest that a killer, after luring Wallace away, would have waited over an hour-and-a-half before committing his crime unless he was well aware of the time that Wallace was due back.

Gannon's theory is an imaginative joining of the evidential dots. It is consistent with many of the key points in the case:

• Assuming his alibi for the night of the murder is sound, Parry could not have killed Julia Wallace.

• Parry is a prime suspect for making the Qualtrough call.

• Assuming the milk boy called at 6:45pm, Wallace had insufficient time to commit the murder himself.

• Marsden was one of a small number of people whom Julia would have let inside her house in Wallace's absence, at least according to Wallace.

• Neighbour Mrs Johnston heard two unusual thumps a little before 8:30pm.

• If Lily Hall was correct, Wallace talked to a man shortly before he arrived home.

• According to John Parkes, Parry had his car cleaned later that evening and a bloodstained mitten was retrieved from it.

153

Gannon accepts at face value the statements made by Olivia Brine, Lily Hall and John Parkes. He interprets Wallace's quest for Qualtrough as an attempt to establish an alibi. Using these as his rock, he sculpts a coherent picture of a conspiracy. But is it plausible?

One question springs to mind immediately. How would Wallace have been able to coerce, not one, but two young men into a murder conspiracy? Gannon believes it was a secret that the two men were desperate to hide and which Wallace exploited as blackmail. This leads to an extraordinary claim. He speculates that Julia was paying the cash-strapped men for sex. This would be consistent with the money in the corset pocket, he argues, allowing either young man to recover his payment covertly during the sexual act. Similarly, the homemade diaper was a convenient and cheap method of post-coital hygiene, easily slipped off and replaced.

Such speculation is controversial, to say the least. Would a diffident woman, a few months shy of her 70th birthday, have been so preoccupied with sex as to pay for it? It should be remembered that Julia Wallace was born in the first half of Queen Victoria's reign, a misogynistic age in which women were not expected to express themselves sexually. Almost certainly, the money in her handbag was for housekeeping and the cash in the corset was more likely her private stash, concealed from her penny-pinching and controlling husband who would have probably found it otherwise. To make a further inference that it was hidden because of sex is unwarranted. Further, given her age, would not a homemade diaper be more likely to be used for incontinence?

Gannon conjectures further that Wallace told the two men that they would be named in his divorce proceedings unless Julia could be eliminated in some other way. There is no evidence that Wallace was considering divorce, but he may have used it as a ruse to ensnare his accomplices. Marsden, who was engaged to be married into a wealthy family, was fearful of exposure and ridicule, and was easy to blackmail, suggests Gannon. Similarly, Parry would most likely have been ostracised by his father and had much to lose. In short, the men were coerced into killing Julia Wallace in return for Wallace's silence.

According to this theory, Marsden was given a particularly raw deal. By his association with a customer called Qualtrough he was connected to the telephone call and he had no secure alibi for the time of the murder. Indeed, Marsden told the police he was in bed with the flu at the time of the killing, which was never confirmed. He must have been truly desperate to agree to such a scheme.

There are other questions. Why would Wallace volunteer the names of his accomplices to the police? Gannon argues that their names would have cropped up when former Prudential employees were questioned by police, and Wallace named his co-conspirators to allay suspicion. But does this explanation stand up to scrutiny? By providing no less than 10 paragraphs of information on Parry and Marsden in his second statement, with the majority devoted to Parry, Wallace was not allaying suspicion but leading the police right to his alleged conspirators. Even more inexplicably, he knew that Marsden could not possibly have an alibi for the night of the murder. Drawing attention to his collaborators in this manner was only likely to result in a trip to the gallows for them all.

Another issue is the timing of the crime. Wallace had a perfect alibi while he was at the chess club on the Monday night. Surely, that was the ideal opportunity to eliminate his wife. Marsden's visit would have been unexpected but, if Wallace is to be believed, he was one of the few people Julia would have let into the house. If there was no problem with Marsden entering the house and Wallace had a perfect alibi for the Monday, why was the telephone call necessary? Indeed, why involve Parry at all? These are important questions because explaining the telephone call is central to resolving the case.

Conspiracy theories make great stories, and this one is no exception. But was the cautious, controlling and obsessive Wallace likely to involve others in a plot to kill his wife? Would he not have sooner poisoned his wife or found some other way of implementing the perfect murder on his own? Apart from an alleged conversation with an unknown man shortly before arriving home, all of Wallace's other suspicious behaviours are consistent with him acting alone or as the result of a prank call.

Of all the theories we have examined, arguably Gannon's conspiracy theory is consistent with the largest amount of testimony taken at face value, but consistency is not the only criterion of a good theory. It also needs to explain plausibly the key features of the case while minimising the number of speculative assumptions. You should also be mindful that murder conspiracies are rare, especially ones involving coerced parties. Furthermore, a strong theory will have critical evidence that uniquely supports it. In this case, the suspicion of conspiracy rests largely on the observation of Lily Hall – whether it can bear the weight of the theory it is being asked to support is for you to decide. It is examined in more detail later {see Exhibit 15}.

Three of the theories (Wallace, Prank and Conspiracy) hold that Wallace wanted his wife dead, two (Parry and Accomplice) reject this view. To even it up, our last theory also suggests Wallace had no involvement in his wife's murder.

10. DISGUISED KING

In the "Disguised King" chess variant, the king plays as a pawn and each player secretly selects one pawn as the king. This "royal pawn" obeys all the usual rules for the king, e.g. it cannot be captured without the game ending, and is identified by a mark on its base or simply by checking the notation at the end of play. This is an appropriate metaphor for our final theory. While every writer scrutinises the behaviour of William Wallace and Gordon Parry, they overlook the unassuming suspect in plain sight: next-door neighbour John Johnston.

The Neighbour theory is controversial, not least because of its origin. In his book, *Merseyside Murders* (2021), Tom Slemen claims that, in the early 1960s, John Johnston confessed to the murder of Julia Wallace. Johnston was suffering from dementia and seemingly told only one person of his crime on his deathbed – a mysterious character named only as Stan. Forty years later, after hearing a radio broadcast about the case, a seriously-ill Stan tells a criminologist about the confession; why the shadowy Stan waited four decades to tell his tale is not revealed. Clearly, in light of these facts, the "confession" has no evidential weight whatsoever. However, I suggest we ignore its dubious source and briefly examine the theory at face value like every other.

The possibility that the culprit was a neighbour was raised at the time of the murder. After Wallace's trial, the police received a letter suggesting that the weapon was not found because it "was taken to a nearby home". Wallace's solicitor also received a signed letter from a different source, who claimed:

The evidence of the Johnstons seems to have been taken by the police without very much question… I think there should have been a closer investigation of those who were first in the house… According to the evidence, it appears just as suspicious for the next-door neighbour, before knowing that anything very serious was the matter, to have so carefully noted the exact movements of Wallace when he was able to gain admittance. Then again, was it not stated in evidence that when Wallace had to admit the police, he had to withdraw the bolt but this Mrs Johnston did not notice.

More pertinently, the writer might have questioned the coincidental meeting between the neighbours in the entry that night. Those who believe Wallace guilty suggest this was a ruse so that there would be a witness to the discovery of the body, but what if we turn the tables? Could it have been a ruse by the Johnstons instead? Did they contrive to bump into Wallace because they wanted to revisit the scene and make sure they had left no incriminating evidence? This is what Slemen believes. His account can be summarised as follows:

• John Johnston was the "Anfield Burglar", responsible for several break-ins in the neighbourhood using a skeleton or duplicate key.

• He made the call to the chess club to lure Wallace away. He knew the Mossley Hill area because a close friend lived at Menlove Gardens West.

• The Johnstons saw William and Julia leave their back yard and believed they were going out together. Julia was wearing a mackintosh and was in fact looking for her missing cat.

• Not seeing Julia return, they nipped into the back of No. 29, raided the insurance money and jemmied open the cabinet.

• Disappointed with the takings they went to the parlour, where flu-stricken Julia was lying on the chaise longue with the mackintosh over her. In panic, John Johnston realised she could now reveal the identity of the Anfield Burglar. As she rose from the chaise longue, he clubbed her with the jemmy.

• The jemmy was taken back to No. 31 and explains why the murder weapon was never identified let alone found.

• The Johnstons intercepted William Wallace on his return to gain access to the crime scene and provide a defence if their fingerprints were discovered.

Slemen points to two postcards sent to Florence Johnston by Julia Wallace when she and William were holidaying in Wales on separate occasions in the late 1920s. He believes Florence was more familiar with her neighbours than she stated at the trial and this, he claims, is suspicious. Further, he believes Florence did not appear shocked by the sight of Julia's dead body and asked peculiar questions. In particular, she seemed anxious to learn more about the box of matches on the table by the chaise longue, asking Wallace if they belonged to Julia, and coldly queried what murder weapon was used. Why would anyone ask such questions with the body of her neighbour sprawled on the floor? Could the matches have belonged to Florence, who inadvertently left them in the parlour after the murder? Slemen thinks so.

Having been told by Wallace that he could not open the back door, John Johnston remarked, "That's funny, try it again and I'll wait" {see Exhibit 13}. Why did he think it was odd? For all he knew, Julia might have always locked it at night. When Wallace rushed outside and informed them that his wife had been killed, rather than being taken aback at Julia's death, he asks a question about how she died: "Has she fallen downstairs?" Perhaps the most important point raised by Slemen is one we have touched on before: if someone else killed Julia, surely the Johnstons would have heard something? The two terrace houses were separated only by a party wall – it was certainly not soundproof. The Johnstons heard Wallace knock on the back door but did not hear Julia fall in the parlour or the cabinet door crash to the ground in the kitchen. According to Slemen, this is because they were actually next door perpetrating the crime.

What can we say of this account? Let's start with the last point. As we discovered in the previous chapter, Florence actually told police that she heard two thuds at about 8:25pm. It is possible that she did overhear the assault, perhaps when Julia fell, weakening one of the planks of the Neighbour theory. Of course, this might have been misdirection by Florence, trying to confuse the police about the real time of the murder. However, no noises or vibrations were noticed by the other next-door neighbours, Mr and Mrs Holme at No. 27. So whoever killed Julia, they did so without the Holmes hearing anything unusual.

What about the Johnstons' behaviour at the crime scene? People often do peculiar things in difficult situations, and they do not come more stressful than a death. What would you say in a similar situation? And how do you know that your reaction would be typical? If anything, you might consider the demeanours of both John and Florence to be too calm and considered to have bludgeoned Julia to death earlier that evening.

The key assertions of the Neighbour theory have little evidential support and, in some cases, contradict fact. For example, there was no need to jemmy the cabinet door – the doors were attached by hooks, the top half repaired after being broken previously. In fact, if Johnston was using a duplicate or skeleton key, there was no need for him to bring a jemmy at all. The theory also raises many questions. Why did Julia retire to the chaise longue in the cold parlour rather than to her comfy chair in the warm kitchen? Perhaps she wanted to lie down, but a close scrutiny of the police photograph of the kitchen reveals another chaise longue behind her chair, making her decision to go to the parlour even less plausible. How did John Johnston know about the cashbox? Even if we assume that the two couples were closer than previously believed, it is difficult to see why Julia would have told Florence about her husband's business, especially the cashbox. Indeed, Wallace never mentioned that any of his neighbours knew of it. Perhaps the Johnstons discovered it when they were looking after the house while the Wallaces were on holiday but, even if that is true, they inexplicably waited several years before getting their hands on its contents. And, perhaps most pertinently, there is absolutely no evidence that the employed John Johnston was a burglar, let alone a serial one. Certainly, he was not an accomplished thief because he missed the easy pickings in Julia's handbag, which was practically in plain sight.

According to the shadowy Stan, the Johnstons had originally planned a distraction burglary. They had purloined Julia's cat and Florence was to distract Julia, perhaps by bringing the cat to the front door, giving her husband a few minutes to enter the property at the back. This neatly explains the disappearance of Julia's cat, Puss. Given that Johnston died in the early 1960s, before this fact was made public by author Jonathan Goodman, this seemingly adds *prima facie* credibility to the account. However, Slemen provides no evidence that Stan actually talked to John Johnston in the early 1960s (apart from stating the care home in which he died, something any acquaintance might have known). Indeed, given that Stan came forward three decades after Goodman's book was published, the relevant information was in the public domain.

Indeed, there is little in this account that could not have been devised by someone with a good knowledge of the case, apart from one interesting aspect: the position of Julia when she was attacked. For decades, the prevailing opinion on this matter – possibly the only opinion – was MacFall's suggestion that Julia was attacked while she sat in the armchair. However, the Neighbour theory suggests Julia was attacked as she rose from the chaise longue, which is consistent with modern forensic views {see Exhibit 5}. However, this potentially corroborating evidence must be evaluated alongside opposing facts, the most problematic of which is the Qualtrough call.

If John Johnston entered the phone box on the Monday night must have known Wallace was on his way to the chess club and Julia was home alone. So why did he rush to a phone box hoping to produce identical circumstances for the following night when he could have struck right then? It makes little sense. Further, if he was responsible for a string of burglaries in the area, the call was entirely out of keeping with the opportunism of the others. The mystery call is the defining characteristic of the case, yet it is reduced to just one line in this account: the dying John Johnston told Stan he was the caller. The lack of any explanation on this point, in addition to its dubious source, surely weighs heavily against the theory's plausibility.

Stan's account lacks coherence with key facts of the case, but we should not lose sight of the fact that a murder victim is far more likely to be killed by someone they know. The theory also explains the appearance of a visitor in the parlour and accounts for the presence of the mackintosh and the absence of a weapon, which was presumably taken away and hidden next door until it could be disposed at a later time. Yet, without a stronger foundation for the claim that John

162

Johnston was a serial burglar, there is no apparent motive. And although the neighbours certainly had opportunity, this is woefully insufficient in itself, not least because they could have burgled the next-door house almost at any time. Too much opportunity is sometimes as problematic as too little. Finally, for heat-of-the-moment killers they were extremely cool and collected. Indeed, their behaviour after Wallace returned to find his wife dead would be worthy of performance art.

Members of the Cold Case Jury, you have been presented with six different theories as to how Julia Wallace might have been murdered. Three assume Wallace was innocent, three claim he was involved. If your head is spinning with all the evidence and permutations, do not worry – later I will review everything and you will also be able to examine key evidence for yourselves. For now, let us see how this unprecedented drama concluded in 1931.

11. THE END GAME

William Wallace was in the frame for murder as soon as Superintendent Moore walked into the parlour that Tuesday night. Keen to prove his mettle, his sole objective was a quick and successful conviction. Rather than spreading the net widely to trawl for all possible suspects, it appears that Moore was simply looking for anything that would confirm his preconceived view. This is not to say that his view was incorrect but, had greater attention been paid to Parry and Marsden, who were named as potential suspects by Wallace almost from the outset, any doubt surrounding the murder might have been dispelled. If we knew where Parry was on the night of the Qualtrough call, and also had cast-iron confidence in his alibi for the night of the murder, we might be able to rule him out from having any involvement in the crime.

At 7pm on Monday 2 February 1931 the inevitable happened: William Wallace was arrested for the murder of his wife. On being arrested, Wallace said, "What can I say in answer to a charge of which I am absolutely innocent?"

The next morning, Wallace appeared before a magistrate in the police court. In outlining the case against the defendant, the prosecuting solicitor made over a dozen errors of fact. Wallace, remanded in custody, selected Hector Munro as his solicitor. Munro was also a member of the Liverpool Central Chess Club. On Thursday 19 February the committal proceedings commenced. The committal determines whether, in the opinion of a magistrate, there is sufficient evidence that a jury could find the defendant guilty. If there is, the defendant is sent for trial.

Munro knew that timing was key to the defence of his client, and interviewed the friends of Alan Close, the milk boy. Before the committal proceedings had finished, Munro spoke to James Wildman, the paperboy who claimed that he saw Close on the Wallace doorstep at a little before 6:40pm. This was the first time that Wildman had been interviewed. The police had not taken his statement as he was not one of the youths who had spoken to Alan Close about the Wallace murder. It was the ever-alert Douglas Metcalf, the other paperboy in the vicinity, who had later spoken to Wildman and realised that his observations were significant. The police subsequently interviewed Wildman but disbelieved his timing, although it was cued by the same church clock used by Alan Close, whose revised timing was accepted.

William Wallace was duly committed for trial, to be heard before Mr Justice Wright in St George's Hall, Liverpool. The trial began at 10am on Wednesday 22 April 1931. After a virtuoso opening speech by the prosecution barrister, Edward Hemmerde, the verdict was almost a foregone conclusion by lunchtime. He painted a picture of guilt with such broad brushstrokes that the finer details of the truth were obscured: "You start here with a case of a woman who had no enemies in the world; you start here with a case where there is no suggestion that anyone could have thought there would be much money in the house, and where not much money was taken; and apparently the person who committed the murder handled the notes in the middle bedroom because there is blood upon them. Therefore, surely it is incredible that money had anything whatever to do with this ghastly tragedy. And when you eliminate money, what are you left with? That someone did this woman to death in that room almost certainly wearing a raincoat and tried to destroy that raincoat. Who would have an interest in destroying it? The person who has done this deed takes upstairs some bloody trace of his deed – of this woman's blood – why should a thief, why should someone have come into that house, and wanting to wash, have not used the running water in the kitchen?"

The prosecution fallaciously assumed that the murderer had touched the treasury notes in the middle bedroom. Yet, according to Florence Johnston's testimony, Wallace had touched his wife's bloodied body before he checked if anything had been stolen upstairs. When he returned, he specifically mentioned that the £5 had not been taken, and Wallace testified that he had probably handled the treasury notes.

The prosecution also suggested that Wallace had tried to destroy the mackintosh in the gas fire, and that only he would have gone upstairs to clean himself. Yet it was ludicrous to suggest that Wallace deliberately set fire to the mackintosh: a gas fire was never capable of destroying the evidence. And the prosecution assumed that the murderer had been in the bathroom, but the only evidence of this was the single clot on the toilet pan, which could have been transferred by an official during the police investigation. In fact, it was never even demonstrated that it was Julia's blood, yet such rhetoric made a strong impression on everyone in the court.

Despite the prosecution's focus on the mackintosh and the money, the issue of time held the heaviest evidential weight, able to tip the jury's verdict one way or the other. The star witness for the prosecution in this respect was milk boy Alan Close, who testified on the first day. The prosecution's questions were cursory. The cross-examination of Close by the defence was far longer and, for both the witness and the prosecution, uncomfortable {see Exhibit 7}.

The key witness on the second day, and perhaps of the entire trial, was John MacFall. We have already covered his evidence regarding the time of death. It is important to note

166

here an exchange that shows how he insisted on pushing his opinion, and on a matter that might have swayed the jury. After the prosecution had finished questioning the pathologist, the defence barrister, Roland Oliver, stood to commence the cross-examination:

Counsel: I want to begin with your last bit of evidence...
MacFall [interrupting, holding up a sketch]: May I put in this before that?

There was a discussion between the barristers and judge. The result was that the prosecution asked one last question of MacFall, who answered it with relish.

MacFall: I formed an idea of the mental condition of the person who committed this crime. I have seen crimes, many of them of this kind, and I know what the mental condition is. I know it was not an ordinary case of assault or serious injury. It was a case of *frenzy*.

Although it was merely MacFall's opinion, the implications were not lost on anyone in the court, not least the jurors. It suggested that the killer raged beyond the influence of reason, someone moved to murder by an unstoppable torrent of emotion or during a moment of insanity. And who else but the husband would be so moved against a shy and diffident woman "with no enemies in the world"? During the ensuing sharp exchanges between the defence barrister and the witness, MacFall strayed into areas of psychology that, author Jonathan Goodman wryly observed, made him appear to be Sigmund Freud's tutor. Most commentators agree that Oliver had the better of the exchanges but, for the defence, it was a case of damage limitation.

The third day saw the prosecution rest. Roland Oliver did not call for the trial to be dismissed due to lack of evidence, much to the surprise of Hector Munro, Wallace's solicitor.

Oliver had already told his team that he was sure the jury was prejudiced and not listening. Was he already thinking ahead to a possible appeal if the verdict went against Wallace? Any motion to withdraw the case from the jury would have entailed the judge having to evaluate the weight of evidence against Wallace. Did Oliver believe that, had Mr Justice Wright ruled against the defence's submission, it might undermine a subsequent appeal that cited insufficient evidence to support a guilty verdict?

In his opening speech to the jury, Roland Oliver took only half-an-hour to make his points. He stressed the importance of the time Julia Wallace was last seen alive: "It must have been a terrible shock to the police – that time of 6:45pm. If Alan Close had delivered the milk at this time, the defendant was clear. The argument of delivering the milk at 6:30pm was that it would give sufficient time for this murder to have been committed. You have only Close's word that he looked at the church clock, but that is not what he said to the children the following evening."

He also emphasised that if Wallace had killed his wife he would have been heavily splattered with blood, and pointed out that there "was no trace of blood on his clothes, hands, face or boots", and that none was chemically detected in the bathroom or back kitchen.

At 2:20pm William Herbert Wallace took to the stand. His testimony lasted three hours, during which time he answered over 700 questions calmly, even during the searching cross-examination. To the jury he came across as highbrow, being too precise with some of his answers, adding qualifications when simple, bold statements would have served him better. The jury could not warm to him, as he seemed cold and aloof. Only when he was asked about the discovery of his wife's body did he show a sign of emotion. "And I looked into her face," he said, his voice trembling, "and saw she was obviously quite dead." He closed his eyes.

Oliver asked Wallace who Julia would admit to the house:

Counsel: Looking at it now, if someone did come and give the name of "Qualtrough" to your wife on that night, do you think she would have let him in?

Wallace: Seeing I had gone to meet a Mr Qualtrough, I think she would, because she knew all about the business.

Counsel: If she had let him in, where would she have taken him?

Wallace: Into the front room. There is no question about that.

Although he personally believed that Julia knew her killer {see Exhibit 10}, Wallace agreed that it was possible that a stranger posing as Qualtrough might have been admitted to the house. During the cross-examination, the prosecution was keen to dispel this possibility. The following are selected exchanges between Hemmerde and Wallace.

Counsel: If you had stayed at home that night, it would have been quite natural that the piano should be open, and the fire lit and you would be having your ordinary musical evening?

Wallace: No, probably we should not have had any music that evening. Her cold would have made her say, "It will be rather cold in the front room; I do not think we should bother tonight with music."

Counsel: Her cold had not been too bad for her to walk out into the yard and see you out?

Wallace: That is so.

Counsel: If you had let your wife know you were going to be in, that is just how the room might have been?

Wallace: If we had decided to have music that is, of course, how it would have been, naturally.

Counsel: This is your theory as outlined by Mr Oliver: someone came there, introduced himself, was allowed to come in, had the fire lighted for him in the parlour and, as your wife leant down, crashed her head. Is that it?

Wallace: That is the suggestion, I think.

Counsel: And having done so, and struck 11 blows in all, he turned off the gas fire and went out?

Wallace: I do not know what he did.

Counsel: Does that strike you as a probable thing that a man would turn off the gas and go out?

Wallace: In view of the fact that the mackintosh had been burned, I would say "yes".

Counsel: Why, because to someone passing it would show a reflection showing the house was inhabited? Why turn it off?

Wallace: I cannot explain his actions at all.

The prosecution also made much of Wallace's problem of entering his house, suggesting it was a charade to make it appear that someone else was inside when he returned home.

Counsel: You see I am putting to you that neither door was bolted or locked, and this suggestion that they were bolted was purely play-acting?

Wallace: You may think that, but you are wrong.

Counsel: What would have happened if your wife had gone to the post?

Wallace: I would have been in the same position: I would not be able to get in, but the chances are she would not have bolted the door.

Counsel: So, this is the position: you are outside your house, your wife may have gone to the post, and you ask the neighbours, "Have you heard anything unusual?"

Wallace: Yes.

Counsel: Do you remember Inspector Gold asking you if you thought anyone was in the house when you got back, and do you remember your answer?

Wallace: No, I do not.

Counsel: "I thought someone was in the house when I went to the front door because I could not open it, and I could not open the back door." Do you remember saying that?

Wallace: No, I do not.

Counsel: Do you still think that, when you returned, someone was in the house?

Wallace: No, I do not.

Counsel: You have given that theory up?

Wallace: Yes.

Counsel: Did you ever believe it?

Wallace: I might have done at the moment.

In his state of anxiety, perhaps Wallace had genuinely thought someone was in the house at the time. On the other hand, he might have originally wanted to give that impression, but could now safely jettison the subterfuge when he realised it had failed. The final phase of the cross-examination returned to the issue of the locks.

Counsel: And now you say that when you returned that night, you are convinced that the front door was bolted but the back door was stiff?

Wallace: Yes, that is so.

Counsel: I put it to you that the front door was in a poor condition for a very long time, and the back door was the same?

Wallace: As far as the locks were concerned, yes, that is so. The back door had been like that for years, sticky.

Counsel: And the front?

Wallace: The front door had been out of order for quite a while, but not seriously. I had not had that experience before.

Counsel: Had you have known before the key not to turn in the lock?

Wallace: No, and we had not been unable to get in with our keys.

Counsel: You could not open the front door?

Wallace: No.

Counsel: But you saw the superintendent open it at the very first attempt?

Wallace: Yes, that is true, but I could not open it because the bolt was on it.

Counsel: But the key?

Wallace: I said the key slipped back.

Counsel: You never told him that?

Wallace: I do not know whether I told him, but I tell you that.

In fact, Wallace had shown surprise when Superintendent Moore informed him about the slipping lock – "It was not like that this morning." Yet, hours later, in his first police statement, Wallace claimed the lock slipped when he tried to enter the second time. At the trial he added that it was the first time this had occurred. Was Wallace slithering around the truth, trying to reconcile his written statement with what he first told Moore? Furthermore, Wallace had failed to tell the superintendent that the door was also bolted. Perhaps he did not think it important at the time but, of all Wallace's testimony, his answers concerning the locks and bolts are arguably the most perplexing. Hemmerde had saved his ace till last.

For Wallace the ordeal of the cross-examination was over. Hector Munro, Wallace's solicitor, believed his client made an excellent witness: he made no errors in his statements and was not pulled up on any facts. However, being factual in the witness box did not mean he cut a sympathetic figure to the jury.

The fourth day, Saturday 25 April 1931, saw the closing speeches and the judge's summing up. Roland Oliver told the jury that there were two factors in determining the guilt of Wallace beyond a reasonable doubt. Who had sent the telephone message? And at what time had it been proved that Julia Wallace was killed? Oliver was scathing about MacFall's evidence, pointing out that the expert was incontrovertibly wrong in his opinion about the time of death: Julia Wallace had been seen alive *after* 6pm. Oliver, yet again, pointed out that the prosecution's case rested on the word of Alan Close.

After nearly an hour's scrutiny of the prosecution case, Oliver finished with a rhetorical flourish: "You have a crime without motive; you have a man against whose character there is not a word to be said; you have a man whose affection for his wife cannot be doubted. You are trying a man for the murder of a woman, who is his only companion, for no benefit. The Romans had a maxim which is as true today as it was then: 'No one ever suddenly became the basest of men'."

Edward Hemmerde closed the prosecution's case with a speech lasting over an hour. He tackled head-on the first question posed by the defence, highlighting the "singular coincidences" of the telephone call. Wallace had departed his house at a time that would have brought him to a nearby telephone box at the precise time that Qualtrough was making his call, leaving a message for Wallace at a place where only Wallace could know that he would pick it up later. It was powerful rhetoric. As for the "vital point" of the time of death, this was "easily established", he claimed. And that was all he claimed. The domineering presence of John MacFall in the witness box days earlier, which had cast a shadow on the defence case, was left well alone by the prosecution. This was probably to avoid reminding the jury of the problems with his evidence. Rather, Hemmerde insisted that Wallace had "practically 20 minutes" to commit murder, which he considered "ample time". This assumed that the milk boy had called at 6:30pm, a disputed point of evidence. Clearly, the logical sin of 'begging the question' is a legal virtue, at least for an advocate.

In his hour's summing-up, Mr Justice Wright called the case a "most remarkable murder", one unrivalled in the annals of crime. He said that no evidence pointed to the murderer: no fingerprints, no conceivable motive, and no eyewitness to the crime apart from its perpetrator. The summing-up was insightful and fair, dealing with all the evidence. He stated that "the most vital part of the case" was the question of time. He told the jury that the testimony of Alan Close was clearly "a reconstructed time", based on the recollection of the time shown by the church clock. He also thought that, if Wallace had only 12 minutes, it was "a very narrow limit of time" for him to do everything that he was alleged to have done.

At 1:20pm the jury was sent away to consider its verdict. An hour later the jurors returned, taking their seats in the jury box in a packed courtroom buzzing with expectation. The verdict was as Roland Oliver had feared: guilty. Two women jurors sobbed as a square of black silk was solemnly placed on the judge's wig. The judge then passed the death sentence, after which Wallace was led down the stairs, away from the emptying court, and driven to the condemned cell. During the following days and weeks, he read books on astronomy and chess. He was visited frequently by Munro, who found Wallace removed and indifferent to his plight. Munro later remembered one conversation in particular and was surprised to discover that Wallace was in favour of capital punishment, believing the death penalty acted as a deterrent.

But it was not the end of the matter. The defence team drew up grounds for an appeal. There were 10 points in total, but the first two were the most important. These stated: "The verdict was unreasonable and cannot be supported having regard to the evidence; and the judge at the conclusion of the evidence should have withdrawn the case from the jury."

The Court of Criminal Appeal had been established in 1907, following disquiet over the conviction of Adolf Beck, who was found guilty of fraud through mistaken identity. Over 24 years it had overturned only two death sentences. One was due to misdirection by the judge and the other because the defence had not been properly presented to the jury. Never before had the Court set aside a jury's verdict on the grounds that it could not be supported by the presented evidence, although Section 4 of the Criminal Appeal Act (1907) did provide such grounds for a verdict to be overturned. Wallace's appeal implied that both the jury and judge had gone awry. It was a tall order.

The appeal against the verdict and sentence was heard over two days. The panel of three judges, led by Lord Chief Justice Hewart, delivered its verdict on Tuesday 19 May 1931. The judges agreed that "the case against the appellant was not proved with the certainty that is necessary in order to justify a verdict of guilty". Citing Section 4 of the Act, the appeal was upheld and the conviction quashed.

Wallace was legally not guilty, but this did not mean he was actually innocent. The Liverpool police strongly believed they had nicked the right man and, two days later, announced that the case would not be reopened. William Herbert Wallace was a free man. And so was the killer of Julia Wallace.

12. SUMMING UP

Members of the Cold Case Jury, the appeal judges ruled that there was insufficient evidence to convict William Wallace beyond a reasonable doubt. But you have a different burden of proof: who *most likely* killed Julia Wallace? There are two decisions to make. First, was Wallace innocent or not? And, depending on your answer to the first, which theory is the best explanation? Three theories hold Wallace was involved in his wife's murder:

Wallace. William Wallace alone murdered his wife.
Prank. Wallace killed his wife after Gordon Parry made a prank telephone call.
Conspiracy. Wallace masterminded a plan to murder his wife.

Three theories hold Wallace was innocent:

Parry. Parry alone murdered Julia Wallace.
Accomplice. An unknown accomplice of Parry's killed Julia Wallace.
Neighbour. The Johnstons killed Julia Wallace.

This list is not exhaustive; there are other possibilities. However, to my knowledge, every major writer on the case would subscribe to one of the theories above. You may already have a verdict in mind, or you may find the evidence overwhelmingly inconclusive and are at a loss as to what to think. I suggest your answers to the following questions will help define your verdict:

- Who made the Qualtrough call and why?
- What does the crime scene tell us about the murder?
- Why was the murder weapon removed from the scene?
- How plausible is the account of Parry's late-night dash to the garage?

Logically, the telephone call is the most important aspect of the case. If you are confident that Wallace made the call, your verdict is Wallace because it is the only theory that places him in the call box; every other assumes that Parry made the call, either intentionally or as a prank. Wallace is certainly in the frame: he had sufficient time to make the call and arrive at the chess club when he did and he was the only person who knew for sure that he would be attending that night. At the club, it appears he had planned in exquisite detail how to respond in front of witnesses if the message was passed on. In particular, he mentioned "Qualtrough" at least three times to emphasise the unusual name; he intentionally stated "West" so that it would be corrected to "East" emphasising the address; and he signalled his intent to pester the tram conductors the following evening. If Wallace made the call, it was a great opening gambit.

Yet why did Wallace fumble in the call box and in particular why did he say, "Operator, I pushed button A but I have not had my correspondent yet"? He was used to making calls from public telephone kiosks and knew that if there was a problem you pushed button B and started over. The expression might be used by someone unfamiliar with the A/B phone box, or a conman who wanted to save on the cost of the call. This is what we would expect of Gordon Parry, who misled the police as to his whereabouts at the time of the call. Indeed, it is the only proven lie in the entire case.

Why would Wallace make the call? Presumably to give the impression that someone wanted him out of his house on the Tuesday night. Yet, he could have killed his wife on the

Monday night and established a decent alibi. If he made a fuss when he boarded the tram to his club, his departure would be time-stamped as he needed. At the chess club he would certainly be remembered, not least by his opponent, and his friend James Caird who accompanied him home. The quality of the alibi would have been the same, perhaps even better. Or was it strengthened by suggesting that someone else wanted his wife dead?

Why would Parry make the call? He wanted Wallace out of the house, either as a practical joke or to implement a burglary. Of course, he would not know if Wallace would act on the message – there were plenty of ways for the scheme to fail. For a prank, it did not matter. For a burglary, Parry might have thought he was smarter than he was, or did not mind if the plan failed so long as it had a chance of success, especially if he had a failsafe working with an accomplice. Indeed, one reason Parry might have tried to fiddle a free call was because he knew there was a possibility of failure and did not want to be out of pocket.

Another crucial part of the case is the crime scene, and especially the involvement of the cashbox. If Wallace planned the telephone call in such fine-grained detail, we can justifiably assume he thought as carefully through the staging of the crime. The raiding of the cashbox that few people knew existed, the suspicion of Parry in his second statement, his insistence that Julia would not admit a stranger into the house while he was away, and his post-acquittal pointing of the finger at his former colleague all suggest that Wallace wanted to frame him for the murder of his wife. No motive is necessary – it is a valid inference from the facts. If we are to believe that Wallace is guilty, we should accept that Wallace killed his wife *and* attempted to frame Parry for it.

But raiding the cashbox is surprising because it appears Wallace reimbursed his company for its losses. It would have been far cheaper to stage some other kind of burglary – he could have said almost anything had been stolen because no one would have known differently. Why did Wallace involve the cashbox? Was he determined to see Parry hang or does it point away from Wallace as the killer?

The most distinctive part of the crime scene is the burnt mackintosh. Why was the raincoat in the parlour and how did it catch fire? You have to decide between two theories: the killer most likely used it as a shield to avoid blood spatter; or it was worn by Julia for extra warmth, pointing to a killer for whom blood transfer was not such a pressing concern. The most likely way Wallace used the mackintosh was as a shield, kneeling beside a prone Julia. If Wallace was innocent then the mackintosh fell into the fire after Julia draped it around her shoulders as an improvised shawl. In either case, it is likely that the raincoat became trapped under Julia and smouldered, and the killer had to move her body to retrieve it.

Numerous blows rained down on Julia's head in a brutal attack – possibly as many as a dozen or more. This is overkill, and typically points to a killer emotionally involved with the victim, such as the husband. However, in this case the husband is a calculating assassin who needs to avoid blood spatter. Even allowing that the mackintosh might have been used as a shield by Wallace, does the nature of the murder point away from him in this case? Further, it appears many blows were struck while Julia's head was by the armchair, yet Wallace is alleged to have wielded none in that location because he was forced to move the body early on in the attack to retrieve the burning mackintosh. Another killer, not using the mackintosh for protection, would not have been immediately concerned about the smouldering raincoat. Any scenario that assumes Wallace delivered several blows in the corner of the room has to explain why he would have done so without the protection of the mackintosh and why he moved the body – surely a reckless manoeuvre in itself for someone keen to avoid blood transfer.

Is there any evidence that a visitor called? In the police photograph, there are plumped-up cushions on the chaise longue that suggest Julia might have used it recently; her box of matches on the table in the bay window suggest she prepared the room; the position of her feet indicate she was hit when she rose from the couch; and it is possible that she would have used a mackintosh as a shawl for extra warmth had she ushered an unexpected visitor into the cold parlour. Of course, Wallace might have staged the room to make it look like a visitor had called; it would be a key reason to kill his wife in the parlour.

According to Wallace, the downstairs was in darkness when he returned home. He could not risk anyone finding the body in the parlour while he was creating his alibi, so would have been motivated to turn off the gas lamps. It is hard to see another killer being so motivated, especially as turning off the lamps risked leaving an incriminating fingerprint. However, a savvy criminal might have used gloves or realised that holding the lever between the knuckles, which are not used in fingerprint identification, would eliminate the risk.

Was the front door bolted? Wallace was adamant that that it had been. If he lied, it was because he wished to imply that the killer was in the house when he returned. However, it is possible that another killer slid the bolt in case Wallace returned earlier than expected. What about the locks? Do you find it suspicious that the only occasion on which he had trouble with his front door lock was when his wife was lying dead on the parlour floor? However, Superintendent Moore did identify a problem with it. And, if guilty, why did Wallace concoct a story that the lock had failed in *two different ways* when he had already told the Johnstons that he believed the door was bolted?

What was the murder weapon? It was assumed to be the iron bar, yet John MacFall stated the wounds were inflicted by "a large-headed instrument" and a modern forensic opinion suggests that an iron bar was unlikely. Whatever was used, it was removed from the scene. Why? An obvious answer is that the killer brought it to the house and feared it might incriminate him if he left it behind. Alternatively, if a visitor had improvised with a household object, such as the iron bar, he may have held it with his bare hands and risked leaving incriminating fingerprints. On the other hand, a guilty Wallace might have wished to suggest that the killer had come to the house.

The testimony of John Parkes links Gordon Parry to the crime, but there has to be some doubt as to its reliability. Why did Parkes wait so long before talking about this important encounter? In fact, he waited until all the people connected to it were dead. On the other hand, it is reasonable to believe the garage hand only became aware of Parry's death through the Radio City broadcasts and feared retribution, most likely legal action, if he had mentioned it earlier. If the iron bar found behind the fireplace a few years after the murder was the one that the cleaner claimed went missing, it falsifies a key assertion of John Parkes' account and undermines his entire claim.

If you suspend judgement on the claims of John Parkes then independent confirmation of Parry's involvement is lost. However, it must be stressed that there is no direct evidence tying Wallace or anyone else to the murder either. Hector Munro, Wallace's solicitor, insisted that if there "had been a scintilla of evidence against Wallace" the Court of Criminal Appeal would have upheld the death sentence. Even so, the appeal court judges and the trial judge were suspicious that Wallace's story was too good to be true. But are the convoluted nature of his alleged plan (e.g. involving the cashbox and the arrival of a milk boy) and his post-acquittal finger pointing at Parry more consistent with innocence? Was Wallace just dreadfully unlucky, as author Jonathan Goodman maintained, or was the series of unfortunate events too remarkable for him to be blameless?

Members of the Cold Case Jury, was William Wallace innocent or not? If you believe he was innocent, your choices are narrowed to three theories. The **Parry** theory assumes the young amateur actor was both the caller and killer and was *not* at Olivia Brine's at the time of the murder. To accept this theory you need to reject Mrs Brine's statement. It is short on detail, but on what grounds would you reject it? Perhaps you find the remarkable account given by John Parkes plausible. You would also need to believe that Parry was capable of bashing the brains out of an acquaintance with whom he had musical afternoons. Although he was described as someone who could "handle himself", there is little evidence he was explosively aggressive. The only known incident in his entire life was a charge of assaulting a young woman in his car, on which he was acquitted. A further problem remains. After seeing Wallace leave for the chess club, would Parry head for a telephone box rather than immediately visiting Julia? Was an extra day's collection really worth a call, a delay and a risk of failure?

The **Accomplice** theory assumes Parry made the call, but accepts he had an alibi for the time of the murder, and Julia was killed by an accomplice of Parry's when a distraction burglary went wrong. The call was made by Parry to provide a pretext to allow the accomplice to enter the house and to lure Wallace away. This theory explains why Parry did not have an alibi for the time of the call, why he might have lied as to his whereabouts after leaving Olivia Brine's, and why he had no blood on his clothes when he visited Atkinson's Garage. On the other hand, if an accomplice called, none of the neighbours heard him knock. Other questions remain. Why did the accomplice turn off the gas appliances downstairs? And how did he manage to do everything without leaving bloodstains or fingerprints? Remember, this was a planned burglary; the murder was an unexpected turn of events. In which case, why did Parry chose the wrong day in the wrong week to maximise the cashbox haul?

The **Neighbour** theory explains why the Johnstons claimed might not have heard anything from the Wallace household that night: they were perpetrating the crime. There is no evidence that John Johnston was a burglar or even knew the location of the cashbox. Its biggest drawback is the call: Johnston implausibly made it when there was no reason to.

If you believe Wallace was involved in the murder of his wife, your choices are narrowed to a different set of three theories. The **Wallace** theory is the simplest: it holds that Wallace made the call as part of a carefully planned murder. He could have aborted his plan at any time until he delivered the first blow; that was the point of no return. He killed using the mackintosh as a shield to prevent blood transfer to himself, and used the delivery of the milk and his tram journeys to show he had insufficient time to commit the murder. He searched for a fictitious address to stay away from his house as long as he could to suggest that another killer had ample time to strike. The problem with the locks was a charade to give the impression that someone was still inside his house when he returned. His fortuitous bumping into his neighbours provided witnesses to the time of his return and the discovery of the body. However, where did he dispose of the weapon? If it was away from his house, he had to transport it, possibly along with bloodied gloves. And would he have planned this murder to pin the blame on Gordon Parry without having the faintest idea whether or not his scapegoat had an alibi?

The **Prank** theory assumes Gordon Parry was the caller and Wallace the killer. Parry is certainly in the frame for making the call: he misled the police as to his whereabouts at the critical time and it appears he had form for making nuisance calls. Parry would have made the call as a practical joke on the way to visit his girlfriend and after watching Wallace leave his house. But how likely is it that Wallace could devise his murder plan in less than a day? Even if he had been thinking about killing his wife, he still had to fit the call into his plan in short order without overlooking any detail. If you have doubts about Wallace being the killer, this theory is arguably less credible than him acting alone.

The **Conspiracy** theory assumes Parry made the Qualtrough call and Joseph Marsden was the killer, following a plan masterminded by Wallace. It accepts that Lily Hall observed Wallace talking to another man on the night of the murder, a claim he denied. Unfortunately, Hall's testimony was not as clear as it could have been. But what other evidence for conspiracy is there? Would Wallace – a loner by all accounts – trust others in a plan to murder his wife, let alone be able to coerce them? And why would he lead the police to his conspirators?

Members of the Cold Case Jury, keeping this in mind, it is now time to turn to the evidence. In Part Two, you will find photographs, witness statements, facts and background information. These are not mere footnotes to the story. They allow us to see the crime scene, hear witnesses in their own words and place events in their full context. Only after seeing the original evidence will you be in a position to decide what happened on that winter night long ago in Anfield. In Part Three, I provide my view on the case.

After examining the evidence, I hope you will deliver your verdict. Visit the Cold Case Jury website (coldcasejury.com) and simply click on 'Your Verdict' for *Move to Murder* and follow the simple instructions. After you have cast your vote, you can view the collective verdict of the Cold Case Jury.

PART TWO

THE EVIDENCE

Our story is not yet finished. It can only be completed by listening to the narrator of every crime – the evidence.

Exhibit List

Many photographs, diagrams and maps are available at the Cold Case Jury website. A subset appears in this book:

A. Wolverton Street Area (Map)
B. Searching For Qualtrough (Map)
C. A Long-Winded Journey (Map)
D. Ground Floor Plan
E. The Forensic Picture

The documentary evidence is provided in 17 exhibits:

1. Annual Timeline
2. Daily Timeline
3. Engineer's Report
4. Post Mortem Report
5. Modern Forensic Views
6. The Mackintosh Clue
7. Close Calls
8. Wallace's Statements
9. Wallace's Life Story
10. "I Know The Murderer"
11. Parry's Alibi
12. Parry's Response
13. The Neighbours View
14. Amy Wallace's Account
15. Conversations In The Dark
16. Forensic Accounting
17. Trial Minutes

Exhibit A. Wolverton Street Area

Monday 19 January 1931

A. Telephone kiosk (Anfield 1627) from where the mystery call was made

B. Tram stop the police claimed Wallace used

C. Tram stop Wallace said he used

Tuesday 20 January 1931

1. Wallace allegedly seen by Lily Hall (about 8:35pm)

2. Harry Greenlees talks to "Stocky Man" (about 8:40pm)

Exhibit B. Searching For Qualtrough

A. Wallace alights from No. 5A tram from Penny Lane
B. Sydney Green says there is no 25 Menlove Gardens East
C. Katie Mather confirms there is no such address
   Had Wallace stopped his search now, he would have returned home by about 8:15pm
D. PC Serjeant advises Wallace to use a street directory in the Post Office
E. Wallace enters Post Office but it has no directory
F. Wallace uses a directory at a newsagent
G. Wallace boards the tram home
   Wallace arrives home between 8:40pm and 8:45pm

Exhibit C. A Long-Winded Journey

Tuesday 20 January 1931 – Parry's journey to see his girlfriend

1. Mrs Brine (Knoclaid Road): Parry stayed here between 5:30pm and 8:30pm.

2. Post Office (Maiden lane): bought the *Evening Express* and cigarettes.

3. Hignetts (West Derby Road): picked up his accumulator battery.

4. Mrs Williamson (Lisburn Lane): talked about a 21st birthday party.

5. Lily Lloyd (7 Missouri Road). arrived at about 9pm and stayed until about 11pm.

A = Recreation Ground

B = Wolverton Street

Exhibit D. Ground Floor Plan (No. 29)

'ENTRY'

GATE

W.C.

COALS

BACK YARD

BACK KITCHEN

BACK DOOR

Cashbox (Top Shelf)

X

Stairs

KITCHEN

Range

Armchair

HALL

Piano

Bloodstains

Fire

PARLOUR

FRONT DOOR

WOLVERTON STREET

Exhibit E. The Forensic Picture

1. Bloodstain in front of the armchair (not shown)
2. Bloodstain, mostly on the hearthrug
3. Two large pools of blood surrounded Julia's head
1-3 are consistent with Julia's head (and torso) being moved during the attack

A. "Blood Spatter Zone" – most blood spatter was in this area – probably due to several blows being delivered while Julia's head was lying at (1)
B. The gas regulator of the Sunbeam fire
C. Box of matches, presumably used to light the fire
F. The position of Julia's feet by the hearth and chaise longue

Exhibit 1. Annual Timeline

The following timeline is placed before the Cold Case Jury to enable a wide-angled view of events that culminated in the murder of Julia Wallace. Events with estimated dates are indicated with an asterisk.

1861
April 28. Julia Dennis born at East Harlsey, Yorkshire
1871
April 19. Anne Dennis, Julia's mother, dies in childbirth
1875
February 19. William Dennis, Julia's father, dies aged 40. Orphaned at 13 years old, not much is known of Julia's life for the next 30 years
1878
August 29. William Herbert Wallace born at Millom, Cumbria
1888
Wallace contracts typhoid in Blackpool, Lancashire*
1892
Wallace starts drapery apprenticeship at Thomas Tenant, Barrow, Cumbria
1897
Wallace is an assistant at Whiteway Laidlaw & Co. in Manchester
1902
Wallace arrives in India, working for Whiteway Laidlaw & Co. in Calcutta
1906
Wallace travels to China; he works for Whiteway Laidlaw & Co. in Shanghai; he is admitted to hospital with a serious kidney condition
1907
March 19. Wallace returns to England
April 7. Wallace admitted to Guy's Hospital, London, for a radical nephrectomy
1908
Wallace convalesces after nephrectomy and is unemployed
1909
January 12. Richard Gordon Parry born in Liverpool

1910
Wallace moves to Harrogate with his father and sister
1911
Wallace appointed secretary and agent for Liberal Party in Harrogate; meets Julia Dennis
1914
March 24. William Wallace marries Julia Dennis
1915
March. Wallace appointed an agent for the Prudential Assurance Company; William and Julia move to Clubmoor, Liverpool
July. William and Julia move to 29 Wolverton Street, Anfield, Liverpool
1922
Wallace joins Central Liverpool Chess Club, which meets at the City Café in North John Street, Liverpool*
1923
Mrs Florence Wilson nurses pneumonia-stricken William Wallace at 29 Wolverton Street*
1926
Gordon Parry joins the Prudential Assurance Company
1928
November 28. Wallace attends his first violin lesson at the home of his supervisor, Joseph Crewe, in Green Lane
December 26. Wallace has final violin lesson with Joseph Crewe
December 30. Wallace bed-ridden with bronchitis
December 31. Parry takes over Wallace's collection round for two weeks; Joseph Marsden also helps
1930
June 9. Wallace admitted to Royal Southern Hospital, Liverpool, with a serious kidney infection
July 10. Wallace discharged from Royal Southern Hospital, and told his condition is probably terminal
December 15. Following a railway accident, Julia is late home from a trip to Southport; Wallace is worried and goes to the local police station to make enquiries
1931
January 19. "R. M. Qualtrough" leaves a message for Wallace at the chess club
January 20. Julia Wallace bludgeoned to death
January 24. Julia Wallace buried at Anfield Cemetery

February 2. William Wallace arrested for the murder of his wife

February 19. Committal hearings begin

March 4. William Wallace ordered to stand trial

April 22. The trial of William Wallace begins

April 25. William Wallace found guilty of murder

April 30. Wallace's lawyers lodge appeal against guilty verdict

May 12. The scheduled date of execution, postponed due to appeal

May 16. The appeal hearing begins in London

May 19. William Wallace's conviction quashed by the Court of Criminal Appeal

May 21. Liverpool Police announce it is not re-opening the case into the murder of Julia Wallace

June. Wallace moves to Bromborough, Cheshire

July. Wallace receives £500 in damages after libel actions against various newspapers

July 4. *Tit-Bits* magazine publishes the first of six weekly articles about Wallace's life story

1932

January 30. Gordon Parry arrested twice (loitering with intent to commit a felony, and later for stealing a car)

February 24. Gordon Parry arrested for stealing money from a telephone kiosk [1]

April 16. *John Bull* magazine publishes the first in a series of weekly articles about Wallace's experiences entitled *The Man They Did Not Hang*

May. Wallace issues libel writ against *True Detective Mysteries* magazine

June. Joseph Marsden marries Sylvia Taylor

1933

February 9. Wallace admitted to hospital with kidney ailment

February 26. William Herbert Wallace dies from uraemia and pyelonephritis

March 1. Wallace buried in the same plot as his wife in Anfield Cemetery

1936

July. Gordon Parry found not guilty of assaulting a young woman in his car

1940

June 19. Alan Close, the former milk boy, dies piloting a Bristol Blenheim during World War II

1951

Superintendent Hubert Moore dies, having retired from the police in 1939

1980

April 14. Gordon Parry dies.

1981

January 20. Radio City broadcasts programme on the 50th anniversary of Julia Wallace's death

February 26. Follow-up programme broadcasts interview with John Parkes

Notes:

[1] Parry committed seven offences during the first two months of 1932: all were connected with theft. It appears that these crimes were petty, impulsive and unplanned.

Exhibit 2. Daily Timeline

In complex murder cases, establishing a reliable timeline of events surrounding the killing is crucial. Based on trial testimony, witness statements and police documents, the following timeline provides a detailed overview of what happened and when. Events with estimated times are marked with an asterisk.

Monday 19 January 1931

19:15. Wallace leaves his house (according to his statement)

19:18. First attempt at calling the chess club; caller complains to the operator that he has not spoken to his correspondent*

19:20. Call placed to the chess club, the time noted at the Anfield Exchange

19:24. Caller leaves message for Wallace at the chess club, giving his name as R. M. Qualtrough*

19:35. Gordon Parry calls at his girlfriend's house; she is giving a piano lesson, so he leaves [1]

19:45. Wallace arrives at chess club (seen by James Caird)

20:45. Parry returns to girlfriend's house*

22:15. Wallace leaves the chess club*

22:55. Wallace arrives home*

23:00. Parry leaves girlfriend's house

Tuesday 20 January 1931

10:30. Wallace leaves for his morning collection round

14:10. Wallace returns home for lunch

15:15. Wallace leaves for his afternoon collection round

15:30. Amy Wallace visits Julia

16:15. Baker's boy (Neil Norbury) delivers bread to No. 29 Wolverton Street

17:30. Parry calls at Mrs Brine's house (according to her statement)

17:55. Wallace leaves the house of his final customer, Mrs Martin*

18:00. Harold Denison calls at Mrs Brine's house and finds Parry already there

18:05. Wallace arrives home from afternoon collections (according to his statement)

18:30. Paperboy delivers *Liverpool Echo* to No. 29 Wolverton Street

18:40. Julia Wallace closes front door after speaking to milk boy Alan Close* {see Exhibit 7}

18:49. Wallace leaves home to keep his appointment with Qualtrough* {see Exhibit 3}

18:55. Wallace boards first tram at Belmont Road*

19:06. Wallace boards second tram at Smithdown Lane

19:16. Wallace boards third tram at Penny Lane*

19:19. Wallace alights at Menlove Avenue* {see Exhibit 3}

19:30. Wallace speaks to Katie Mather of 25 Menlove Gardens West*

19:45. Wallace speaks to PC James Serjeant

19:55. Wallace enters Allerton Road newsagent and speaks to manager Lily Pinches

20:00. Wallace boards tram in Allerton Road to return home [2]

20:25. Florence Johnston hears two thumps, possibly coming from No. 29*

20:30. Gordon Parry leaves Mrs Brine's house, buying cigarettes and papers from a local newsagent

20:35. Lily Hall claims to recognise William Wallace talking to a stocky man in Richmond Park*

20:40 Harry Greenlees talks to "Stocky Man" in Richmond Park {see Exhibit 15}

20:45. William Wallace talks to his neighbours John and Florence Johnston in the entry behind his house; Gordon Parry visits Mrs Williamson about her son's 21st birthday party

20:50. The Johnstons see Julia Wallace lying dead on the parlour floor*

21:00. Gordon Parry visits his girlfriend's house

21:10. PC Fred Williams arrives at crime scene

21:50. Professor John MacFall arrives at crime scene

22:05. Superintendent Hubert Moore arrives at crime scene

22:10. MacFall makes initial estimate of time of death (as 8pm)

22:25. Sergeant Harry Bailey arrives at crime scene

22:30. Inspector Herbert Gold arrives at crime scene

23:00. Gordon Parry leaves his girlfriend's house

23:45. Parry allegedly drives to Atkinson's Garage and asks John Parkes to clean his car inside and out*

23:55. Wallace taken away to give his first police statement*

Wednesday 21 January 1931
12:00. Professor MacFall conducts post-mortem

Thursday 22 January 1931
10.45. Wallace gives police second statement, naming Parry and Marsden among others

Notes:
[1] Based on Lily Lloyd's statement. Her mother stated that Parry left earlier {see Exhibit 11}.
[2] Based on Wallace's trial testimony. He stated he entered the shop a little before 7:55pm and boarded the tram at 8pm.

Exhibit 3. Engineer's Report

Wallace's legal team hired civil engineer Julian Maddock to examine the timings of the tram journeys Wallace said he took on 19 and 20 January 1931. Maddock produced an 18-page report, dated 16 April 1931, which presented the results of the eight tests he performed. This document, along with other files relating to Wallace's legal defence, is held by law firm Hill Dickinson LLP in Liverpool. I am grateful to Hill Dickinson LLP for granting me permission to present a summary of the report. My conclusions are italicised. See Exhibit A and Exhibit B for the relevant maps.

1) The Night of the Call

In his statement, Wallace said he departed his house at 7:15pm and arrived at the chess club "at about 7:45pm" on 19 January 1931. He stated he walked from his house in Wolverton Street to a tram stop at the junction of Breck Road and Belmont Road, boarded the No. 14 tram there and travelled to North John Street, where he alighted and walked the short distance to the City Café. I will refer to this as Route One.

The prosecution alleged he departed his house at 7:15pm, went to a nearby telephone kiosk to make the Qualtrough Call before boarding the No. 14 tram at a stop 25 yards from the kiosk. I will refer to this as Route Two.

Tests A and B replicated the entire journey, door to door, using Route One, the one Wallace claimed he took. Maddock found that the quickest time for this journey was 23 minutes 50 seconds, approximately 24 minutes, excluding any waiting time at the tram stop.

Maddock was informed by Liverpool Corporation Tramways that on, Monday 19 January between 7pm and 8pm, the only tram running this route was the No. 14 with a frequency of every 8 or 9 minutes [1]. The maximum wait time at the stop would therefore be 9 minutes. Adding this to the time recorded in Test A, the longest journey time would be 33 minutes. If Wallace left his house at 7:15pm, he would arrive at the chess club between 7:39pm and 7:48pm.

Test C replicated the walk from Wolverton Street to the telephone box (Anfield 1627), a distance of 400 yards. The average time for this was 3 minutes 50 seconds, approximately 4 minutes.

Test D replicated the entire journey, door to door, using Route Two. Maddock found that the quickest time was 24 minutes exactly, almost identical to the times recorded using Route One. Maddock noted that even though the tram had a slightly longer journey on Route Two, there was also less walking compared to Route One. Hence, the times are similar.

Maddock reported that, "With reference to Mr Wallace's journey on 19 January... the time he states as 30 minutes is reasonable and consistent. It is also possible to go round by the telephone box and, provided one takes a tram direct from there, and there is one available immediately, it is possible to arrive at the City Café in about the same time, but this does not allow any time for making the telephone call."

Maddock did not investigate the last point further. However, we know from the record at the Anfield Telephone Exchange that the call was put through at 7:20pm. As Gladys Harley answered the call first and then fetched Samuel Beattie, who spoke to the caller and took down details, it is reasonable to assume the call lasted approximately four minutes.

According to **Test D**, the time taken from boarding the tram at the stop by the telephone kiosk to arriving at the chess club (which included a short walk) was 20 minutes 20 seconds. If Wallace boarded the tram at 7:24pm, the earliest he could arrive at the chess club was 7:44pm. The latest time of arrival would be 7:53pm, after waiting 9 minutes to board the No. 14 tram.

Based on Maddock's tests, it is possible that Wallace arrived at the chess club at approximately 7:45pm by either route.

If we knew that Wallace arrived at the chess club at 7:45pm or before [2], we could say that it is more likely that he took Route One. However, we know only that he arrived "at about 7:45pm".

2) The Night of the Murder

Tests E and F measured the time the journey took from 29 Wolverton Street to the Menlove Avenue tram stop following the route Wallace claimed he took on the night of the murder.

Excluding waiting times, the quickest test time was 26 minutes 45 seconds.

Wallace's journey was divided into seven phases:

1. Walk to Belmont Road
2. Ride on No. 26 tram
3. Alight at Smithdown Lane
4. Ride on No. 5 tram
5. Alight at Penny Lane junction
6. Ride on No. 5A tram
7. Alight at Menlove Avenue

The fixed point in the timeline is at phase 4 – we know the No. 5 tram left Smithdown Lane at 7:06pm {see Exhibit 17}. Maddock found that the first three phases took, on average, 16 minutes 30 seconds, close to the average of the six police tests of a little over 17 minutes. Therefore, if it took Wallace the same amount of time on the night of the murder, he left his house *before* 6:50pm.

The tests showed that the second tram (4) took, on average, 9 minutes 38 seconds, or approximately 10 minutes. Therefore, we can assume Wallace would have arrived at Penny Lane junction (5) by 7:16pm. He boarded the final tram here with little waiting time – assume no more than a minute. According to the tests, the average journey time for the final tram (6) was 2 minutes 15 seconds. So, taking all this into account, Wallace would have arrived at Menlove Avenue (7) by 7:19pm.

Based on Maddock's tests, it is likely that on the night of the murder Wallace departed 29 Wolverton Street before 6:50pm, arriving at the tram stop in Menlove Avenue at 7:19pm.

This conclusion is consistent with Wallace's statements to the police and at his trial: he departed his house at about 6:45pm and arrived at about 7:20pm.

Tests G and H timed the return journey that Wallace used on the night of the murder. It took between 33 and 38 minutes, depending on waiting time. If Wallace boarded the tram at precisely 8pm, as he claimed, he would have arrived home by about 8:38pm.

Notes:

[1] Maddock remarked that on 19 January 1931 there was tunnel subsidence under Dale Street in central Liverpool, causing disruption to normal tram services.

[2] In his police statement, Thomas McCartney believed Wallace arrived at the chess club at 7:30pm. However, Samuel Beattie later told the police that no member recalled seeing Wallace arrive before 7:45pm. It appears McCartney changed his mind, perhaps after talking to other members. Wallace stated he arrived at the club "at about 7:45pm".

Exhibit 4. Post Mortem Report

Below is the initial post-mortem report by John MacFall, which was discovered among the case files at Merseyside Police. The report is produced faithfully, except I have broken it down into six numbered sections for ease of reference. My comments are italicised.

[1] On 21.1.31 at Princes Dock Mortuary, I made a P.M. examination of the body of Julia Wallace. Woman about 55 years, 5' 3/4", lightly built, prominent abdomen. No linea abicantes [*stretch marks on the skin that often follow pregnancy*]. The external genital orifice was quite clean with no evidence of blood.

[2] There was a small recent bruise mark on the inside of the left upper arm. There were no other marks of violence on the trunks or limbs. The hair was matted with blood and brain tissue. The hair was removed. Two inches above the zygoma was a large lacerated wound 2" by 3" from which brain and bone were protruding. On the back of the head on the left side were ten diagonal apparently incised wounds.

[3] On removal of the scalp the left frontal bone was driven into the front of the brain corresponding to the external wound. The whole of the left side of the back of the skull was driven in and broken into pieces. The injury extended into the middle and rear fossae, fracturing and breaking up the rear part of the cerebellum bursting the tentorium cerebelli and breaking up the left part of the cerebellum. The left lateral sinus was broken across, also the meningeal arteries.

[4] The appearance was as if a terrific force with a large surface had driven in the scalp, bursting it in parallel lines, with the appearance of several incised wounds, but the edges of these wounds was not sharp.

[5] The lungs, heart, kidney and spleen were normal. The stomach contained about four ounces semifluid food consisting of currants, raisins, and unmasticated lumps of carbohydrate. The small bowel was normal, the caecum ascending and transverse colon were enormously and chronically distended – typical constipation bowel. Uterus virginal and clean. The vagina clean and no evidence of bleeding. The right ovary normal, the left 3½ by 2½ fibroid.

[6] I am of the opinion that death was due to fracture of the skull by someone striking the deceased three or four times with a hard large-headed instrument.

A different report – one that appears to never have been seen by any other researcher – was published in James Murphy's *The Murder of Julia Wallace* (p. 56). It contained minor stylistic differences in sections 1-3 but major changes were incorporated into the final sections. Section 6 is expunged and section 4 is replaced with the following: "The appearance was as if a terrific force with a hard instrument had driven in the skull in 11 places... The edges of the wounds were not sharp. Death was due to the fracture of the skull by someone striking the deceased 11 times upon the head with terrific force with a hard instrument. From my findings, in my opinion, one blow was harder and more severe than the rest. This one blow produced the front, open wound, and caused death, which took place in one minute."

In the initial report, death was caused by as little as three blows of a large-headed instrument, bursting the scalp in parallel lines. Yet, in his trial testimony, MacFall was certain that Julia Wallace died as a result of 11 distinct blows to her head. Without an explanation for the change of opinion, we can only assume the wounds were consistent with either conclusion, but the difference is crucial. Based on the higher number, MacFall described the attack as "frenzied".

In a separate document, titled *The Report of Dr MacFall*, the medical examiner stated: "On 20.1.31 at 9:50pm, I was called to Wolverton Street, Anfield. In the parlour I saw the dead body of a woman... The hands were cold but the body warm; rigor mortis now present only in the upper parts of the left arm but by about 1 o'clock had extended to the right arm and right leg, but on no part was there any marked rigidity. From these two observations, it was most likely that death had taken place two hours before my arrival."

Therefore, the estimated time of death was 7:50pm. By the time of the trial, MacFall had changed his mind – Julia Wallace had died before 6pm. He also wrote in this report that Julia was most likely sitting in the armchair when she was struck – and this opinion did not change for the trial: "There was no blood staining of the hands and nothing was clutched in the hands, nothing beneath the fingernails... As the brain substance was found only round the head, it would seem as if this was the last smashing blow made while the head was on the ground, the back of the skull having been smashed in before.

"It was possible for the woman to have been sitting in the chair in the corner with the head lowered and turned to the right. A smashing blow on the left side of the back of the head would produce part of the multiple wound as seen, and a large bursting of the head would produce blood splashes as found. I do not think they were produced by the whirling round of a blood stained weapon [cast-off] as careful observation of the direction of the "soda water bottle" spots, partly diagonal spots and round spots in the corner, shows them to concentrate or focus on a point just in front of the chair, like hitting and bursting a bag with a wet sponge in it. It is evident there was a great burst of blood..."

If Julia was struck while leaning forward in the armchair, one would expect her body to have crumpled to floor to the left of the fireplace when she was struck. Yet Julia's body was found with her feet to the right of the fireplace and her body lying diagonally in the centre of the room. Further, there was an arc of three large bloodstains on the floor – the first in front of the chair, the last surrounding Julia's head in the centre of the room {see Exhibit E}. Neither fact is explained by MacFall's account.

Exhibit 5. Modern Forensic Views

John MacFall had a reputation for being cavalier, certainly among some of his colleagues. Because of his perfunctory investigation, we have little reliable forensic insight into the Wallace case. Can a modern perspective help? Below is the view of a contemporary forensic scientist who has read widely on the case and received crime scene images and the post-mortem photographs and reports.

Dr Greg Schmunk has practiced forensic pathology as a Medical Examiner since 1988, and is certified by the American Boards of Pathology and Medico-legal Death Investigation. He is — in layman's terms — an expert in death and murder. He has performed over 6,000 forensic examinations and testified in civil and criminal courts over 500 times. In 2013, he gave testimony before the US Senate hearings in Advancing the Science and Standards of Forensics. For over a decade he was a technical consultant to CBS Studios working on the TV shows *Crime Scene Investigation* and *CSI: Miami*. He currently runs an Iowa-based consulting company called Urbandale Forensics. His full interview is published at the Julia Wallace Murder Foundation website {see Part Three}.

Where in the parlour was Julia attacked?
MacFall believed that Julia was situated to the left of the fireplace sitting on the corner armchair because of the blood spatter in that area of the room. What bothers me about this supposition is the position of Julia's feet. If the attacker hit her while she was near the armchair, and then dragged her (possibly by the hair) to her final position, he would have lifted her feet and legs and moved them to the right of the fireplace. This would be highly unusual behaviour during a violent assault.

The chaise longue appears to have pillows arranged for someone who is reclining, but there is no record of any blood spatter in that corner of the room. It is reasonable to conclude that Julia was not attacked while she was sitting or relaxing here. She was most likely standing, or bending down, by the fireplace. However, it makes little sense that she was turning on the gas fire because it needed to be on for some time to make the bars hot enough to cause the three parallel burn marks on her skirt. In this case, she would most likely have been shoved inside the fireplace fender. However, she did not hit the hearth with any force because no hair, blood or tissue was found there. It is possible she was pushed towards the fire and received a blow to the head which stunned her.

Julia has no known defensive injuries and no injuries to the front of her head. This seems to point to a sudden attack from behind. One blow could have knocked her out and many of the blows could have been inflicted when she was on the floor. The cast-off on the wall behind the armchair is consistent with some blows being delivered in this area of the room.

How many blows did Julia likely receive?
There are multiple blows on the back of the head, just above the posterior hair line, which mainly line up in a diagonal orientation from left lower to right upper. There also is a linear contusion or abrasion on the right upper back in the same orientation. Above and behind the top of the right ear there are at least two or three impacts parallel to each other in a horizontal to slightly upper-posterior (back) to lower-anterior (front) orientation. On the back portion of the right parietal scalp there appear to be at least four impacts. In total, I believe she was struck up to 15 times (although the autopsy images are poor quality to say with a high degree of confidence).

What was the likely weapon?
The injuries shown in the post-mortem photographs are consistent with a single, heavy blunt object. There is a repeating pattern in several of the injuries which would be inconsistent with a metal bar or crowbar unless it had a patterned surface. Julia's injuries are abrasions (scrapes) due to a non-smooth object.

How bloody was the attack?
There is significant spatter in the corner of the room by the armchair from cast-off. This happens when a bloody weapon casts blood from its end as successive blows are struck. Direct spatter is generated when a weapon strikes an already bloody surface. In other words, had only one blow been struck, there would be neither cast-off nor direct spatter. Looking at the autopsy photos,

it seems clear that there would be a reasonable amount of direct spatter from the weapon striking a now bloody surface. I would expect blood on the assailant.

If the attacker wore the mackintosh over his clothes, it would largely protect the underlying clothing. However, I see no way that anyone could have committed the murder without getting seriously bloodstained, even if the mackintosh was worn, because there would still be spatter on the attacker's face, neck and hands (unless wearing gloves), lower legs and shoes.

In my view, the mackintosh was never placed over Julia's head during the attack. If it covered the head for some of the blows, the city analyst [William Roberts] should have been able to detect defects – most likely true tears – in the material. The burn to Julia's skirt and the mackintosh would suggest these had both caught on the fire in the same way, so the more likely scenario would be the mackintosh was on or close to Julia and fell under her during the attack.

What is your overall impression of the murder?
The more blows struck generally indicates less control and organisation by the attacker. For example, someone who wields this number of blows would be less concerned with avoiding blood spatter. It seems to be either a crime of passion or an offender who panicked with overkill. In my opinion, neither type of offender plans well.

*

To complement Dr Schmunk's view, summaries of two other forensic scientists' opinions are provided – again each was supplied with diagrams, reports, photos and background information. These have been abridged from longer interviews at the Julia Wallace Murder Foundation website {see Part Three}.

Forensic Scientist No. 2 (UK)
• Cause of death is blunt force trauma to the head from multiple blows (exact number uncertain)
• It highly likely that the first blow would have been the strongest
• The concentration of the blood spatter to the left of the fireplace suggests Julia's head was struck in this area
• There would be a lot of blowback blood spatter, meaning the attacker would have blood on his clothes even if the mackintosh was worn

• If the mackintosh was worn while kneeling, more blood would have been expected on the coat's lower half than described

• The mackintosh and skirt were probably burned at the same time, suggesting it is more likely that the mackintosh was on Julia rather than being worn by her attacker.

Forensic Scientist No. 3 (UK)

• The lack of downward blood runs on Julia's cardigan suggest she was prone when blows struck the back of her head

• The blood stains to the left of the fireplace are cast-off and impact spatter

• Julia possibly stood to the right of the fire and facing the centre of the room when she knocked to the floor

• She fell onto the floor in the position she was found [1]

• Once flat on the ground, multiple blows rained onto the back of her head

• The mackintosh and skirt were probably burned at the same time

• The assailant would have little or no blood upon them from carrying out this attack [2].

[1] The analyst does not account for the two pools of blood on the floor by the armchair (which were shown on a trial exhibit and reproduced in Exhibit E). Also, in my view, Julia falling into the room – and away from the fire – does not adequately explain the scorching of her skirt.

[2] The analyst believes the assailant stood on Julia's left near the circular table when he bludgeoned her {see Exhibit E – the table was situated just to the left of the word "FENDER"}. As there was no reported blood spatter radiating from the body to where the assailant might have stood and beyond (e.g. on the chaise longue), the scientist concludes little or no blood would have been found on the killer. However, the analyst's assertion is dependent on the precise position of the killer, which is unknown. For example, blood was found on items on a chair by the piano and on the wall by the door, which might be blowback spatter if the killer stood in front of the piano.

Comment: Two scientists suggest the killer would have been bloodstained after carrying out this attack even with the use of the mackintosh as protection, and one dissents from this opinion. All three agree that multiple blows were struck, possibly a great number, to account for the blood spatter in the room. All agree that the burning of the skirt and mackintosh probably occurred at the same time, and two experts explicitly state that it was more likely that the coat was on Julia when it fell into the fire.

Exhibit 6. The Mackintosh Clue

One of the most distinctive and puzzling features of the case is the presence of the burnt mackintosh in the parlour. Here are some quotes from key witnesses about it.

Florence Johnston
Statement to police: Mr Wallace said, "Oh, they have finished her. Whatever is she doing with my mackintosh and her mackintosh around her."

Statement to Hector Munro: Before the Police arrived, Mr Wallace and I went back into the front room, and I said to him "Whatever have they used?" He said "What was she doing with her mackintosh? And my mackintosh?" I looked, and saw the mackintosh tucked round her body, behind her, and touching the body. She looked as if she was lying on it. It looked as though a knock had come to the front door, and she had pulled the mackintosh round her shoulders, as she had a cold, before answering the knock. I said "Why, is it your mackintosh?", and he just stooped down and pulled out the folds, and said "Yes, it's mine". There was only one mackintosh there, so far as I know. We then went back into the back room.

Trial testimony: Well, it appeared to be something roughed up, you know; I did not know really what it was. It was almost hidden under the body, you see.

Detective Sergeant Bailey
Deposition: In the parlour I saw the dead body of Julia Wallace. Tucked up against the body at the back I saw the mackintosh. It was much bloodstained. On looking closely at the mackintosh I saw burnt matches inside of a fold. I then observed the mackintosh was burnt down the right side.

Detective Inspector Gold
Deposition: When I first saw it by the body, it seemed to me that it would be almost impossible for anyone to identify it as a particular mackintosh, or as a mackintosh at all, because it was in such a

crumpled condition. It might have been a piece of mackintosh material, a cycling cape or an old army ground sheet.

Detective Superintendent Moore

Deposition: Close up against the deceased's body was a mackintosh in a crumpled condition and bloodstained condition. I called Wallace into the room, and said to him, "Is this your mackintosh?" Wallace did not answer. I said, "Had Mrs Wallace a mackintosh like this?" Wallace remained silent. I said to Detective Sergeant Bailey, "Take it up, and let us have a look at it," which he did. I got hold of the right sleeve and, on stretching it out said, "This is a gents." Wallace then got hold of it and, after a short examination, said, "If there's two patches on the inside, it's mine. It's mine, I wore it this morning, but the day turning out so fine I wore my fawn coat this afternoon"... The mackintosh was very much burned on [one] side extending around to the centre of the skirt at the back.

William Wallace

Wallace said little about the mackintosh in his police statements but he was questioned about it during his cross-examination at his trial:

Counsel: Just listen to what you said [in your first statement]: "When I discovered my wife lying on the floor, I noticed my mackintosh lying on the floor at the back of her."
Wallace: I cannot remember whether it was my first or second visit [to the parlour].
Counsel: Then, when Mrs Johnston is there later with you, you say to her... "Whatever is she doing with my mackintosh" as though you were making a discovery... Mr Johnston says he never saw it at all; Mrs Johnston says that she never saw it until you pointed it out; Constable Williams says that he never saw it until the second light was lit... but you noticed it at once, according to your statement that night?
Wallace: Yes, I accept that.

Also see Exhibit 9.

Exhibit 7. Close Calls

The precise time at which Alan Close delivered milk to 29 Wolverton Street is critical to the case against William Wallace. The time ranges from 6:30pm to 6:45pm. Given that Wallace left his house before 6:50pm, the earlier time gives Wallace a maximum window of almost 20 minutes, the latter only four. In this window, Wallace killed his wife; checked himself for blood spatter (possibly cleaning himself); staged a robbery; and possibly disposed of the murder weapon and any other equipment (e.g. gloves). No one thinks this is possible in four minutes, especially if he also washed himself, dried, dressed, and cleaned the bathroom. If the milk boy called at 6:45pm, as Alan Close told his friends, William Wallace was innocent.

A few days after the murder, when the police already knew that the case against Wallace turned on the timing, Superintendent Moore and Sergeant Bailey accompanied Close in a re-enactment of his delivery. Close was timed as he walked his round from the Holy Trinity Church to 29 Wolverton Street: it took six minutes. A second took five minutes. Close also claimed he remembered the time on the church clock was showing 6:25pm, meaning the earliest time Close arrived was 6:30pm.

At the trial, Close denied he told friends that he had delivered the milk to 29 Wolverton Street at 6:45pm. He was interrogated on this point by the defence barrister:

Counsel: On the evening of the 21st did you have a conversation with Elsie Wright and Douglas Metcalf?
Close: Yes.
Counsel: Were you asked at what time you were at the Wallace's the night before?
Close: I don't remember.
Counsel: Did you say "at a quarter to seven"?
Close: No.
Counsel: I suggest you said that you were there at a quarter to seven.
Close [much quieter, mumbling]: No, between half-past six and a quarter to seven.
Counsel: Did you say that?

Close [almost whispering]: I think so.

Counsel: You were there between half-past six and a quarter to seven?

Close: Yes.

Counsel: In the presence of the other children, you said it was quarter to seven when you were at Mrs Wallace's. Is that not right?

Close [shaking his head]: [No reply].

After an interjection from the judge, Close eventually resorted to stating the less precise time, replying "between half-past six and a quarter to seven". Yet, his friends remained steadfast in what they had been told, especially Douglas Metcalf:

Counsel: Did you hear Alan Close say what time he had seen Mrs Wallace alive?

Metcalf: Yes. He said it was a quarter to seven.

Counsel: Have you any doubt about that?

Metcalf: No.

Kenneth Caird also confirmed that Close had said "quarter to seven". Even if Close had genuinely changed his mind about the time, it does not alter what he told his friends, so why did he deny it? One can only assume the young lad was giving his answers under duress.

Is there corroboration for the milk being delivered at 6:30pm? Florence Johnston, the neighbour at No. 31, stated that her milk was delivered that night "at about 6:30pm". If hers was delivered at this time, so was the milk next door. The neighbour at No. 27, Mr Holme, believed he heard the Wallaces' front door closing at 6:35pm. On this basis, it appears the milk was delivered between 6:30pm and 6:35pm.

However, when she spoke to Wallace's solicitor {see Exhibit 13}, Florence rowed back on the specific time in her statement: "The milk boy, Alan Close, called at my house that evening, but I cannot remember the exact time. He might come at any time between ten past six and seven, but recently he had been very late." If he delivered milk to Florence between 6:10pm and 7pm, it naturally suggests a late delivery time would be closer to 7pm and not 6:30pm. Indeed, piecing together his trial testimony, Alan Close completed his round that night at about 6:55pm. Wolverton

Street was one of his last deliveries – the two remaining streets being Richmond Park and Redford Street. He did not have many deliveries to make – there is only so much milk you can carry on foot. Even allowing 10 minutes for him to finish his round, Close would have been in Wolverton Street at about 6:45pm, the time he originally stated.

In his police statement, Alan Close said he looked at his watch at 6:45pm in Redford Street, which is a 200 yard walk from 29 Wolverton Street (via an entry at the bottom of Redford Street). That would take about two minutes at a brisk 4mph, a pace we might expect of a young lad who was running late. Even allowing for a delivery in Richmond Park, Alan Close would have left the Wallace's after 6:40pm.

Other evidence supports a delivery time of around 6:40pm. James Wildman, a paperboy, claimed he was at No. 27 when he glanced across and saw a milk boy standing at No. 29. It had to be Alan Close, because no one else delivered milk to the house that night. The milk boy was still standing there, with the front door wide open, when Wildman left. He was sure the time was a little before 6:40pm: "I passed Holy Trinity Church clock at 6:35pm and it takes me two minutes to walk to Wolverton Street, so it would be 6:37pm when I got there." When Wildman glanced across, Close was standing on the doorstep. Presumably, Julia was in the kitchen emptying the milk into her jug. She then returned to the front door, handed back the empty can to Close and spoke to him. This would have taken about a minute. If Wildman's timing is accurate, the door would have closed at 6:38pm.

In *The Murder of Julia Wallace*, James Murphy argues that Wildman was probably mistaken about the time he delivered the evening papers. He claims that the distance and angle from which Wildman saw the church clock made an accurate reading unlikely. Murphy fails to consider, however, that Wildman's timing is consistent with the evidence of Douglas Metcalf, who was at a community hall when he asked a local for the time. He was told it was 6:35pm. He then went to a nearby dance hall, talked to some boys for a short while, and then headed down the entry into Wolverton Street, from where he saw Wildman walking down the street having delivered his papers. Another friend, Elsie Wright, stated that at about 6:40pm she passed Alan Close in Letchworth Street as he was heading towards Wolverton Street.

Alan Close died during World War II and the truth perished with him, but the preponderance of evidence suggests that he did not make his delivery at about 6:30pm. In fact, after considering all the evidence, it seems clear that Julia Wallace closed her front door for the last time at about 6:40pm.

Exhibit 8. Wallace's Statements

The police statements of William Herbert Wallace are presented to the Cold Case Jury so his own words can be read. His first recorded comments were given to PC Williams – Exhibit 17 provides the full text – which the constable reconstructed from memory about two hours later. The first statement was taken several hours after the murder. My comments are italicised.

The First Statement *Tuesday 20 January 1931.*
I am 52 years old and by occupation an insurance agent for the Prudential Assurance Company, Dale Street. I have resided at 29 Wolverton Street with my wife Julia (the deceased), age believed to be 52 years, for the past 16 years [*Wallace appears unsure of her true age*]. There are no children of the marriage and my wife and I have been on the best of terms all our married life.

At 10:30am today I left the house, leaving my wife indoors doing her household duties. I went on my insurance rounds in Clubmoor, my last call being 177 Lisburn Lane shortly before 2pm. I then took a tram car to Trinity Church, Breck Road, arriving at my house at 2:10pm. My wife was then well and I had dinner and left the house at about 3:15pm. I then returned to Clubmoor and continued my collections, finishing at about 5:55pm, my last call being either 19 or 21 Eastman Road. I boarded a bus at Queens Drive and Townsend Avenue, alighted at Cabbage Hall and walked to my house at about 6:05pm.

I entered my house by the back door, which is my normal practice, and then had tea with my wife, she was quite well, and I then left the house at 6:45pm leaving by the back door. I caught a tram from Belmont Road and West Derby Road and got off at Lodge Lane and Smithdown Road, and boarded a Smithdown Road car to Penny Lane. I then boarded another car up Menlove Avenue, looking for Menlove Avenue East where I had an appointment with Mr A. M. Qualtrough at 7:30pm in connection with my insurance business. [*Two interesting slips. Wallace incorrectly states both the address and the first initial of his putative customer*].

I was unable to find the address and I enquired at 25 Menlove Avenue West [*it was Menlove Gardens West*] and I also asked, at the bottom of Green Lane, a constable [*PC Serjeant*] about the address. He told me [*as had Sydney Green about 20 minutes previously*] there was no such address. I then called at the Post Office near the Plaza Cinema to look at the directory, but there was none there, and I was unable to find the address. I also visited a newsagent where there was a directory, but I was unable to find the address. It was then 8pm and I caught a tramcar to Lodge Lane and then a car to Belmont Road and West Derby Road, and walked home from there.

I arrived at Wolverton Street at about 8:45pm. I pulled out my key and went to open the front door, and found it secure and I could not open it with my key. I knocked gentle (SIC) but got no answer. I could not see any light in the house. I then went round the back, the door leading from the entry to the back yard was closed but not bolted. I went to the back door of the house and I was unable to get in, I do not know if it was bolted or not, it sticks sometimes [*this last point was confirmed by Sarah Draper, the cleaner*], but I think the door was bolted, but I am not sure. There was a small light in the back kitchen, but not in the kitchen. I then went back to the front.

I was suspicious because I expected my wife to be in and the light on in the kitchen. I tried my key in the front door again and found the lock did not work properly. The key would turn it, but it seemed to unturn without unlocking the door. I rushed around the back, and saw my neighbours, Mr and Mrs Johnston, coming out of 31 Wolverton Street. I said to them: "Have you heard any suspicious noises in my house during the past hour or so?" Mrs Johnston said they had not. I said then, I couldn't get in, and asked them if they would wait while I tried again. I then found the back kitchen door opened quite easily.

I walked in by the back kitchen door, found the kitchen light out, lit it, and found signs of disturbance in the kitchen – in the kitchen a wooden case in which I keep photographic stuff had been broken open and the lid was on the floor. I then went upstairs and entered the middle bedroom but saw nothing unusual. I then entered the bathroom and this was correct. I then entered the back room and found no disturbance there. I then entered the front room, struck a match, and found the bed upset, the clothes being off. I don't think my wife left it like that. I then came down and looked into the front room, and after striking a match, I saw my wife lying on the floor. I felt her hand and concluded she was dead.

I then rushed out and told Mr and Mrs Johnston what had happened, saying something, but cannot remember what I did say. After my neighbours had been in, Mr Johnston went for the police and a doctor, I asked him to go. I afterwards found that about £4 had been taken from a cashbox in the kitchen, but I'm not sure of the amount.

When I discovered my wife lying on the floor, I noticed my mackintosh lying on the floor at the back of her. I wore the mackintosh up to noon today, but left it off owing to the fine weather. My wife has never worn the mackintosh to my knowledge. You drew my attention to it being burnt, but it was not like that when I last saw it, and I cannot explain it.

I have no suspicion of anyone.

Comment: *Although on the night of the murder Wallace harboured no suspicions of anyone, when he arrived at the police station on Thursday morning, Inspector Gold pressed him about who Julia would admit to the house. His response was the basis of his second statement, which he duly signed.*

The Second Statement *Thursday 22 January 1931.*
Mr Gordon R. Parry [*actually R. Gordon Parry*], of Derwent Road, Stoneycroft, is a friend of my late wife and myself. He is now an agent for the Gresham Insurance Company, although I'm not quite sure of the company [*he stated later that it was the Standard Life Assurance Company*].

He was employed by the Prudential up to 12 or 15 months ago, and he then resigned to improve his position. Although nothing was known officially to the company detrimental to his financial affairs, it was known he had collected premiums which he did not pay in and his supervisor Mr Crewe of Green Lane, Allerton, told me that he went to Parry's parents who paid about £30 to cover the deficiency [*Supervisor Crewe would later deny the deficiency was this great*].

Parry is a single man about 22 years of age. I have known him about three years and he was with my company about two years. I was ill with bronchitis in December 1928 and Parry did part of the collecting for about two or three days a week for about three weeks. I discovered slight discrepancies and I spoke to him about it. He was short of small amounts when paying in and he had not entered in the book all the amounts collected. When I spoke to him he said it was an oversight and that he was sorry and he put the matter right [*there is no suggestion that Wallace informed Crewe of the discrepancy*].

Previous to Parry doing my work he had called at my house once on business and left a letter for me which he wrote in my front room. I was not in at the time and my wife let him in. While he was doing my work in December 1928 he called very frequently to see me about my business, and he was well acquainted with our domestic arrangements. He had been in the parlour and kitchen frequently and upstairs in the middle bedroom a number of times to see me while I was in bed. I do not think he called to see me after I resumed duty in January 1929, but if he had called my wife would have had no hesitation in admitting him.

I have often seen him since he has been working for his new company and have spoken to him. About last November I was in the City Café one evening, I think it was on a Thursday evening playing chess, and I saw Parry there. He was not playing chess. He was by himself walking across the room. I said "Good evening" and he returned my greeting. I think that was the last time I saw him. He is a member of an amateur dramatic society which holds its meetings at the City Café on Thursday evenings. I do not think he drinks. He is engaged to Miss Lloyd of 7 Missouri Road, Clubmoor [*evidently Wallace knew Parry well enough to know to whom he was engaged*]. He would be on a weekly salary from his company plus commission on business, and his earnings would be about £4 per week.

There was another man named Marsden who also did part of the work for me while I was ill in December 1928. I do not know his address. He was an agent for the Prudential Company for two or three years and had left before he did my work. I gave him the job because he was out of work. Parry recommended him. I have heard that Marsden left the Prudential on account of financial irregularities [*it is unclear whether Wallace knew this before he gave him the job. It is hard to believe he would have done so had he known*].

While Marsden was working for me he often came to my house on business [*Marsden could have only covered Wallace's round for a few days*]. He also knew the interior arrangements of my house. I have seen Marsden several times since he worked for me. I do not know if he is working now [*Marsden was working at a bookmaker in Birkenhead*] and I do not know anything about his private affairs. If he had called at my house my wife would have asked him in.

Both Parry and Marsden knew the arrangements of my business with regard the system of paying in money collected to the head office in Dale Street. There is a definite order of the company's that money must be paid in on Wednesdays, although this is not strictly enforced, and I paid it in on a Thursday usually. I have had the cashbox, from which the money was stolen, for about 16 years. I always put the company's money in that box, and it is always kept on the top of the bookcase in the kitchen during the daytime. At night I always took it upstairs to my bedroom. Parry and Marsden know I kept the money in the box because while they worked for me I always put the money into it when they called to pay over to me their collections. They had both seen me take it down and put it back to the top of the bookcase often.

Marsden is about 28 years of age, about 5 foot 6 or 7 inches, brown hair, and fairly well dressed. Parry is about 5 foot 10 inches, slim build, dark hair, rather foppish appearance, well dressed and wears spats, very plausible. I believe Mr Parry owns a motor car or has the use of one, because I was talking to him about Christmas time in Missouri Road [*no doubt Parry was seeing his girlfriend, Lily Lloyd*] and he had a car then which he was driving. He gave me one of his company calendars.

Superintendent Crewe, his assistant Mr Wood (26 Ellersley Road), Mr J Bamber, Assistant Superintendent (43 Kingfield Road) are employees of the company who would be admitted by my wife without hesitation if they called. [*If these colleagues also knew of the location of the cashbox in the kitchen then presumably Wallace had no suspicions about any of them*]. There are personal friends of ours who would also be admitted if they called: Mr F. W. Jenkinson, his son Frederick, his daughter, his wife, they live at 12 Moscow Drive. Mr James Caird, his wife and family (Letchworth Street). He has two grown-up sons. Mr Davis, music teacher of Queens Drive, who is teaching me the violin. Mr Hayes, my tailor, of Breck Road.

221

When I left the house at 6:45pm on Tuesday night last my wife came down the back yard with me as far as the yard door, which she closed. I do not remember if she bolted it. On Monday night I left home at 7:15pm to go to the chess club. I got there about 7:45pm and started to play a game of chess with a man whose name I think is McCarthy, but I am unsure of him and I do not know his business. [*It was actually Thomas McCartney; Wallace seems to have a poor memory for names*]. He is a member of the club. We had been playing for about 10 minutes when Captain Beattie came to me and told me there had been a telephone message for me from a Mr Qualtrough asking me to go and see him at 25 Menlove Gardens East at 7:30pm on the Tuesday 21 [*it was Tuesday 20 January*] on a matter of business. Captain Beattie had the name Qualtrough and the address 25 Menlove Gardens East and the time and date of the appointment written on an envelope and I copied it into my diary. Mr Caird was present and we discussed how to get to Menlove Gardens.

When I left on Monday night to go to the chess club I think I walked along Richmond Park to Breck Road and then up to Belmont Road, where I boarded a tramcar and got off at the corner of Lord Street and North John Street.

When I was at Allerton looking for the address 25 Menlove Gardens East, in addition to the people I have already mentioned, I enquired from a woman in Menlove Gardens North. She came out of a house near the end by Menlove Gardens West. She told me it might be further up in continuation of Menlove Gardens West. I went along as suggested by her and came to a crossroad, I think it was Dudley Road [*Dudlow Lane*], and I met a young man about 25 years old, tall and fair [*Sydney Green*] and I enquired from him but he could not inform me. I walked back down the West Gardens to the South Gardens and found all even numbers. I came out onto Menlove Avenue itself, when I saw a man waiting for a tram by a stop where there was a shelter. I went up to him and asked if he could tell me where Menlove Gardens East was, and he said he was a stranger to the area and did not know. I think these are all the people I spoke to that night at Allerton.

When I got back home and after getting into the house and making the discovery of my wife's death, Mr Johnston went for the doctor and the police. Mrs Johnston and I stayed in and, sometime after, a knock came to the front door. I answered it and it was thus found that the front door was bolted. The safety catch was not on the latch lock. I opened the door and admitted the constable. This was the first time I went to the front door after getting into the house [*although he would have had the opportunity to go to the front door when he first entered the house alone*].

When I left my house at 6:45pm my wife was sitting in the kitchen, that is when I got my hat and coat on ready to go, and as I have already said, she came down the yard with me. The tea things were on the table. When I got back the table had been cleared of the tea things [*although they were not washed, according to Florence Johnston*].

There is a Mr Thomas, a member of the chess club, and a Mr Stan Young, who used to be an employee of the company, who would be admitted by my wife if they called. I do not know their addresses. My wife had no friends unknown to me as far as I know.

The Third Statement. *Friday 23 January 1931.*
Before I got on the tram at Smithdown Road on Tuesday night, I asked the conductor whether it went anywhere near Menlove Gardens. The conductor [*Thomas Phillips*] said I had better go to Penny Lane and have a transfer. I then boarded the car and sat inside on the first seat on the right. A few seconds later a ticket inspector [*Edward Angus*] entered the car and he told me to get off at Penny Lane and then take a 5A, and he told me the numbers of other cars which I cannot remember, and that either of those cars would take me to Menlove Gardens.

I took a penny ticket and got off at Penny Lane. The conductor pointed to a tram, a 5A, which was standing there, and told me that would take me to Menlove Gardens. I boarded it and took a penny ticket and asked the conductor to put me off at Menlove Gardens, and he did so. I remember looking at my watch and noticing that I had 10 minutes to spare before the appointment was due at 7:30pm. So it must have been about 7:20pm when I got off the tram.

Comment: *Tram conductor Thomas Phillips testified that he told Wallace he could "get on a No. 5, 5A, 5W or a No. 7 car". In his statement, however, he said that he saw Wallace hurrying to a No.*

5 car and shouted to him, "No not that one — a No. 7 in the out loop." Wallace moved towards the No. 7 but actually boarded a 5A. It appears Wallace was following the instructions of the ticket inspector rather than the conductor.

Fourth Statement *Thursday 29 January 1931.*

On Monday night the 19th when I left home to go to the chess club I think I went out by the back door and up the passage to Richmond Park and then up Breck Road and got the tram at Belmont Road. I do not remember seeing anyone I know. I am not sure but I have an idea that I posted a letter in the pillar box opposite the library in Breck Road. I have a lot of correspondence and I have no special reason for remembering about whether or not I did post a letter that night because I post so many.

When I returned home at 8.40pm on Tuesday the 20th I went to the front door because it was my usual practice if I was out late at night. It was my usual practice to use the back door in daylight and if I went out by the back way after dark my wife usually came down the yard and bolted the yard door after me when I went out.

As far as I can recollect I do not know anyone named Hall [*a reference to Lily Hall*] living in the neighbourhood of Wolverton Street or Richmond Park or any of the streets adjacent, but I have an idea that I have heard my late wife mention of that name in connection with Holy Trinity Church, but my recollection of that is very hazy. In the summer of 1929 I remember my wife and I had been out for a walk. I had forgotten to take my key and we had to borrow a key from Mr Gosling who lives on the opposite side of Wolverton Street and his key opened our front door. Some years ago a man named Cadwallader, who lived at 33 Wolverton Street, had a key that opened our door, because he used to drink and on several occasions he made a mistake and came into our house instead of his own. He has been dead several years and his widow and son still live at 33 Wolverton Street.

Comment: *It appears that at least one neighbour, possibly more, could enter 29 Wolverton Street by simply using their own front door key. However, the burnt mackintosh tells us that the parlour fire was lit at some point, weighing against an uninvited neighbour entering her house. In fact, had someone entered the house with a* *duplicate or skeleton key, we would most likely expect Julia to have been attacked in the kitchen, where she was sewing.*

Exhibit 9. Wallace's "Life Story"

After the trial, Wallace wrote a 55-page memoir, which was the foundation of six articles that appeared in *Tit-Bits* magazine in the summer of 1931. The document is kept by Hill Dickenson LLC, Liverpool, who gave permission for the following extracts to be published. I have selected a few passages that add to our knowledge of the man and particularly his thoughts on the murder. The section headings and italicised comments are mine; the words are those of William Herbert Wallace.

Wallace's Interests

My work, which was not particularly arduous, suited me admirably; the open air and exercise improved my health, and I had sufficient leisure to devote to those scientific pursuits which had always meant so much to me from my earliest years.

I had taken certificates at technical schools for electricity and chemistry. I was expert in the grinding of lenses for my microscopic hobby, and my greatest ambition was that I might make some discovery which would be of benefit to science.

At the Liverpool Technical College I resumed my chemical researches and after two years was appointed part-time demonstrator and lecturer in chemistry. I continued lecturing for five years. My fees I shared with my wife, classifying the additional income as pocket money for us both. My share I spent on scientific books and instruments!

Microscopic photography was an additional interest and earlier botanical studies I extended, making hundreds of slides. In all of these hobbies my wife proved an encouraging and devoted helper, entering wholeheartedly in every one of my pursuits.

The Quest

This '25 Menlove Gardens East' proving to be an entirely fictitious address, I spent a good deal of time making enquiries from various people because I felt that there might be some error in the taking down of the phone message and, also having come some four miles from my home, I would not leave the district until I had definitely established that no such person or place existed. And why such action on my part should have been construed by the police later as an effort to establish an alibi I cannot imagine. To me it seemed, and still seems, a perfectly natural procedure.

Locked Out

Until I returned home I did not suspect the message was a deliberate fake because I was almost certain that some stupid blunder had been made. But on attempting to enter at my front door and finding it would not open, I immediately had a sensation of uneasiness. It was so unusual to find the door bolted. I knocked because I had every reason to believe my wife was in the house, either upstairs or sitting in the kitchen as was her habit. The back yard door would certainly have been bolted for this was my wife's custom if I was out of the house.

Receiving no answer to my knocking, I went round to the back and found that though the back yard [gate] was shut it was not bolted. I could not, however, gain entrance to the back kitchen door. Again I knocked and still there was no reply. The thought crossed my mind that my wife might have gone out to the post but then I recollected she had rather a heavy cold and certainly would not have risked going out of the house. Thereupon, my uneasiness increased. It was such a totally unusual experience that I could not enter [the house] that a vague alarm seized me.

Again, I tried the front door with no better result. Coming once more round to the back, my neighbours, Mr and Mrs Johnston, came out of their house, apparently to take a stroll.

"Good evening," I said, "Have you heard any unusual noise or anything in our house during the last hour or so? I've been out on a business call and I find both doors locked against me and I can't get into the house."

Comment: *In their statements, the Johnstons confirmed that Wallace told them he could not get into his house by either the front or back door. According to PC Williams, Wallace told the constable that he "returned home, being suspicious that something had happened". At the trial, he said he felt no uneasiness when he initially went to the back door, thinking his wife might have gone to the post. Cross-examined on this point, Wallace said prior to returning home he had become a little uneasy, largely because of the rash of burglaries that had occurred recently in the area, but not unduly alarmed. He also testified that,* *by looking through the back kitchen door, he could see no light coming from the kitchen and then became suspicious.*

The Masquerade
It was clear as daylight to me that whoever had sent the phone message to the chess club had done so purposely to get me out of the house the following night when I was likely to have a substantial sum of money in my cashbox. It was equally clear that he must have been well known to my wife, for otherwise she would not have admitted him. I could imagine this man of mystery, who masqueraded under the name of Qualtrough, watching me leave my house on the Monday night and board the tram going city-wards, then slipping into the nearby telephone booth and sending that message to await my arrival. This fact convinces me, also, that his voice must have been familiar to me because, evidently, he was not risking my being at the other end of the line.

Again, the next night he would be lurking outside my house and again he would watch me leave and board a tram. My movements would convince him I was off to that fictitious address, 25 Menlove Gardens East, and that I was safely out of the way for a length of time sufficient for his purpose.

The Trial
Mr Hemmerde outlined the case against me. It all sounded so futile, so absurd, so much a waste of time. The very idea that I could raise my hand to any woman, and particularly my wife, was monstrous. The main contention of the police was that I had sent the telephone message to myself at the chess club to set up an alibi the following night. That, without the shadow of any conceivable motive, I had murdered my wife using an iron bar or a poker which couldn't be found...

Another puzzle was the fact that my mackintosh was found under the shoulders of my wife, badly burnt at the bottom and heavily bloodstained. The front of my wife's skirt was also burnt and the prosecution saw no way out except that my wife, being struck, had fallen onto the gas fire. But if the murderer was wearing the mackintosh how had it become burnt also? I was surprised as much as anyone and could not agree with my counsel that my wife had thrown it around her shoulders to go to the door to admit – whoever she did admit. It was a thing I had never known her to do and could not imagine her doing. But I confess my poor brain could invent no other possible alternative to that theory. I can't imagine what the murderer was doing with it or how it came to be burnt unless it was worn in some way by my wife...

I had to sit in that dock and listen to this weaving of coincidences, suggestions, theories, and ifs – none of which had the slightest weight of evidence – without being able to reply in any way or protest. A hundred times I wanted to shout out a refutation of some vile suggestion. It seemed to me then, and still is, a firm conviction that the prosecution was vindictive and pressing every conceivable and inconceivable point with malevolence... every point in what was called evidence against me fitted the alternative theory of the crime having been committed by some other man whose motive was, obviously, robbery.

Making History
My case, I understand, is now the only one on record in which a jury's verdict in a murder trial has been reversed on point of fact. I am, too, I believe, the only man condemned to death for whom prayers have been offered in an English Cathedral. So perhaps my sufferings have been worthwhile. At least, I have made history!

Comment: *This passage, and indeed the entire memoir, reveals an egocentric and serious person who wanted to be noticed.*

Murder Will Out
I am free to live, to take up – if it were possible – the thread of my life. But there is a brutal murderer at large. Who is he? Where is he? Who was that man of mystery in the telephone box? Who was this masquerader, Qualtrough? Who was this man of blood whose face must have been familiar to my poor wife and whose voice would have been recognised by me? Who was it who knew the routine of my business and exactly where I kept my weekly collections of cash? Who plotted this vile crime and was content to let an innocent man go to the gallows in his stead? There is an old saying that 'murder will out'... Time alone will tell.

Comment: *With these words, the memoir ends. Interestingly, there is no mention of Marcus Aurelius or Stoicism in the entire* *document. In a later article, Wallace suggested he was found guilty because his Stoicism made him appear callous. He believed he should have been credited with showing fortitude and strength of character.*

Exhibit 10. "I Know The Murderer"

In the summer of 1931, Wallace's his life story was serialised by *Tit-Bits* magazine. The narrative followed his Life Story memoir quite closely, even ending with same lines, but it appears the copy had been spiced up a little by a journalist. The articles were:

- 4 July 1931. Innocent But Condemned To Death
- 11 July 1931. The Mysterious Mr "X"
- 18 July 1931. Death Called By Telephone
- 23 July 1931. In The Condemned Cell
- 1 August 1931. Escape From The Scaffold
- 8 August 1931. A World Of Whispers

Six months later, *John Bull* magazine also ran six articles on Wallace's ordeal titled "The Man They Did Not Hang". They followed similar themes but were ghost-written; the style is florid with greater sensationalism, especially compared to his memoir. The articles were:

- 16 April 1932. The Most Amazing Document Ever Written
- 23 April 1932. The World Refuses to Have Me Back
- 30 April 1932. Women's Poison-Tongues Pursue Me
- 7 May 1932. In The Condemned Cell I was Less Lonely
- 14 May 1932. Three Dreaded Days in My Life
- 21 May 1932. I Know the Murderer

In this last article, Wallace claimed he knew the identity of the killer and provided more of his thoughts on the crime than in the earlier serialisation. He insisted the murderer was known to both him and his wife, was familiar with his business affairs, frequented the City Café and had recently been convicted of theft. In other words, it was Gordon Parry, although he could not name him. Below are some key extracts, providing us with an insight on Wallace's thoughts on the murder.

"Now let me say this: *I know the murderer...* I feel bitter because, since my acquittal, [the police] refuse to give my lawyer or myself, any information as to whether or how far they have carried on any investigation."

Comment: *Wallace appears to want to track down the killer, or at least give that impression. The police stated after the acquittal that they would not be pursuing the case further, insinuating that they had put the correct man in the dock.*

"I must have been well known to the man who took my wife's life... Even after my liberty was given back to me, it was some time before I would connect my suspect to the crime... Then, at last, I discovered why he went to my house and killed my wife... the murder took place on a Tuesday night. Often I had in my house on Tuesdays as much as £100 of my employer's money, which I paid in weekly on Wednesdays. He must have got to know this, and also that the money was usually in a cashbox and where that box always was."

Comment: *If Wallace wrote this, he was disingenuous. He usually paid his remittances on a Thursday, and said so at the trial. He would not have anything like £100 in his house during a normal collection week {see Exhibit 16}. Indeed, he testified that it would be between £20 and £40 pounds, which is accurate. The passage in* John Bull *reads as if someone had looked at the trial transcript and replayed the arguments of Wallace's barrister.*

"It was my wife's rigid rule not to admit strangers into the house while she was alone, and to this day it has been some speculation how the man actually made his way inside. He must have been ready with some pretext to be allowed to wait until I returned."

Comment: *This is consistent with his memoir and earlier* Tit-Bits *article, in which he claimed the killer "was known to my wife, otherwise she would not have allowed him to enter the house. Indeed, the fact she had taken him into the sitting room and lit the gas fire pointed conclusively to her having had utter confidence in the caller that night." However, Parry claimed he was admitted on his first visit {see Exhibit 12}.*

"He followed my wife into the sitting room and, as she bent down and lit the fire, struck her, possibly with a spanner... She must have been felled as soon as she lit the fire and before she could regulate the flow of gas. It would have been at full blaze and as he bent down at the fireplace the flame set light to the mackintosh."

Comment: *See Chapter 5 and Exhibit 6 for a discussion about the mackintosh.*

"Only now do I know that at the time of the crime he was in desperate straits. And I have found that he has been convicted for offences involving money."

Comment: *The last point is true – Parry was charged with stealing money from telephone boxes in February 1932. If the first is accurate, Parry clearly had a motive for burglary. An anonymous typed letter sent to Wallace's solicitor claimed that, at the time of the murder, Parry was asking colleagues and insurance agents to loan him money.*

Wallace quoted MacFall from the trial (it was almost verbatim): "[Wallace's] demeanour was abnormal. He was quiet – too quiet – for a person whose wife had been killed in that way. He was not so nearly as affected as I was myself." Wallace then remarked: "What relevance, I asked myself, had this to forensic science? What could this professor possibly know about my normal demeanour, my quietness in emergency? And how could he judge to what extent I was affected?"

Comment: *One has to agree: MacFall was speaking without knowledge and outside his expertise. If Wallace had cried uncontrollably would MacFall have said that he was too much affected and faking it? We should conclude – regardless of whether Wallace was actually guilty or not – that MacFall gave prejudicial testimony.*

Exhibit 11. Parry's Alibi

The statements of key witnesses are being placed before the Cold Case Jury because they provide important testimony given to the police when memories of events were fresh. This section deals with statements relating to Gordon Parry, who claimed to be at Lily Lloyd's house on the night of the Qualtrough telephone call. As you will see, his girlfriend refutes this. Parry's alibi for the night of the murder was provided by Olivia Brine. My explanatory comments are italicised.

Richard Gordon Parry *Friday 23 January 1931*.

I live at 7 Woburn Hill and I am an inspector employed by the Standard Life Assurance Company. I have known Mr and Mrs Wallace of 29 Wolverton Street since September 1926, by being in the employ of the Prudential Assurance Company of which Mr Wallace was an agent [*Parry had known Wallace for over four years at the time of the murder*]. In December 1928 Mr Wallace was off duty ill, and I did his work for two weeks. On the Thursday of the first week and on the Wednesday evening of the second, I called at his house to hand over the cash and settle the books. The first time I called Mrs Wallace gave me a cup of tea and some cake while I was waiting for Mr Wallace to come downstairs. It was about 10am and I waited in the kitchen. I had been to Mr Wallace's house on several occasions prior to December 1928 on business matters for my superintendent, Mr Crewe, and had also called several times after that date on similar business.

I always looked up to Mr and Mrs Wallace as a devoted couple. The last time I called at Wallace's was about October or November 1929, and then I called on business for Mr Crewe. The last time I saw Mr Wallace was about three weeks ago on a bus from Victoria Street. I got off at Shaw Street. I know that Mr Wallace is very fond of music, he plays bowls, and I have seen him at the City Café in North John Street – he is a member of a chess club there.

I am a member of the Mersey Amateur Dramatic Society and previous to the production of John Glaydes Honour on 17 November 1930, at Crane Hall, we were rehearsing at the City Café every Tuesday and Thursday. It was during these rehearsals that I saw Mr Wallace at the City Café on about three occasions. I did not know previously that he was a member of the chess club there.

On Monday evening [*19 January 1931*] I called for my young lady, Miss Lilian Lloyd of 7 Missouri Road, at some address where she had been teaching, the address I cannot remember, and went with her to 7 Missouri Road at about 5:30pm and remained there until about 11:30pm when I went home [*this is not true, according to the statements of Lily and her mother – see later*].

On Tuesday [*20 January 1931*], I finished business at 5:30pm and called upon Mrs Brine, 43 Knoclaid Road. I remained there with Mrs Brine, her daughter Savona [*13 years old*], her nephew Harold Denison, until about 8:30pm. I then went out and bought some cigarettes – Players No. 3 – and the *Evening Express* from the post office in Maiden Lane, on the way to my young lady's house. When I was turning the corner by the post office I remembered I had promised to call for my accumulator at Hignetts in West Derby Road. I went there and got my accumulator and then went down West Derby Road and along to Mrs Williamson, of 49 Lisburn Lane, and saw her. We had a chat about a 21st birthday party for about 10 minutes, and then I went to 7 Missouri Road, and remained there till about 11pm to 11:30pm, when I went home [*note the reference to the 21st birthday party*].

I have heard of the murder of Mrs Wallace and have studied the newspaper reports of the case and naturally, being acquainted with Mr and Mrs Wallace, I have taken a great interest in it. I have no objection whatever to the police verifying my statement as to my movements on Monday 19th and Tuesday 20th.

Miss Lilian Lloyd *Monday 26 January 1931.*
I am 20 years of age and reside with my parents at 7 Missouri Road. I am a music teacher. I am keeping company with R. G. Parry of 7 Woburn Hill. On Monday 19 I had an appointment at my home with a pupil named Rita Price. I cannot remember properly but either Rita was late or I was. It was not more than 10 minutes. I gave my pupil a full 45-minute lesson and about 20 minutes before I finished Parry called. That would be about 7:35pm [*this would be approximately 10 minutes after the Qualtrough call was made from the Anfield telephone box, which was about one mile away*]. I did not see him and when I finished the lesson he had

gone. I know he called because I heard his car and his knock at the door and I heard his voice at the door. I do not know who answered the door. He returned between 8:30pm and 9pm and remained until 11pm. He told me he had been to, I think, Park Lane [*which is near North John Street, the location of the City Café*].

On Tuesday 20 Parry called between 8:30pm and 9pm, but I think it was near 9pm. He told me in answer to a question he had been to a Mrs Williamson. I know Mrs Williamson, she is a friend of mine. He told me that he had got an invitation for myself and him to Leslie Williamson's 21st birthday party in April. I do not remember whether or not he had told me he had received the invitations that night but I got the impression that he had. He remained until about 11pm and then went home. He came in his car. I think Parry wore striped trousers on the Monday night and his blue suit on the Tuesday and Wednesday, and I think he has worn his striped trousers every day since, but I'm not sure about Friday or Saturday.

Comment: *Lily states that Parry told her he had seen Mrs Williamson, yet there is no statement from the latter to corroborate this.*

Mrs Josephine Lloyd *Monday 26 January 1931.*
I am the wife of Reginald Lloyd and have a daughter Lilian. My daughter is a music teacher. She is keeping company with R. G. Parry of 7 Woburn Hill.

On Monday 19 January 1931 Mr Parry called at my house at about 7:15pm as near as I can remember. I can fix the time as about 7:15pm because my daughter has a pupil named Rita Price of Clifton Road who is due for a music lesson at 7pm or a bit earlier every Monday. Last Monday [*the night of the Qualtrough call*] she was a few minutes late and she had started her lesson when Parry arrived in his car. He stayed about 15 minutes and then left because he said he was going to make a call to Lark Lane [*it appears that Parry never intended to stay long*]. He came back in his car at about 9pm to 9:15pm and stayed until about 11pm, when he left.

On Tuesday 20 January Mr Parry called at 9pm and remained here until about 11pm. He came in his car which he left outside.

On Monday and Tuesday nights of last week Parry was dressed in a black jacket and vest and striped trousers and spats when he called. On Wednesday and Thursday, or Thursday and Friday, he was wearing a navy blue suit. I think it was Thursday and Friday because on Saturday he had his striped trousers again.

Comment: *There is disagreement between mother and daughter as to whether Parry arrived at 7:15pm or 7:35pm on Monday 19 January 1931. The significance of the timing could not have been lost on the police: if it was 7:15pm then Parry could not have made the Qualtrough call.*

An impartial analysis of the two statements should conclude that Lily's account contains more detail concerning the fixing of the time. If Rita normally arrived at about 7pm but was running 10 minutes late, this would imply she had arrived at 7:10pm. If Parry had arrived 25 minutes into the lesson, this puts his arrival time at 7:35pm, as the daughter suggests. If Parry had arrived at 7:15pm, he would have arrived just after the beginning of the delayed lesson, something one would expect Lily to have remembered. Mother and daughter also have conflicting memories of what Parry was wearing on the night of the murder.

One thing is certain: Parry had certainly not arrived at 5:30pm and stayed six hours, as he asserted in his statement. The police never resolved why he had misled them and, more importantly, where he was at the time of the call.

To fully corroborate his alibi for the night of the murder, the police should have interviewed Mrs Olivia Brine, her nephew Harold Denison, her daughter Savona Brine, Phyllis Plant, the staff at the post office, the staff at Hignetts, and Mrs Williamson. It appears the police only took statements from the first two, which are reproduced below.

Mrs Olivia Brine *Monday 26 January 1931.*
I am a married woman, my husband is away at sea. I have known R. G. Parry about two years. Just before last Christmas he commenced calling with my nephew William Denison [*Harold's older brother*]. At about 5pm to 5:30pm on Tuesday 20 January Parry called at my house. He came in his car. He remained till about 8:30pm when he left. While he was here a Miss Plant called. My nephew Harold Denison also called.

Mr Harold Denison *Monday 26 January 1931.*
I have known R. G. Parry for two years. I called at 43 Knoclaid Road on Tuesday 20 January at about 6pm. My aunt Mrs Brine lives there. When I called Mr Parry was there. He remained till about 8:30pm when he left.

Comment: *Parry, Mrs Brine and her nephew all stated that Parry departed at "about 8:30pm" but none gave any indication of how they fixed that time (contrast with the Lloyds). Could Parry have left at, say, 8:15pm?*

Exhibit 12. Parry's Response

In 1933, *The Trial of Herbert Wallace* was published. It carried extracts from Wallace's private diaries and, although blanked out for publication, Wallace named the man who he believed had killed Julia. This prompted a man to come forward and talk to *Empire News*. The anonymous interviewee could only be Gordon Parry, but there is a suspicion that the article was ghost-written and largely fabricated, perhaps as a publicity stunt by the book publisher [1]. However, some of the details ring true, and I have included it so you can decide for yourself.

In the article, Parry cited three grievances that he believed Wallace held against him:

- Parry had spread gossip about his home life at the office
- He was jealous of Parry's business success
- Parry was too familiar with his wife.

Below are key extracts from the article "Wallace Accused Me" (5 November 1933). I have taken the most relevant quotes, occasionally re-ordering them for easier reading. The headings are mine.

Coming Forward

"I am the man Wallace suspected, and even accused. And I feel it is up to me to come forward with my version... Wallace, in his business capacity, his social life and his personal pleasures was a fine man... it is plainly my duty to place before the public certain facts concerned with the private and intimate life of Wallace."

Private Life

"Wallace had three grievances against me. He was worried about his physical condition... and only I knew that he had consulted specialists and had been given certain serious advice."

"Mrs Wallace was a good and pure woman who had suffered disappointment. Wallace, poor fellow, was not to blame. But his wife appeared to lose heart as the years went by. Perhaps of all their acquaintances, I knew the circumstances."

"...it took a bit of time, and much persuasion, to bring his wife to the door. Eventually, I was admitted to the house, and the first thing that struck me was an unpleasant smell. I stood and could not help sniffing, and Mrs Wallace explained that it was the drains... After I had explained that I was a friend of her husband and one also interested in insurance, I got as far as the parlour. Here I took a seat, and here I discovered that the smell I had got at the door was more pronounced. I said nothing, but used my eyes... The woman herself was, to my mind, untidy. The house was without doubt neglected... Piles of dishes lay all over the room – unwashed."

"I stood up as he entered the room; his wife was reclining on the couch. There was a look of sneering discovery in the eyes of the man and my reply was a glance at the untidy figure on the couch... The woman had not moved from the couch, and there was not the slightest indication of a meal [for Wallace]..."

Spreading Gossip

"Unfortunately, in a spirit of sympathetic friendship I mentioned what I had seen, and within a few days gossip spread all over the office. Wallace heard this and blamed me. I tried to undo what my tongue had started, quite innocently, but the story grew, and Wallace's anger and hatred grew with the story."

Jealousy

"I told Wallace on a certain occasion that I would let him know when certain stocks would be a profitable investment and called around to his house to give him some useful information... I still do quite a little business on 'chance'. Wallace discovered I was a lucky punter and had asked me to give him some tips... Wallace hated me because I was successful in business where he failed... My success added fuel to the fire of his hatred, and he never tried to hide this from me."

Comment: *By the time this was published, Parry's self-proclaimed business acumen had led him to thieving from telephone boxes and attempting to steal cars.*

Too Familiar

"Gradually, Wallace began to look on me as an enemy – not only as an enemy but as a persistent danger to his home life. He could not see the utter absurdity of his conclusions in this respect, for of all the women I have ever met, his wife, at the time I knew her, was to me the least attractive."

Confrontations

"Soon after the tragedy… I met [Wallace]. He looked at me and grew red and then pale. His jaws set in a terrible struggle with the unspoken words, but all his efforts could not hold him dumb, for as we passed he turned his head and said, 'They'll get you – you devil.'

"After he came back to Liverpool, I managed to see him. He smiled grimly as I stopped him, and a look of utter hatred came over his face… he went livid, and turning down an alley, beckoned me to follow. When we were alone, he turned upon me saying: 'Do you want to add another to the crime you have committed? Try – try, you cur! I have taken all precautions against you. I know you want me out of the way and that you will do your best to get me. I have told the police, and if I am found murdered as was my poor dear wife they (the police) will know who to place in the dock.'"

Mortal Dread

"…on the advice of my lawyer I told the police. It was about that time that he put in all the gadgets at his house – switches that illuminated the outside and the interior. He was, I do believe, in mortal dread of being murdered – and that he regarded me as the only possible assassin."

Notes:

[1] The opening paragraph of the article included the lines: "I am not the man detained by the police and questioned. That man proved his absolute innocence…" Parry was the only other suspect questioned by the police. Were these lines included because *Empire News* was concerned it might be sued by Parry who actually had *not* cooperated? However, it is also possible that Parry wanted a smokescreen to fully protect his identity, especially if he had promised his father not to talk about the case.

HIS FINAL WORDS

In the 1960s, Jonathan Goodman tracked down and spoke to "Dick" Parry. The notes of the interview were published by Roger Wilkes in *The Final Verdict*, and reveal that Parry:

• Denied that Wallace named him as prime suspect [*which we know he did*]

• Adamantly refused to talk about the case because he had promised his father he would not. [*Why was William Parry so concerned about his son talking?*]

• Claimed the "worry of it all" shortened his mother's life

• Recalled that the police were satisfied of his innocence when he was able to show that he had spent the evening with some people "arranging a birthday celebration". [*This must be the three hours he spent with Olivia Brine. It's a shame the police could not elicit this detail from Mrs Brine or her nephew in their statements*]

• Said the incident broke up his engagement with Lily Lloyd. [*Did Lily discover that Parry had lied about his whereabouts at the time of the call? Or that he had been at the house of a married woman for three hours on the night of the murder?*]

• Claimed that he would often have tea with Julia and they would have musical evenings – alone. [*Was Wallace at his chess club? And, if he called after dark, did Parry have a particular knock to indicate to Julia that it was him at the door?*]

• Admitted that he was "a tearaway" and his expenditure exceeded his income.

Exhibit 13. The Neighbours' View

Below are statements given by Florence and John Johnston, both eye witnesses to the discovery of Julia Wallace's battered body.

Florence Johnston (Police Statement) *21 January 1931*
I live with my husband at 31 Wolverton Street. I have known Mr and Mrs Wallace about 10 years. I have never known them to quarrel. I did not see Mr and Mrs Wallace on Tuesday the 20th January 1931. At about 4:30pm on that day I heard Mrs Wallace speaking to the window cleaner at the back. We have the same window cleaner.

I was in my house up to 8:45pm and I did not hear any unusual noise in Wallace's house until about 8:25 to 8:30pm. I was then in my kitchen and I heard two thumps which I thought was my father in my front parlour taking off his boots [*there is no record of whether this was confirmed by her father*]. My father lives in our front parlour. I took no notice of the noises and at about 8:45pm me and my husband went out of the back door.

As my husband opened our yard door, Mr Wallace was passing, walking hurriedly, towards his back door and I said, "Good evening Mr Wallace", and he said "Have you heard anything unusual?" I said, "Why? What has happened?" He said he could not get in either back or front. He went to his back door and opened it and said to us "It opens now." My husband said "We will wait a minute. I'll see if everything is all right." He said "I know she won't be out. She has a bad cold."

I saw there was a light in the back bedroom and a minute or two afterwards it went up. I then saw the light of a match in the other back bedroom. A minute or two later he came to his back door and said, "Oh come in and see. She's been killed." He was hurried and his voice was raised but not to a shout. His tone was distressed.

Whilst I was waiting at the entry door when Mr Wallace first went in the house I did not see any light in the kitchen but they have a dark green blind over the window so that I would not be able to tell if the gas was lit. When I went into the house with Mr Wallace the gas in the kitchen was lit, and the parlour light was lit too.

My husband went away for the doctor and the police and I stayed with Mr Wallace. I then again went with Mr Wallace into the parlour where the body was. He knelt down by the side of the body, on the window side, and we both felt her hand. She seemed to have gone colder in about 10 minutes. Mr Wallace said, "Oh. They have finished her. Whatever was she doing with her mackintosh and my mackintosh round her."

Before he said this about the mackintoshes he had moved round the body on the sideboard side and he stooped down and felt the mackintosh and looked at it. I said, "I wonder what they have used" and he felt under the hearthrug but only just under the edge, and he patted it as if he was feeling underneath for anything. We then went into the kitchen. The kitchen fire was nearly out and Mr Wallace and I put some wood on and he helped me to get it going by stirring the few live embers at the bottom. Mr Wallace put the coal on after the chips had caught. From the appearance of the fireplace when I went in it looked as if there had been a good fire and that it had burned out.

I was in the lobby by the front door with Mr Wallace when the Constable came and knocked. I tried to open the door but it is a different type of lock to ours. To open ours the knob has to be turned and Wallace's had to be slid along. I couldn't open Wallace's and I turned to Mr Wallace and said, "Oh. You had better do it." He opened the door. I cannot say whether it was bolted or not.

About five minutes before I saw Mr Wallace in the entry I had heard someone knock on his back door. I had heard Mr Wallace knock in a similar way many times before and recognised the knock as his. As far as I can recollect I did not hear any noise in Wallace's yard or back [of the house] between the time I heard the knock and when I saw him.

My milk that day was delivered from Mr Close of Sedley Street [at] about 6:30pm. I had my jug in the lobby and my front door open. The boy put my milk in the jug and shut the door after him. I heard the door shut and I fetched in my milk at once.

F.S. Johnston

The following are excerpts from a long statement given by Florence to Wallace's solicitor, Hector Munro. I have selected quotes that add to her police statement.

Florence Johnston *14 February 1931*

"I and my husband lived at 31 Wolverton Street, Anfield, for about ten years until we moved to my daughter's house early this February. I was very friendly with Mr and Mrs Wallace, but more so with Mrs Wallace, who was very kind to me. They were both delicate and the winter months tried them very much."

"They were a very devoted couple and I remember that Mr Wallace was agitated when his wife did not return in the evening from Southport just before Christmas. Mrs Wallace told my daughter how worried he had been, and said that when she got in about 1am they sat up quite a long time talking and having tea together. I never saw any quarrels between them, and do not believe that Mr Wallace would have ever thought of doing any harm to his wife."

"When I first went into the front room, I saw a box of matches lying on the table, and asked Mr Wallace if those were her matches, and he said they were. There were also two dead matches lying by the body."

"Before my husband had left Mr Wallace said 'See, she hasn't had time to wash up the tea things'. There were a few coins lying on the kitchen floor, and Mr Wallace said 'See, they've broken that off.'' We looked, and saw the door of a cabinet lying on the floor."

"The police talked together in the Hall, and Mr Wallace and I were in the Hall by the stairs. We were all very agitated and could not sit down for long. Then we all sat in the kitchen, and Mr Wallace sat in the chair, and was very, very distressed, half collapsed. He has a sallow complexion, and I would not notice any pallow. His shoulders heaved, and he was sobbing. I had sent my daughter for Mrs [Amy] Wallace in Ullet Road. Mr Wallace could hardly speak for emotion."

"Whenever the Police came into the kitchen, Mr Wallace pulled himself together, but when they were out, and he was alone with me and my husband, he broke down several times and sobbed. He leaned his face on one side of his hand. Once, when one of the policemen came in, he asked to see Professor MacFall, who was examining the body. When Mrs Amy Wallace [and Edwin, his nephew] arrived, he just said 'Tell them, please. I can't'. He sat crouched over the fire, sobbing occasionally. He broke down momentarily on two occasions that I remember."

"Before the police arrived, Mr Wallace and I went back into the front room, and I said to him 'Whatever have they used?' He said 'What was she doing with her mackintosh? And my mackintosh?' I looked, and saw the mackintosh tucked round her body, behind her, and touching the body. She looked as if she was lying on it. It looked as though a knock had come to the front door, and she had pulled the mackintosh round her shoulders, as she had a cold, before answering the knock. I said 'Why, is it your mackintosh?' and he just stooped down and pulled out the folds, and said 'Yes, it's mine'. There was only one mackintosh there, so far as I know. We then went back into the back room. The first policeman arrived about ten past nine."

"The milk boy, Alan Close, called at my house that evening, but I cannot remember the exact time. He might come at any time between ten past six and seven, but recently he had been very late."

John Johnston (statement to Hector Munro) *14 February 1931*
I lived at 31 Wolverton Street Anfield for about 10 years and had known Mr and Mrs Wallace for a long time. They were a devoted couple. At 8:45pm on Tuesday 20th January I and my wife were just stepping out of our back door to go out. As I opened the door, my wife stepped out and at the same time Mr Wallace passed our door.

My wife said "Good evening, Mr Wallace." I thought by the sound of his voice that he was anxious. He said "Have you heard anything unusual tonight?" My wife said "No, what has happened?" He said "I've been out and find I can't open the front door. It's been bolted against me." I asked him "Have you tried the back kitchen door?" He said "Yes, I couldn't open it." I said "That's funny, try it again and I'll wait."

He then went up the yard, and opened the door without any effort, and shouted to me "It opens now." I said "I'll stop here while you have a look round." I cannot say if the light was on in the kitchen when he went in. The next thing I heard was Mr Wallace calling a name twice. I do not know what the name was, and as soon as he had called the name the [middle] bedroom light was turned up. After that a match was struck in the doorway of the back bedroom.

Shortly afterwards he came to the back kitchen door into the yard and said "Come and see; she's been killed." I said "Has she fallen downstairs?" We (my wife, Mr Wallace and myself) went through the kitchen to the front sitting room, and there saw Mrs Wallace lying on the floor. The gas had already been lit, and I saw a matchstick on the floor. I stooped down and saw her head all battered and her brains on the floor. My wife took hold of her hand and said "Oh, you poor darling", and I asked "Is she cold?" and my wife replied "No."

I said "Don't disturb anything I'm going for a doctor and the police." Mr Wallace stooped down and felt her hand. He mentioned something about her rings being missing, and I presume when he took hold of her hand he felt to see if they were missing, and Mr Wallace said, "Perhaps she hadn't them on." He was very distressed and appeared to have had a very severe shock.

We then went into the kitchen and I asked him if he wanted any particular doctor and he said "The nearest one." Mr Wallace pointed out that a wooden lid was on the floor by the recess in the kitchen and said "see they have broken that off." He then reached up to a top shelf and took down a cashbox and opening it I asked him, "Is anything missing?" and he said, "About £4 but I can't say I'm certain till I check my books." He then replaced the cashbox, and I asked "Is everything all right upstairs before I go for the police?" He went upstairs and came down almost at once and said "Everything is all right up there; there's £5 there in a dish." I at once left leaving my wife and Mr Wallace in the home.

I called at Dr Dunlop and told him of the happening. He lives at Lower Breck Road which is the nearest doctor to this address. He said it was a case for the police surgeon and I at once went to Anfield Police Station and arrived there at about 9:05pm. I informed the sergeant and he at once sent a constable with orders to stay there until other officers arrived.

I waited in the police station till 9:30pm. And during that time the police ambulance arrived and reported that the woman was dead and cold. I then returned to the house and informed the police there. Mr Wallace kept breaking down crying and saying, "If Julia saw this she would go mad." I asked the police later on if I might go and I went home. The police came and took my statement at 2am. The front room did not appear to be disturbed.

J.S. Johnston

Exhibit 14. Amy Wallace's Account

William Wallace's sister-in-law does not have a major role in our story. However, her police statement reveals that Wallace told Julia about the Qualtrough call.

Amy Wallace *21 January 1931*
I am married and live at 83 Ullet Road. My husband is abroad. Mrs Wallace of 29 Wolverton Street is my sister-in-law. At about 3:30pm on 20 Tuesday 1931 I called at 29 Wolverton Street to see my sister-in-law. She was in and I stayed there until 4pm or shortly after. She wanted me to stay for tea but I refused because I had no time to stay.

She was in her usual health apart from her cold. We talked about various matters and she told me that her husband, Mr Wallace, had a telephone message while he was at the chess club the previous night to call somewhere in the Calderstones district sometime that evening, that is the Tuesday evening. She told me that neither she nor her husband knew anyone in the district.

The bread boy called while I was there but no one else. We were alone in the house. She did not mention she expected anyone to call. I left sometime between 4pm and 4:30pm.

Amy Wallace

Comment: It appears Julia did not mention the distinctive name "Qualtrough" to Amy – if she had, one would expect Amy to have remembered it. Wallace stated at his trial that Julia "knew all about it [the appointment]. As a matter of fact, we had discussed it during the day and it was really because we discussed it together that I decided to go" and they also "discussed it at tea". Asked whether he had told her the man's name and where he was going, Wallace replied: "Yes, everything about it. I might say I never made a decision if I was in difficulty without conferring with my wife on any point." So, it appears Wallace talked to Julia about the phone call on two occasions, possibly briefly over breakfast or lunch, and again at tea when more information might have been provided, including the caller's name.

Amy Wallace also gave an interview to a press reporter. Although she later claimed that she did not know it would be published, she did not complain about its content. The *Nottingham Post* ran the following brief article:

Mr W H Wallace's only relative in Liverpool is a sister-in-law, a Mrs Wallace, who lives in a flat in the south end of the city. In an interview with the Post, *she said: "Mrs Wallace was one of the most peaceful and lovable of women. In fact, her kindness was her only fault. Her husband, my brother-in-law, was perhaps nervous of her being all alone in the house at night, as they had no family, and had told her more than once not to open her door to strangers. I expect she did not like to keep them out in the cold, and this terrible business may have been the result of her kindness. I am sure she had no personal enemies. The motive must have been robbery."*

Comment: Amy Wallace implied that Julia would let a stranger into her house; Wallace was adamant she would not. However, we know Julia had admitted strangers connected to her husband's business because Parry was allowed into the parlour on his first visit {see Exhibit 12}.

Exhibit 15. Conversations In The Dark

The following statement was given by Lily Hall, who claimed she saw Wallace talking to another man at about 8:40pm on the night of the murder. It is significant because, if she is correct, it raises the possibility that Wallace was involved in a conspiracy (see Chapter 9). See Exhibit A for the map of the area in question.

Miss Lily Hall *Sunday 25 January 1931.*
I am a typist employed at Littlewoods, commission agents, and I live with my parents at 9 Letchworth Street [*this is 100 yards from 29 Wolverton Street as the crow flies*].

I have known Mr Wallace for three or four years by sight and about a fortnight ago, I learned his name from Mr Johnston Junior of 31 Wolverton Street. I was there visiting them.

On Tuesday 20 January 1931, I left Charles Street soon after 8pm and took a tram home at the corner of Lord Street and Whitechapel. I got off the tram at the tram stop in Breck Road at the corner of Walton Breck Road. I had arranged to go to the pictures that night if I got home in time, and when I got off the tram I looked at the Holy Trinity Church clock, which is near the tram stop, and saw it was then 8:35pm by that clock.

I walked straight home along Richmond Park and as I was passing the entry leading from Richmond Park to the middle of Wolverton Street, I saw the man I know as Mr Wallace talking to another man I do not know. Mr Wallace had his face to me and the other man his back. They were standing on the pavement in Richmond Park opposite to the entry leading up by the side of the Parish Hall. I crossed over Richmond Park and up Letchworth Street and home. When I got into our house, our clock was just turned 8.40pm but it is always 5 minutes fast. It takes me not more than 3 minutes to walk from the tram stop to our house.

The next morning I heard Mrs Wallace had been murdered and when I got home that night I told my parents that I had seen Mr Wallace the previous night. Mr Wallace was wearing a trilby hat and a darkish overcoat when I saw him talking to the man in Richmond Park on Tuesday night. The man he was talking to was about 5 foot 8 inches tall and was wearing a cap and dark overcoat; he was of stocky build.

In her statement, Hall does not say that she observed the men parting. She introduced this fact at the committal hearing and trial. Below is an extract from the trial transcript:

Counsel: As you crossed over the road [*Richmond Park*] towards Letchworth Street, what was the last thing you saw?
Hall: They parted.
Counsel: And where had they gone?
Hall: One went straight along [*Richmond Park*] and one down the entry.
Judge: Which entry are we talking about?
Hall: The one I was standing by.

Hall's answer was ambiguous – only she knew which entry she was standing by – and it caused confusion in court. To clarify matters, the prosecution counsel asked if the entry in question was located on the same side of the road as Letchworth Street. Hall affirmed it was. The judge sought further confirmation, asking whether the entry was the one to the south of Richmond Park. Counsel confirmed it was. These facts tell us the entry that one of the men used was adjacent to the Parish Hall. This is consistent with Hall's unambiguous answer at the magistrate's court when she stated that Wallace was standing "at the bottom of the entry by the Parish Hall". In which case, both men were walking *away* from the entry to Wolverton Street, suggesting neither was Wallace.

The police made three appeals in the local press for the men to come forward. On 29 January, the *Liverpool Express* reported that the police were anxious to talk to two men, one of whom was believed to be a resident of Wolverton Street, "who at about 8:35pm on Tuesday 20 January were standing in conversation on the pavement in Richmond Park opposite the entry between Letchworth Street and the Parish Hall. It is thought by the police that the two men may be able to provide certain information regarded as vital in connection with the line of enquiry now being conducted by the detectives."

No one came forward. Perhaps the men did not hear about the appeal or were nervous about having "vital" information in an unspecified "line of enquiry" in case they were suspects. Or perhaps, if author John Gannon is correct, they refused to come forward because they were involved in a murder.

A few days after the final police appeal, Hall picked out Wallace as "the man whom she saw talking to another man in Richmond Park" from a police line-up. If Hall believed she saw Wallace having a conversation in the dark, she was obviously going to identify him in daylight, having known him by sight for several years. The line-up changed nothing. It was not even mentioned when Hall testified at the trial.

But is there anything to support Hall's claim? From a detailed analysis of everything she said, Hall observed the two men at some time between 8:34pm and 8:37pm [1]. Wallace claimed he boarded the tram home at about 8pm. We know from the engineer's timing tests that it took between 32 and 37 minutes to reach the Parish Hall [2], therefore Wallace would have been standing where Hall claimed to have seen him between 8:32pm and 8:37pm; a remarkable degree of similarity. But it assumes that the times stated by all the witnesses were correct.

Hall was not alone in claiming she saw a stocky man in Richmond Park that night. Wallace's solicitor Hector Munro took a statement from Harry Greenlees, who lived at 95 Richmond Park, a stone's throw from Lily's house. He claimed he spoke to a stocky man minutes after Hall's sighting.

Henry Harrison Greenlees

I am 38 years of age. On Tuesday 20 January last I was returning from a Choir practice at St Georges Church, Everton, accompanied by a Mr Leak, my Choirmaster. He left me at Anfield Road. I walked down towards the end of Walton Breck Road, and looked at the clock of Holy Trinity Church which is brightly illuminated. It was then 8.35 p.m.

I walked along Richmond Park and when opposite No 26 but on the other side {see Exhibit A} I was accosted by a stockily built man in a felt hat who had crossed over from the bottom of Letchworth St. He asked me to direct him to No 54 Richmond Park. I told him that number did not exist. I know both Mr Wallace and Miss Hall, and did not see either of them that night. It was 8.40pm when I stepped into my house.

*

Greenlees would have spoken to Stocky Man at about 8:39pm as the encounter was very near to his home. Is it likely that there were two stocky men in Richmond Park that night, close to the same place and just minutes apart? Were they in fact the same person? If so, it is improbable that Stocky Man was the killer of Julia Wallace. An assassin would not be casually asking for directions moments after his hit and so close to the scene, and certainly not *after* he had allegedly spoken to his alleged client, William Wallace. Perhaps Stocky Man first asked directions of a stranger, which was observed by Lily Hall at about 8:35pm. He then walked a little way along Richmond Park, before backtracking to near Letchworth Street, all the time searching for his address. He then asked directions of Harry Greenlees just before 8:40pm. Given all the facts, it is a plausible interpretation, especially as it is consistent with Wallace's first and fourth statements in which said he arrived home between 8:40pm and 8.45pm, meaning he could have crossed Richmond Park when neither Lily Hall nor Harry Greenlees were there [3].

There are reasonable grounds to believe that Hall did not see Wallace, but it is surprising nonetheless. It is far easier to misidentify a stranger than someone you know by sight, especially someone as distinctive as Wallace. If you believe Hall observed Wallace, Conspiracy has to be a leading contender. If not, all theories remain on the table.

Notes:

[1] Hall said that she returned home at 8:35pm (her five-minute-fast clock showed 8:40pm) and also that she was at the end of Walton Breck Road at exactly the same time. Clearly, she is mistaken about one, but assume for the moment she returned home at 8:35pm. As it is only a short distance to her house from when she saw the two men, she would have first seen them at about 8:34pm. On the other hand, if she was correct about the time when at the end of Walton Breck Road, she would have arrived home at 8:38pm (assuming it was a three minute walk as she claimed). In this case, she would have first approached the men at about 8:37pm. So we have a specific window of time when Hall could have seen the two men: between 8:34pm and 8:37pm.

[2] The timing tests revealed it would have taken 33-38 minutes for Wallace to get home, and I have allowed one minute for him to walk the short distance from the Parish Hall to his house.

[3] This would also be consistent with the Johnstons claim that they bumped into Wallace at about 8:45pm. It means Wallace took the tram home at about 8:05pm.

Exhibit 16. Forensic Accounting

The following analysis examines Wallace's financial returns to the Prudential and what they can tell us about the crime.

A. Time To Steal

William Wallace usually collected premiums on Saturday morning, Monday, Tuesday, Wednesday and Thursday. Typically, he did not collect on Friday and every other Monday he collected only in the morning. Every four weeks, without exception, there was a special collection round, taking monthly premiums from customers. There were three types of premium to collect – Industrial, General and Ordinary. The Industrial collections were weekly and penny premiums, typically for sickness insurance, while General might include other types of cover, such as motor or fire insurance. These two made up the bulk of his remittances. The so-called Ordinary business usually netted £1 or £2 per week, and I will ignore it.

The record of Wallace's remittances for 1930 shows that he paid in his collection money at the Prudential District Office on a Thursday or Friday. He always paid the monthly round collections on a Friday, while the normal round was on either the Thursday or Friday, later than other agents [1]. On average, he paid in £43 a week during a normal round and £92 on a monthly round. These are significant sums; in today's money they amount to nearly £3,000 and £6,500 respectively.

In January 1931, Wallace's monthly round was the week before the murder. He paid in £89 on Thursday 15 January 1931, not the Friday, which was unusual. If you suspect Wallace, the departure from his routine so close to the murder will probably only deepen your misgivings, but there might be an innocent explanation. Wallace was ill with a fever on the Saturday – he missed his morning round – and it is possible he was unwell on the Friday. If he was coming down with something on the Thursday he might have decided to submit his remittances earlier than usual.

If the murder of Julia Wallace was connected to a burglary, the thief struck a week too late to hit the jackpot. The obvious candidate, Gordon Parry, knew Wallace's routine when he worked for him in December 1928 [2] and would have known that to get his hands on a bumper haul he had to target Wallace's collection box on a Thursday evening during a monthly collection week. If he planned a burglary, it appears Parry chose the wrong night and the wrong week to maximise his return.

It should be noted that Wallace did not play chess on Monday 12 January 1931, the monthly collection week. If Parry wanted to leave a message at the chess club, he could not have done so that week, perhaps leading him to postpone his plan to the following week.

B. Low Haul

The cash haul was probably much lower than a thief was expecting. Wallace collected £14 on the previous day and a half (he did not collect on the Monday morning that week) and paid out about £10 in sickness benefit, leaving £4 in cash.

C. Remittance Riddle

Wallace did not work on the morning of Wednesday 21 January, the day after the murder. In fact, he was with the police all day from 10am to 10pm (according to his deposition). Therefore, after the burglary, you would expect him to return no remittances that week. Yet according to Prudential records, he paid in £10 11s in premiums that afternoon [3].

We have two mysteries. Let us first examine the timing. His nephew Edwin stated that he accompanied his uncle to Joseph Crewe's office on Thursday 22 January, which fits with Wallace being unavailable on the Wednesday. It appears his payment was back-dated, possibly by Crewe, to the normal remittance day, Wednesday. Wallace did not return to his normal collection routine until the next day, leaving us with the second mystery – where did the £10 11s come from? Author John Gannon suggests it was premiums from the previous week, yet company records show Wallace paid in £89 on the previous Thursday 15 January and he did not collect on the Friday (normal practice) or the Saturday morning (illness) that week. This cannot be correct.

Let's look again at the cashbox. Wallace stated to police that about £4 in cash, a postal order for 4s 6d and a cheque for £5 17s [4] had been stolen. The cash comprised: one £1 note, three 10s notes, and 30 to 40 shillings in silver. If the missing coins actually amounted to 39 shillings and an odd sixpence, the lost cash was £4 14s, and the overall loss, including the postal order and cheque, totalled £10 11s – the exact remittance paid in by Wallace on the Thursday. Was the dutiful Wallace simply repaying – out of his own pocket – the money lost by the Prudential? If so, it shows a remarkable sense of duty.

D. Conclusions
If a guilty Parry wanted a bumper haul of cash, he chose the wrong night. If a guilty Wallace voluntarily reimbursed his company for the stolen money, it is surprising that he involved the cashbox at all; he could have simply claimed that personal money had been taken and he would not have been out of pocket.

Notes:
[1] Although most agents submitted their remittances on Wednesday afternoon, Wallace testified that his usual paying-in day was Thursday. He paid in on a Friday for a normal round on a few occasions in 1930, all below average remittances.

[2] The monthly round was the week commencing 17 December 1928. This date tallies with entries in Wallace's diaries – on Tuesday 18 December Wallace wrote that he had been warned to keep an eye on Parry's accounting.

[3] It was logged in the accounts as Industrial business only – there were no General or Ordinary business premiums paid in that week.

[4] The cheque was made out to Wallace from the Prudential. There appears to be no record of what this money was for, and might have been some kind of advance by his employer to cover expected claims.

Exhibit 17. Trial Minutes

The following provides a succinct summary of the main points of testimony given by all the trial witnesses.

Venue: St George's Hall, Liverpool.
Date: Wednesday 22 April 1931.
Duration: Four days.
Judge: Mr Justice Robert Wright.
Prisoner in the Dock: William Herbert Wallace, 52 years old.
Counsel for the Crown: Edward Hemmerde, assisted by Leslie Walsh.
Counsel for the Prisoner: Roland Oliver, assisted by Sydney Scholefield Allen.

First Day – Wednesday 22 April 1931

Arraignment
The *clerk of the Assize* read the indictment of murder and asked the defendant how he pleaded.
Wallace: Not guilty.

The Case for the Crown
The opening speech for the Crown, delivered by Edward Hemmerde, is a pivotal moment of the trial. He outlined briefly the events of 19 January, about the telephone call, ending with this rhetorical flourish: "That is how we leave it that night: a message from a call box 400 yards from his house, asking him to meet a man he had never seen, and whose name was not familiar to him, at a place which did not exist... you may think that the prisoner wanted people to believe that someone wanted to get him out of the way the next night."

Next, the events of 20 January were sketched, emphasising Wallace's behaviour on the journey to keep his appointment, the seemingly transient problem with his door locks, the burnt mackintosh and the missing iron bar. Hemmerde conceded that the prosecution could advance no motive for the murder, but this was irrelevant if the facts pointed to the prisoner's culpability. It was stressed on several occasions that the deceased "had no enemies in the world", inviting the jury to ask the question, "Who else could have killed her but the husband?"

Hemmerde also raised the issue of the prisoner's emotional reaction on finding his dead wife: "Did he show signs of the broken-hearted husband" or was he "extremely cold and collected"?

Harry Cooke, police photographer, provided details of the images he had taken at 29 Wolverton Street. [*Cooke would have dusted for, and taken photographs of, any latent fingerprints discovered at the scene. He was never asked any questions on this topic*].

William Harrison, surveyor, produced plans of the house and surrounding vicinity.

Leslie Heaton, telephone electrician, stated that, apart from Anfield 1627, all other telephone kiosks near to Wallace's house were in public places, such as the library. Unless it was broken, the light in the kiosk would remain on. [*In his police statement, committal hearing evidence and trial testimony, Heaton never said there was a telephone fault with Anfield 1627*].

Louisa Alfreds, telephone operator, stated that she received a call from an ordinary-sounding man from Anfield 1627 asking for Bank 3581. She connected the call. [*In her police statement, Alfreds remarked that she remembered the caller's voice particularly because of the way he pronounced the word café, and remarked to Lilian Kelly that it was a "funny thing to say"*].

Lilian Kelly, telephone operator, recalled taking a call at about 7:15pm on 19 January from Anfield 1627 to Bank 3581. The male voice said, "Operator I have pressed button A, but have not had my correspondent yet." After conversing briefly with Louisa Alfreds, she asked the caller to push button B to retrieve his money and she "observed an indicator light which showed the money had been returned". She was unable to connect the call and summoned her supervisor, Annie Robertson.

[*In her police statement, Kelly also remembered the manner in which the caller stressed the word café. She stated the second call was logged because the caller complained about not getting through with his original call*].

Annie Robertson, telephone exchange supervisor, testified that she was referred a call by Lilian Kelly at about 7:20pm on 19 January and noted the time. The caller told her that he had received no reply. She connected the call and returned the handling of it to Lilian Kelly.

Gladys Harley, waitress at City Café, recalled that she answered a telephone (Bank 3581) between 7pm and 8pm on 19 January. It was an ordinary male voice. She then handed the call over to Samuel Beattie. Under cross-examination, she affirmed that chess club notices were pinned on a board close to the telephone kiosk and they provided details of which members were scheduled to play and on which dates. [*According to her interview with Hector Munro, Wallace's solicitor, Harley heard the operator ask the caller to "put the pennies in". If there was an attempt to scam a free call, it appears it failed*].

Samuel Beattie, chess club captain, stated that the club met every Monday and Thursday evening at the City Café. He had known Wallace for eight years and had last seen him at the club sometime prior to Christmas. He arrived at the café at 6pm on 19 January and took the telephone from Gladys Harley shortly after 7pm. The speaker was a man with a "strong, gruff voice". At 7:45pm he relayed the phone message to Wallace, who was absorbed playing a chess game. Wallace asked, "Who is Qualtrough?" and "Where is Menlove Gardens East?" Beattie asked a fellow player about the address.

At 10:20pm on Thursday 22 January, Beattie recalled, Wallace asked him if he could be more specific about when the telephone call was received. Beattie replied he could not. Wallace said the timing was important, and pressed him again, but Beattie repeated only that it was about 7pm or shortly after. Wallace also told Beattie that the police had cleared him of any involvement in the crime.

Under cross-examination, Beattie confirmed the chess noticeboard was near the café entrance and in public view. Regarding the call, he said the voice was confident, answering his questions without hesitation. He asserted it was certainly not like Wallace's normal voice.

James Caird, chess club member, testified that he arrived at the chess club on 19 January at 7:35pm, about 10 minutes before Wallace. He was present when Samuel Beattie relayed the message to Wallace. Nobody in the club knew the location of Menlove Gardens East. On the way home from the club Wallace talked about his chess match victory and only briefly mentioned the message. Under cross-examination, Caird stated he had known Wallace for 15 years and he was an intellectual and placid man. As regards playing the violin, he was a beginner. Caird believed that the Wallaces were a happy couple.

James Rothwell, police constable, recalled seeing Wallace on the afternoon of 20 January. He was dressed in a tweed suit and a light-coloured mackintosh and was distressed, dabbing his eye with his coat sleeve. Under cross-examination, Rothwell denied that Wallace's eyes might have been watering in the cold and said that he would never shift from his interpretation of the incident.

Alan Close, 14-year-old milk boy, testified that he had delivered milk to the Wallaces for two years. At 6:30pm on 20 January, he made a delivery to Mrs Wallace. He remembered the time because he had looked at the church clock at 6:25pm and, after tests with the police, he knew it took him five minutes to get to 29 Wolverton Street. Under-cross examination, Close was grilled over the route of his round, the timing of his delivery that night, and comments he allegedly made to other children. He denied telling his friends that he delivered the milk at 6:45pm. [*Close's testimony is presented in greater detail in Exhibit 7*].

Thomas Phillips, No. 5 tram conductor, testified that Wallace boarded his tram at either 7:06 or 7:10pm on Tuesday 20 January. He had three short conversations with Wallace, who was anxious to know the way to Menlove Gardens East. [*The time of departure could not have been 7:10pm because this tram, which took nearly 10 minutes on average to travel to Penny Lane junction, would not have arrived in time for Wallace to board the subsequent one (see next witness). Therefore, the tram left at 7:06pm*].

Arthur Thompson, No. 5A tram conductor, stated that Wallace boarded his tram at 7:15pm at Penny Lane and, after asking about Menlove Gardens East, he advised Wallace to get off at Menlove Avenue, which he did.

Katie Mather, occupant of 25 Menlove Gardens West, stated that Wallace rang her doorbell during the evening of 20 January. He asked if Mr Qualtrough lived at the address and the whereabouts of Menlove Gardens East.

Sydney Green, a clerk, informed Wallace that there was no Menlove Gardens East.

James Serjeant, police constable, also informed Wallace there was no Menlove Gardens East and suggested he tried Menlove

Avenue. Wallace asked for the nearest post office, and commented on the time. The witness also looked at his watch: the time was 7:45pm.

Lily Pinches, newsagent, stated that Wallace entered her shop at about 8:10pm asking for a street directory. Wallace mentioned "25 Menlove Gardens East" but not "Qualtrough".

Joseph Crewe, insurance superintendent, confirmed he had been Wallace's supervisor for 12 years. Wallace used to remit his weekly takings, which might exceed £100, typically on a Wednesday [*although Wallace said it was usually a Thursday in both his police statement and trial testimony*]. He was only permitted to collect weekly premiums in his allocated district but had the right to collect an endowment policy wherever he wished. He stated that Wallace was "an absolute gentleman" who never exhibited any anger or ill-temper, and had visited his house five times for violin lessons. He believed that Wallace and his wife had the best possible relations.

Lily Hall, typist, had known Wallace by sight for at least three years. She saw him last talking to another man in Richmond Park about 8:40pm on 20 January. She had no doubt it was the accused. The two men parted as she passed them, one heading along the road, and the other going down an entry by the Parish Hall {see Exhibit 15}. She did not tell the police of her evidence until a week later, partly because of illness.

Second Day – Thursday 23 April 1931

The Case for the Crown (continued)
John Johnston, next-door neighbour, described the discovery of the body. He believed the Wallaces were "a very loving couple, very affectionate" and had never heard any quarrelling. On the night of the murder, he told Wallace that he and his wife would wait outside while he looked around the house to check everything was all right. [*Both John and Florence Johnston originally told detectives that Wallace said, "Wait here a minute. I'll see if everything is all right." This is consistent with Wallace's statement. Later they changed their minds, claiming they told Wallace they would wait outside while he checked the house. The police statements were amended by hand to reflect the change*].

263

Florence Johnston, wife of the previous witness, also recalled the night of 20 January. She described Wallace's emotional state as "collected" but he had broken down twice, sobbing, in the kitchen when no one else was present. He seemed to be on the verge of breaking down on several other occasions but managed to pull himself together. She speculated that Julia might have thrown the mackintosh around her shoulders, perhaps to open the front door.

Frederick Williams, police constable, was sent to 29 Wolverton Street shortly after 9pm on 20 January. He felt the dead body – it was slightly warm. He accompanied Wallace around the house and was shown the broken cabinet, the cashbox and his wife's handbag, which still contained money. He was present when the treasury notes were found in the middle bedroom. He said Wallace touched the notes but stated that he had seen no blood on the prisoner. He testified that on the night of the murder Wallace had told him: "At 6.45pm I left the house in order to go to Menlove Gardens, and my wife accompanied me to the back yard door. She walked a little way down the entry with me, and she returned and bolted the back yard door. She would then have been alone in the house. I went to Menlove Gardens, to find the address that had been given me was wrong. Becoming suspicious, I returned home, and went to the front door. I inserted my key in the front door to find I could not open it. I went round the back, round to the back yard door; it was closed but not bolted. I went up the yard, and tried the back kitchen door, but it would not open. I again went to the front door, and this time found the door was bolted. I hurried round to the back, and up the back yard, and tried the back kitchen door, and this time it would open. I entered the house."

Sarah Draper, cleaner, said she last visited 29 Wolverton Street on 7 January. When she accompanied the police she found a poker from the kitchen and an iron bar from the parlour were missing.

James Sarginson, locksmith, stated the front door of 29 Wolverton Street had been defective for some time. The back door lock was rusty and required pressure to open it.

John MacFall, professor of forensic medicine, estimated the time of death to be 6pm or before. The blood spatter in the parlour indicated that the victim was sitting in the chair by the fireplace. He found Wallace's demeanour most unusual – he entered the parlour smoking a cigarette and flicked ash into a bowl on the sideboard. He volunteered the opinion that the fatal blows were frenzied.

Under cross-examination, he stated that the victim might have been struck while bending down to light the fire. The assailant would have had blood on his left hand from pulling the bloodied hair of the victim [assuming he was right-handed and was holding the weapon at the same time]. After further questions, he also accepted that blood would be on the assailant's face and lower legs even if he had worn the mackintosh. He conceded that the police might have inadvertently transferred the blood clot to the toilet rim.

Hugh Pierce, medical examiner, judged that the time of death was 6pm with a margin of error of two hours either side.

William Roberts, analyst, testified that the mackintosh was heavily bloodstained on the right side, inside and outside. If worn by an assailant during an attack, he would not expect much blood transfer to that person. The victim's skirt was heavily bloodstained and burned at the front [or side, depending on how it was worn]. There were bloodstains on the hearth rug consistent with the assailant rubbing his feet or boots. There was a blood smear on the middle note in the bundle of four £1 treasury notes, but none on any of the others. There were no bloodstains on the cashbox.

[Roberts was not asked whether the bathroom pipes were tested for the presence of blood].

Hubert Moore, detective superintendent, conceded that a visitor might have been admitted to the house given the parlour fire had been lit. He insisted there was no need for Wallace to strike a match by the parlour door, as there was sufficient light from the kitchen to see into the parlour. Wallace did so, he claimed, because he knew there was a dead body on the floor and wanted to navigate his way around it without stepping into the pools of blood. He agreed that the police had searched everywhere for the murder weapon, including the waste ground by Wolverton Street, without success.

Third Day – Friday 24 April 1931

The Case for the Crown (continued)
Harry Bailey, detective sergeant, gave evidence about the police time tests with Alan Close.

Herbert Gold, detective inspector, had asked Wallace about his journey home. Wallace informed him that his return journey was the same route as the outward, and the first people he spoke to were John and Florence Johnston. He found Wallace "calm and collected" and observed no "sign of emotion in him at all at the death of his wife". When he first saw Wallace, "he had the cat on his knee and was stroking it, and he did not look like a man who had just battered his wife to death". He examined the prisoner's clothing, hands and boots but found no sign of blood.

The analyst **William Roberts** was recalled and gave details about the blood clot found on the toilet.

The prosecution informed the judge that all the evidence for its case had been presented. The clerk of the Assize read Wallace's answer to the charge of murder he gave at his committal hearing. "I plead not guilty… I would like to say that my wife and I lived together on the very happiest of terms… The suggestion that I murdered my wife is monstrous; that I should attack and kill her is, to all who know me, unthinkable, and the more so when it must be realised I could not possibly obtain one advantage by committing such a deed, nor do the police suggest I gained such an advantage. On the contrary, I have lost a devoted and loving comrade, my home life is completely broken up, and everything I hold dear has been ruthlessly parted and torn from me."

The Case for the Defence
The opening statement for the defence, made by Roland Oliver, began by examining the personality of Wallace and the lack of motive. There was no evidence that Wallace made the telephone call. The victim was last seen alive at 6.45pm, according to the original view of Alan Close and corroborated by his friends, which meant Wallace was innocent. He dismissed Lily Hall's evidence as mistaken. The blood found on the toilet and one treasury note was transferred by one of the 12 police officers or two medical examiners in the house that night. There was no advantage for him pretending to be locked out of his own house, as the

prosecution alleged. Oliver also proposed an alternative theory — the killer had called at Wallace's house, after watching him leave, and was admitted by Julia Wallace into the parlour when he explained it was a business call.

William Wallace, the defendant, was questioned about his marital and financial position. After tea, on the night of the murder, he prepared for his meeting and washed his face and hands in the bathroom. His wife accompanied him down the back yard as far as the gate and he told her to bolt it, although he did not hear her do so. [*This contradicts the statement of PC Williams, who testified that Wallace had told him that his wife accompanied him a little way down the entry, returned, and bolted the back yard gate*].

He described in detail his movements on the night of the murder and the night before when he received the phone message. He agreed that Julia might have ushered Qualtrough into the parlour, had he called, because "she knew all about the business" having talked about it during the day and at tea time. [*Wallace consistently refers to the meal taken in the evening as "tea" or "tea time". We know from the statement of Amy Wallace that he must have discussed Qualtrough with his wife before then. Perhaps they discussed it at lunch, an understandable slip of the memory on Wallace's part, but it is possible he first mentioned the call with his wife the night before*].

The cross-examination probed for any inconsistencies in Wallace's account. In particular, the prosecution alleged that the first time he mentioned his attempt to call on Joseph Crewe was at the trial. The prosecution contrasted Wallace's uneasiness when he realised the address was incorrect with his calmness when he could not enter his house, thinking his wife might be posting a letter. He said he felt both.

Wallace denied telling PC Williams that his wife accompanied him down the entry. The prosecution also highlighted another alleged discrepancy. Wallace told the constable that the front door was bolted but in his statement, after Superintendent Moore had examined the lock, Wallace said the lock mechanism was faulty. [*Wallace told the Johnstons that the front door was bolted, which he confirmed when he admitted PC Williams into the house*].

The prosecution asked questions about the missing iron bar, to which Wallace replied that he had never seen it. It was also pointed out that, while in the parlour with the dead body, Wallace looked around the room and asked, "Whatever have they used?" He thought this was a natural response. [*In her police statement, Florence Johnston affirmed that she said, "I wonder what have they used". The prosecution wrongly attributed this to Wallace*].

James Dible, pathology professor, testified that rigor mortis by itself is an extremely unreliable method of establishing time of death. He believed the assailant would be spattered with blood, and the blood clot was at least one hour old when it fell onto the toilet pan because there was no splashing.

Robert Coope, lecturer in clinical chemistry, confirmed the last point. He told the court he had performed over 100 tests to confirm that the blood was not fresh when it fell on the toilet.

James Wildman, 16-year-old paperboy, said that he delivered a paper to 27 Wolverton Street and saw Alan Close standing on the step of No. 29. He estimated the time to be 6:37pm because he remembered seeing the time on the Holy Trinity Church clock, which he had passed two minutes previously.

Douglas Metcalf, paperboy, said he was in Wolverton Street between 6:40pm and 6:45pm and saw James Wildman leaving the street. Alan Close told him that he had seen Julia Wallace at 6:45pm.

Kenneth Caird, 14-year-old son of James Caird, confirmed the last point.

David Jones, paperboy, delivered the *Liverpool Echo* to 29 Wolverton Street at 6:35pm and saw nobody at the house. [*In his police statement, Jones said he delivered the paper at "about 6:30pm"*].

Louisa Harrison, a customer of the Prudential, saw Wallace at 3:30pm on 20 January. He joked with her and was not visibly distressed.

Amy Lawrence, another customer, said Wallace exhibited his usual demeanour on the afternoon of 20 January. Her husband made him a cup of tea.

Margaret Martin, another customer, confirmed that Wallace called after 5:30pm on 20 January. He was "calm" as usual.

Fourth Day – Saturday 25 April 1931

The Closing Speeches

The closing speech for the defence dismissed the testimony of John MacFall, claiming that his estimate of the time of death was unreliable. Attempting to establish when Julia Wallace was seen by Alan Close, attention was drawn to the newspaper delivered by David Jones at 6:35pm. It was found open on the kitchen table. It was not being read by Wallace because, if the prosecution was correct, at precisely this time he was killing his wife and clearing up. It could only have been read by Julia Wallace, which shows her time of death was later than the prosecution was claiming.

If the mackintosh had been worn by the assailant it would have contained much 'soda bottle' or cast-off blood spatter, the type found on the walls. But there was none. The inference was that Julia Wallace was wearing it around her shoulders during the attack and the prosecution's theory was false. It was pointed out that a criminal had much to gain by feeding Wallace a false address: it bought time. Similarly, the assailant might be expected to turn off the gas lamp – if someone knocked on the front door, perhaps a neighbour or friend calling, and observed the parlour light was lit but received no reply, the alarm might have been raised sooner. A criminal was also likely to extinguish the gas fire when the mackintosh caught fire – an instinctive reaction.

The first point addressed in the closing speech for the Crown was the telephone call. Only Wallace knew he would be at the chess club that night – he admitted that he told no one he was going and could think of no one who knew. Wallace could have been at the telephone box at about 7:15pm to make the call. The prosecution claimed that Wallace tried to create an impression that he was unable to enter his house. When Wallace let PC Williams into the house he told the constable that he had unbolted the front door, yet when Superintendent Moore examined the front door lock, and diagnosed a fault, Wallace failed to mention it was bolted, saying only, "It was not like that this morning".

The prosecution also suggested that Wallace never told his wife he was going out [*Julia was aware of the telephone message, according to Amy Wallace's statement*], but asked her to prepare the music room as usual and went upstairs to prepare for murder.

269

Whether the milk boy delivered milk at 6:30 or 6:35pm, he had ample time to commit the murder and leave for his appointment. It was also stressed that a wrong address was essential for the alibi. If a proper address had been given, Wallace would have quickly established there was no Qualtrough and would have no need to ask further witnesses for assistance.

Summing Up

In his summing up, Mr Justice Wright said that 7:20pm on 19 January was a fixed datum in the case. It was the time, noted by Annie Robertson at the telephone exchange, when the call was put through to the café. Could the jury be reasonably certain it was the prisoner who made that call? As to the night of the murder, the judge ran through the arguments. He explained that the most vital part of the case was the time available for the prisoner to commit the crime. Even if the milk was delivered at 6:35pm, the prisoner was seen half an hour later boarding a tram, some distance from his house, seemingly composed. Was this window of time so restricted as to make it improbable or impossible for the prisoner to have done what was alleged? The judge also considered the murder weapon. There were few places the prisoner could have disposed of it, and these had been combed by the police. Could he have boarded the tram carrying a poker or iron bar, without drawing attention to it?

The court adjourned while the jury retired to consider its verdict.

Verdict

After deliberating for an hour, the jury returned and delivered its verdict: guilty.

PART THREE

THE VERDICT

You have read the story. You have sifted the evidence.
Who murdered Julia Wallace? Here is my view.

All that concerns the case which you are supporting must be clearly brought forward; what concerns your own feelings should be left unsaid.
Marcus Aurelius

MY JUDGEMENT

The time has come for me to state my opinion. In my summing up, I posed two questions. Was William Herbert Wallace innocent or involved in the murder of his wife? And, depending on your answer to the first, which is the best explanation of what happened?

Let's examine the case through a wide-angled lens. If Wallace was guilty, he must have planned the entire murder in great detail:

- He used the phone box nearest to his house and boarded a tram in his neighbourhood, both of which carried a high risk of being seen by someone who knew him. Presumably, he had a failsafe: if he believed that he had been observed by an acquaintance, he could abandon his plan.

- When the message was relayed to him at the chess club, he cleverly ensured the customer's unusual name and fictitious address were repeated.

- He created reasonable doubt that he was in his house when the murder was committed by killing Julia and leaving as soon as possible after the milk had been delivered. He obtained another independent timestamp by pestering tram conductors so that they would remember him.

- By killing Julia in the parlour, rather than any other room in which she might have disturbed a burglar, he made it appear that a visitor had called while he was out. He must also have ensured that light from the room could not be seen by anyone on the street.

- He used a mackintosh to keep blood spatter off his body and clothes. This was crucial because he would be in the public eye from the moment he left the house.

- He removed the murder weapon from the scene and disposed of it in a location where it would never be found, presumably somewhere he had carefully reconnoitred and possibly prepared. If the location was away from his home, he secreted it about his person as there is no suggestion that Wallace carried a briefcase or holdall with him that night.

- He disposed of the cashbox contents, including a large number of coins, where they could not be found. Presumably he did this in advance to save time, or hid them in the same place as the weapon.

- By raiding the cashbox, phoning the chess club and insisting that Julia would not admit strangers into the house in his absence, he was able to point the finger at a fall guy: Gordon Parry. We know Parry was the intended victim of this set-up because of Wallace's post-acquittal behaviour in attempting to pin the blame on his erstwhile colleague.

Despite careful planning, a guilty Wallace made at least three mistakes:

- He forgot that, if there was a problem when using a public telephone, you pushed button B to retrieve your two pennies and then reconnected to the operator. He pushed button A, lost his money and started over. This allowed the call to be logged.

- He forgot to keep up his pretence about the fictitious address: he told Katie Mather "It's funny, isn't it, that there is no East?" This allowed the police to claim that the rest of his search – for at least half an hour – was a charade.

- He could not have known if Parry had an alibi for the night of the murder, a critical error.

And Wallace relied on three pieces of luck over which he had no control:

- No witness recalled him boarding the tram by the telephone kiosk. Had anyone remembered, he would have been caught lying.
- The milk boy arrived at the Goldilocks moment – not too early and not too late but just at the right time – to allow Wallace to have tea, prepare for his fictitious appointment, ready everything for the murder and arrive at Menlove Gardens with about 10 minutes to spare, the time many would allow to find an address in a small district.
- His neighbours heard no disturbance when he killed his wife at about 6:45pm, not even a fall or a thump.

In the final paragraph of *Checkmate*, Mark Russell concedes that the entire plan was so fraught with danger and risk of failure that no one but Wallace would have carried it out. But one should immediately ask: why would the cautious and meticulous Wallace have done so? With his chemical knowledge and introverted personality, you would have thought that Wallace would opt for poison, a proposition that Russell summarily rejects on the grounds that Wallace would be the only suspect when the cause of death was discovered. However, a post mortem would have been undertaken only if the family doctor refused to issue a death certificate because death was suspicious. As there was widespread influenza in Liverpool during January 1931, and Julia was frequently unwell, Wallace had an ideal smokescreen; a large dose of arsenic, easily sourced at the time, presents with almost identical symptoms as gastric flu. One is at a loss to see how a poisoning would have been fraught with greater danger than bludgeoning his wife before immediately leaving for a bogus appointment. If Wallace was guilty, he surely opted for a riskier option.

Looking at his alleged plan, one thing leaps out: the staging of a burglary involving the cashbox. It more or less reduced the suspect pool to three people, including him. If the scheme was devised well in advance, possibly years, as Russell suggests, why wasn't the staged burglary given the same amount of thought? The only reasonable conclusion is that Wallace intended to frame Gordon Parry. Yet he must have realised that if Parry had an alibi his plan was sunk and he would most likely go down with it. He had to plan for the worst case scenario – Parry having an alibi – and would have been reckless to proceed otherwise. And there is nothing to suggest that Wallace was a reckless man.

Turning to the crime scene, surely the simplest explanation is that a visitor actually called rather than it was staged by Wallace. The parlour was undoubtedly the room in which Julia would have ushered a guest, especially an unexpected visitor. The plumped up cushions on the chaise longue, clearly visible in the police photograph, suggest it might have been used recently, and we know from Gordon Parry that Julia reclined on the couch when guests were present. The scorching of her skirt suggests the gas fire was on at least for a few minutes to reach a high temperature, just as it would have been if there was a visitor and she spent some time talking to them. The position of her feet is exactly where you would expect her to stand if she had just risen from the chaise longue, perhaps to show the visitor out. The fact that the mackintosh was in the room is consistent with Julia placing it around her shoulders while the cold room warmed up, something she might do if an unexpected guest called. The fact that the mackintosh was burnt suggests it accidentally fell into the fire; its burning is harder to explain if it was critical to Wallace's plan to avoid blood spatter.

The case against Wallace largely rests on his suspicious behaviour, but there is an alternative interpretation. On the Monday night, he went to his chess club as he said he did. He made a genuine mistake in reciting the address to Beattie, as he did later when he gave his first police statement. Nobody at the club was sure about the address, so Beattie advised that he should get on a tram and enquire. On the following night, he did just that.

When he arrived home at 6:05pm on Tuesday night, he glanced at the mantelpiece clock to see if he had enough time to have tea, prepare, and leave in time to make the appointment on time. He was upstairs washing when the milk was delivered at about 6:40pm and did not hear the milk boy. He departed at about 6:45pm because this would allow sufficient time to find the address and arrive promptly for his meeting. When he left, Julia did not bother trailing into the cold hall to grab a coat because she was outside for only a few moments accompanying her husband to the back gate as usual. She then returned promptly to her warm kitchen.

Having used a different tram route to get to Joseph Crewe's house on previous occasions, Wallace asked the second and third tram conductors how to get to Menlove Gardens East. When he started his search for the address on foot, he was told by the first person he met that she had not heard of it but advised him where to look. He followed her instruction. He was then told by a passer-by that the address did not exist and was advised to try 25 Menlove Gardens West. He also followed this instruction. There, he told the owner that it was strange there was no East. Nevertheless, as he had invested his time and money in an hour's return journey, he wanted to be absolutely certain it did not exist and continued his search.

When he returned home there was a problem with the front lock: the key would not turn. Naturally, he went to the back door. The back yard gate was unlocked, Julia having forgotten to bolt it or the killer unbolted it during his escape. To his growing unease, Wallace found the back door would not open either; it sometimes stuck, as the cleaner later confirmed. He returned to the front. Although the key now half-turned, he was convinced the door was bolted, which he told the Johnstons as soon as he encountered them. He confirmed it when he let PC Williams into the house.

The temperamental back door lock now worked. When he stepped inside, Wallace found the kitchen in darkness. He lit the gas lamp and headed to where he believed his wife would be: the upstairs bedroom. Not finding her in the bedroom, he started a room by room search, naturally staying upstairs for convenience. This meant the parlour was the last room he entered. There, he found the battered body of his wife. He turned on the gas lamp and fetched his neighbours. If he was the killer, there was no need to go upstairs: he could have easily entered the parlour directly from the kitchen, claiming he was searching the rooms in order.

In my view, this is a plausible version of events consistent with innocence, but what of Mark Russell's claim that some of Wallace's actions, particularly on the tram journey to Menlove Gardens East, could only be those of a guilty man? The three appeal judges certainly did not agree. The Court of Criminal Appeal was loath to overturn a jury decision, and had the judges believed that any of Wallace's actions had no other reasonable interpretation than guilt, they would have upheld the verdict. While I agree that Wallace's pestering of the tram conductors appears out of character, and therefore suspicious, it is only a pointer to his guilt that has to be weighed against other evidence. It is striking that the appeal judges also did not believe the cumulative effect of the evidence pointed to guilt beyond a reasonable doubt.

Wallace might have been able to kill his wife in short order, but a bloody assault points away from an organised killer desperate to avoid blood transfer, even with the use of a mackintosh. And the blood spatter and stain by the armchair combined with the moving of the body makes me sceptical that Wallace had the protection of the raincoat for the entire time. For me, his plan was at the same time so sublimely nuanced and obviously flawed that it is difficult to reconcile.

Overall, I do not believe Wallace acted alone, discounting the **Wallace** and **Prank** theories, but could there not have been a **Conspiracy**? This theory largely pivots around one question: did Lily Hall see Wallace on the night of the murder? I believe the same stocky man she described also asked Harry Greenlees for directions a few minutes later. In my view, this is not the behaviour of an accomplice or hitman, but someone searching for an address. I believe it is more probable that Hall was mistaken in identifying Wallace.

The putative sexual relationship between Julia Wallace and Parry and Marsden strains credibility. I understand why it is an important part of the theory; without it, there appears no obvious way Wallace could coerce the two young men into his scheme. Yet, even if it were true, I find it difficult to believe they would have agreed. I think it far more probable they would have called his bluff, perhaps even threatened him. It is also highly unlikely that Wallace would involve them only to point the police in their direction two days after the murder.

I also struggle to see why the Qualtrough call was necessary in this scenario. Wallace could have used his attendance at the chess club as a watertight alibi and blackmailed only Marsden, who Julia would readily admit to her house. Writer John Gannon is the only author who builds a theory around the testimonies of Hall, Olivia Brine and John Parkes. I admire his approach and research but, in my opinion, the resulting theory is not the best explanation for the murder of Julia Wallace. The evidential dots are joined by conjectures that I have difficulty in accepting.

For me, the decision is close – I do not share the conviction of many commentators who declare that Wallace was evidently guilty or obviously innocent. The scales, although finely balanced, tip away from Wallace. Modern forensic analysis seems to suggest he was not the killer and, rather than attempting to frame him, I believe Wallace suspected Parry was the culprit. Therefore, my verdict is William Herbert Wallace was **innocent**, but which of the three remaining theories is the best explanation?

The **Neighbour** theory holds that John Johnston made the Qualtrough call, which I cannot accept. There was simply no reason for him to go to such effort when, living next door, he was able to strike whenever an opportunity arose. Nor are there any grounds to believe that he was a burglar, let alone a serial one. The Johnstons were not shown to have lied in their statements and testimony, and I believe an over-critical examination of their behaviour does not produce a strong enough foundation on which to build a case for their guilt. The neighbours can be ruled out.

The revelations of John Parkes point to Parry's involvement and are consistent with the **Parry** and **Accomplice** theories, but there have to be doubts over their reliability given they were aired half a century after the event. I have taken them into account but given them less weight than other evidence. In fact, I have given more weight to the fact that Parry was guarded and evasive about the murder for his entire life, suggesting he had something to hide. It is quite clear that his alibi should have been investigated more thoroughly by the police, not least to understand the nature of his relationship with Mrs Brine. Without such information, however, there is no reason to suspect she was covering for Parry. I find the alibi suspiciously short, but can find no reason to reject it.

For the **Parry** theory, I do not see why the Qualtrough call was necessary. Parry needed no pretext to visit Julia and his easiest option was to strike on the Monday night when he allegedly watched Wallace leave for the chess club. In addition, I do not believe he would have risked being the only suspect when his thievery was inevitably discovered. My view is that Parry was less a killer and more a chancer, a swindler and a thief. He might have been intimidating and able to defend himself but if Parry was the killer he was easily provoked to extreme violence. Such a dysfunctional personality would have shown itself on other occasions, yet Parry appears to have no record or reputation for such brutal aggression. On the contrary, a friend claimed he was squeamish. These factors, taken with the alibi, provide good grounds for believing Parry was not the killer, but he might have been the caller.

Indeed, the **Accomplice** theory assumes just that. If he was initiating a robbery, I believe Parry might have attempted a free-call scam; indeed, the whole idea of using a telephone in a criminal scheme fits Parry's wide-boy character far more than the bookish Wallace. For a burglary, Parry's plan had little to lose if it failed to lure Wallace away and much to gain if it did.

Working with an accomplice involved more planning and the reward was divided, but there was virtually no risk for Parry. A smooth talker, I expect he easily persuaded someone with criminal inclinations to agree to his plan, especially during an economic depression. Yet, unexplained details remain like missing pieces from a jigsaw puzzle: I am surprised an accomplice-turned-killer bothered to turn off three gas appliances in two rooms and managed to flee without transferring any blood to the hall or kitchen.

All the theories we have examined are imperfect. All have holes or raise further questions. On balance, however, I believe the **Accomplice** theory is the best explanation for one of the most puzzling murder cases in British criminal history. If true, Gordon Parry would have been shocked and upset by Julia's murder, but having made the Qualtrough call, he knew he was as responsible as the killer. Is this why his father insisted he never discuss it? In a case of doubt and dual interpretation, I believe one thing is certain: Parry could have brought closure. Decades after the event, when personal confidences would not have been so important, he could have easily proved he played no part, refuting the suspicions of many writers during his lifetime. Yet he refused to do so. Instead, he dutifully kept his vow of silence and took his secrets to the grave.

I have spent a great deal of time gathering the facts, but I do not pretend to have found all the answers. My view is but one. I look forward to seeing the verdict of the Cold Case Jury.

OTHER VERDICTS

Below are my thoughts on the major books and articles published on the case, listed in chronological order. I have concisely summarised them and, where appropriate, stated the author's verdict on the case. All were used as sources in writing *Move to Murder*.

Wyndham-Brown, W. F. *The Trial of William Herbert Wallace* (1933)

Inexplicably, the *Notable British Trials* book series failed to cover the Wallace trial: the quashing of the jury's guilty verdict due to lack of evidence by the appeal court surely makes it extremely noteworthy. In its place is this similar book, which was published by Victor Gollancz within two years of the trial. It has a comprehensive introduction by the author, an edited transcript of the trial, and a brief summary of the successful appeal. The book is out of print, and is difficult to obtain, with booksellers often charging high prices for it.

Sayers, Dorothy L. *The Murder of Julia Wallace* (1936)

This article was published in *The Anatomy of Murder*, an anthology of six famous cases considered critically by famous crime writers of the day. Arguably, this is the standout article in the volume; indeed, of all the early articles on the case, it is probably the best. Sayers summarises the case admirably and provides many insights regarding motive, the murder weapon, and the locked doors. When Sayers wrote her account the identity of Gordon Parry was not known (he was not called as a witness at the trial), and she referred to him as "the unknown man whom Wallace named as the murderer".

Conclusion: Until a strong case is made to the contrary, William Wallace was the killer.

Lustgarten, Edgar. *William Herbert Wallace* (1949)
Edgar Lustgarten, one of the master crime writers, turns his attention to the Wallace case in his book *Verdict In Dispute*, which examines six celebrated trials (the other cases are Florence Maybrick, Steinie Morrison, Norman Thorne, Edith Thompson and Lizzie Borden). Lustgarten is unrivalled as a commentator of the courtroom trial – he provides deep insight as well as compelling drama in all his true-crime writings, and this one is no exception. He believes that Edward Hemmerde, the lead counsel for the prosecution, had an immense impact on the verdict, masterfully pitching five points of Wallace's alleged guilt to the jury in his opening statement.
Conclusion: William Wallace was not guilty beyond a reasonable doubt.

Jesse, F. Tennyson. *Checkmate* (1953)
The great niece of the famous poet, after whom she was named, Jesse was a novelist and well-respected criminologist, editing six volumes of *Notable British Trials*. Her account is a good summary of the case, although there are a few errors in the detail. She believed Wallace was conceited and pretentious and looked down on his wife, thus providing some sort of motive. When she asked Edward Hemmerde how Wallace disposed of the weapon, he "picked up a ruler which lay upon his desk and slipped it up his sleeve", which leaves us with more questions than answers. Clearly, Hemmerde had lost none of his penchant for dramatic allusion.
Conclusion: William Wallace was the killer.

Bridges, Yseult . *Two Studies In Crime (1959)*
No doubt inspired by Hemmerde's comparison of William Wallace to François Courvoisier at the trial, Bridges parallels

both cases in this book. She appears in no doubt that Wallace was guilty, and that the only interesting questions are: How did he do it? And why? She answers the former with a detailed look at Courvoisier's killing of Lord William Russell, and believes Wallace similarly killed his wife while naked. As for the second question, Wallace hated Julia because she was a constant reminder of his failure, and this moved Wallace to murder. Like all Bridges' crime books, this one is enjoyable and well researched, but at crucial points there is a tendency to treat conjecture as fact.

Conclusion: William Wallace was the killer.

Goodman, Jonathan. *The Killing of Julia Wallace* (1969)
Almost every early work on the case assumed Wallace was guilty. John Rowland, writing in 1949, was the first writer to adopt the contrary position in a book-length examination of the case, but it was Goodman's seminal work that robustly argued for Wallace's innocence. Goodman claimed it could be *proved* that Wallace was innocent, although this view is mistaken. He believed that Gordon Parry killed Julia Wallace, a view strengthened after he interviewed him, although he could not name him for legal reasons at the time. Perhaps because of this, the case against Parry is thin; most of the book is dedicated to showing that Wallace was not the killer. This richly detailed and well-written book is a must-read for anyone interested in the case.

Conclusion: William Wallace was innocent.

Hussey, Robert F. *Murderer Scot-Free* (1972)
This book is often overlooked by readers interested in the Wallace case, yet it provides a plausible account of how Julia Wallace was murdered by someone other than her husband. Hussey was the first writer to suggest that the intention was not murder but sneak-thievery. Unlike other accounts, he is prepared to confront the detail and show how events might have unfolded. Hussey is scathing about the police

investigation, the lack of forensic evidence and the lacklustre defence of Wallace by his lawyers. Although not named in the book, there is no doubt that Hussey believes Parry was the culprit.

Conclusion: Gordon Parry murdered Julia Wallace.

Wilkes, Roger. *Wallace: The Final Verdict* (1984)

Wilkes took over where Goodman left off. His two radio programmes about the murder in early 1981, the first on the 50th anniversary of the murder, add to the folklore of the case. It seemed to be fact mirroring fiction, because the shows were broadcast at a time when the popularity of *Shoestring*, a TV series about a radio detective, was at its height. In an immensely readable book, which is more journalistic in tone than Goodman's, Wilkes weaves the story behind the broadcasts with that of the murder. For the first time, Gordon Parry is named as the killer. The book was written before the police files were released, and the statement of Olivia Brine, which provided Parry with an alibi, remained out of sight.

Conclusion: Gordon Parry was the killer.

Murphy, James. *The Murder of Julia Wallace* (2001)

Murphy's book was a reaction to the case against Gordon Parry. It is well researched and argued, and his analysis claims it was possible for Wallace to do everything that he is alleged to have done. He believes that Julia Wallace closed her front door as early as 6:33pm, giving Wallace at least 15 minutes. However, Murphy also makes two key assumptions: the caller and the killer were the same person and the verdict is dichotomous – Wallace or Parry. Both are unwarranted. He is also selective with the evidence when discussing Parry's possible involvement in making the call.

Conclusion: William Wallace was the killer.

Gannon, John. *The Killing of Julia Wallace* (2012)

At the time, this was the most thoroughly researched book in the Wallace cannon since Goodman. For someone who wants every fact on the case, especially about the people involved, this is one of the best books. There is a lot of detail, however, which sometimes intrudes on the reading and obscures the essential flow of the subject matter. For example, almost every time a new character is discussed the reader is given a genealogy; appendices would have been welcomed. For all his research, Gannon's conspiracy theory is speculative with little evidence to place Marsden in the frame for murder.

Conclusion: Wallace conspired with Parry and Marsden to kill his wife.

James, P. D. *The Perfect Murder* (2013)

The bestselling novelist made a foray into true crime shortly before she died. Writing in the *Sunday Times*, she said she had been intrigued by the Wallace murder. When she was invited to give a talk on the case, a solution suddenly came into her mind "with the strength of absolute conviction". Certitude is arguably an incorrect response to any proposed solution – the case is compelling because of the doubt that envelops it like a swirling mist that never lifts. I believe her solution is the most original, and I can see why a novelist would be attracted to its ironic but dramatic storyline: the perfect murder is devised after receiving a chance call. Nevertheless, this does not necessarily mean it is the best explanation based on the evidence.

Conclusion: Wallace killed his wife after Parry made a prank call.

Russell, Mark. *Checkmate* (2021)

The connoisseur of the case will savour the rich detail in this book, although it may be too much for the more casual reader. In fact, 20% of the book is footnotes. The magistrate hearings and appeal court proceedings are covered particularly well. Throughout the chronological narrative the tone is measured and objective, but this changes in the conclusion, where the author provides his analysis. The tenor is more strident, needled with hyperbole as unfavoured ideas are dismissed as "half-baked", "idiotic", "nonsensical" and "insane", to provide a small sample. Russell relies heavily on the arguments of James Murphy and inherits many of the same mistakes, the biggest being the assumption that the caller must also be the killer. This might have been "generally accepted" during the last century but the result is that modern theories are glossed over or ignored. Unfortunately, as the author has strong opinions on the verdict, the analysis suffers from inconsistency and confirmation bias. Two brief examples. First, in dispensing with the idea of a conspiracy, Russell says it would have been "idiotic" of Wallace to meet an accomplice (Lily Hall's sighting) before admitting later that "murderers do actually commit idiotic actions". Second, Russell proclaims that only Wallace would have removed the weapon from the scene. But if it was pre-mediated murder, another killer would surely have brought his own weapon and taken it away; if spur-of-the-moment, the killer might have feared leaving fingerprints on an improvised bludgeon and removed it. The assertion lacks cogency. A more comprehensive and balanced analysis would have complemented the detailed historical narrative to provide a classic reference.

Conclusion: William Wallace acting alone killed his wife.

Wilkes, Roger. *Britain's Most Baffling Murder* (2021)
There was great expectation when it was announced that Wilkes was publishing a second book on the Wallace case. However, it is simply a reprint of *The Final Verdict* from 1984 with a new introduction. To read the author's thoughts on Parry's guilt in light of the released police files should have been instructive. It is not. There is no new analysis and

no contextualising of key claims in the book which are now known to be false – e.g. that Lily Lloyd provided Parry with an alibi for the time of the murder. If you don't have a copy of *The Final Verdict* then this is worth buying for its historical importance to the case. Otherwise, it can be ignored.

The Julia Wallace Murder Foundation

Not a book, but almost a complete digital record of the case. A treasure trove for the researcher and serious "Wallace buff", it covers everything from the police files to the full trial transcript and much more. Can be quite difficult to navigate around, but almost all relevant information pertaining to the case has been collected.

www.williamherbertwallace.com

Research Sources

In researching this book I have relied heavily on primary sources – trial transcript, police reports, witness statements and prosecution files – held at The National Archives (refs: HO 144/17938 and 17939) and Merseyside Police. In addition, I have used the original files of Wallace's solicitor, Hector Munro, held at the Liverpool office of Hill Dickinson LLP. Almost all of these resources are now online at the Julia Wallace Murder Foundation.

EPILOGUE

THE INDIGNITIES OF MURDER

Like most murder victims, Julia Wallace was robbed not only of her life but dignity in death. With her warm body sprawled on the parlour floor, strangers stepped over her and poked about her life in every room. Wallace sighed, "Julia would go mad if she could see all this." Her home was invaded first by the police and then by a ghoulish world, invited inside by the police photographer. There are more images of Julia Wallace in death than there are of her in life. Her private affairs were cruelly exposed; not even her underwear escaped the attention of strangers. The manner of her death even denied her a normal burial. Wishing to avoid gawping crowds, her funeral was kept secret, and only attended by three mourners. Such are the indignities of murder.

If William Wallace was innocent, he also suffered the ignominy of ostracism. Despite having his guilty verdict quashed by three judges, the local community believed the verdict of the 12 jurors. Customers who had known him for years refused to speak to him, their disapproval signalled only by the twitching of net curtains. Children drew the hangman's gallows on his back gate, while others peered into the parlour to glimpse the scene of the infamous crime. Everywhere there were whispers of condemnation.

Some voices were louder. Wallace won several libel actions against publications that did not accept the decision of the appeal court. But Liverpool was lost to him. A few months after his trial, alone and disillusioned, he moved to a bungalow in Bromborough, eight miles away, to spend the final months of his life.

After the Wallace case, Richard Gordon Parry was arrested for several theft offences and also for an alleged assault on a girl. He married twice, finally settling in North Wales, where he died in April 1980. Although he appears to have taken an active interest in the Wallace case – he knew key witnesses had died – he refused to talk about it.

Joseph Marsden died in October 1967. Even though he was named by Wallace on his list, Marsden appears to have avoided the suspicion that followed Parry like circling vultures. From start to finish, we know virtually nothing about him. In terms of this case, he is a shadowy figure, a silent cameo in a play which, according to one script, sees him perform in the pivotal scene and nowhere else.

Wallace would never escape his shadow of ill health. By February 1933 he could no longer tolerate the agony caused by the pyelonephritis in his remaining kidney. Admitted to hospital, an emergency operation was unsuccessful. On drugs to ease the pain, he slipped into long bouts of unconsciousness and finally into a coma. He died in the early hours of 26 February 1933. Four days later, he was buried next to his wife at Anfield Cemetery.

If William Herbert Wallace was involved in her murder, Julia Wallace forever rests in silence next to her killer – perhaps the greatest indignity of all.

PART FOUR

YOUR SUMMONS

I hope you will again take your seat on the Cold Case Jury.

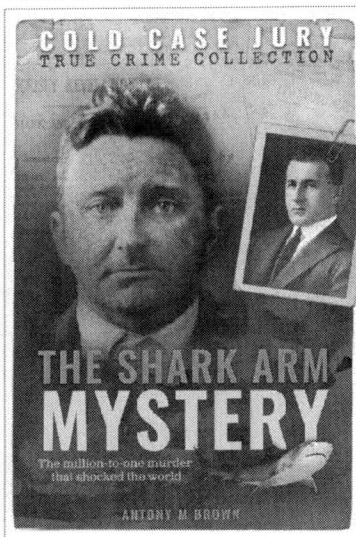

THE GREEN BICYCLE MYSTERY
The shooting of Bella Wright, 1919
It is a case that could have been taken from the memoirs of Sherlock Holmes. In the summer of 1919, a young woman is found dead in a lonely country lane. She is last seen with a man on a green bicycle, who seemingly vanishes into thin air... Now, dramatic evidence is revealed for the first time, including a vital statement hidden in a police safe for decades and the forgotten testimony of a key witness. But does it solve the case or deepen the mystery? Take your seat on the Cold Case Jury.

DEATH OF AN ACTRESS
The disappearance of Gay Gibson, 1947
A luxury liner steams across the equator off the coast of Africa. A beautiful actress disappears from her first-class cabin and a dashing deck steward is accused of her murder. Although the evidence against him appears damning, he vehemently protests his innocence. Found guilty and sentenced to death, remarkably he is saved from the gallows. Using recently discovered police files, the full story is told for the first time with new evidence never brought to trial. Was it murder, or does the new evidence point to a different verdict?

POISONED AT THE PRIORY
The notorious death of Charles Bravo, 1876
When a dying barrister is told by his doctors he has ingested a rare poison he is strangely indifferent to his plight. It looks like suicide, but a coroner's inquest finds he was unlawfully killed. Over a century later debate still rages: was Charles Bravo responsible for his own death or was his life taken by a sinister hand unseen? Nobody was accused, nobody was brought to trial. Now the Cold Case Jury must deliver its

verdict on how Charles Bravo died. With five suspects and four possible verdicts, this is one of the most intriguing cold cases ever.

THE SHARK ARM MYSTERY

The million-to-one murder, Australia, 1935

A scuttled yacht. A missing person. A captured shark. The three events appear unrelated, but when the shark coughs up a human arm in a Sydney aquarium, a one-in-a-million coincidence quickly turns into a murder inquiry. The police have two prime suspects, but one is gunned down in his car by Sydney Harbour Bridge, and the other is soon acquitted at trial. Others are suspected, but the case turns cold. It remains unsolved to this day. Now, the Cold Case Jury must reach a decision on who most likely killed the missing man in one of the most sensational crimes of the 20th century.

OR IF YOU FANCY SOME CRIME FICTION...

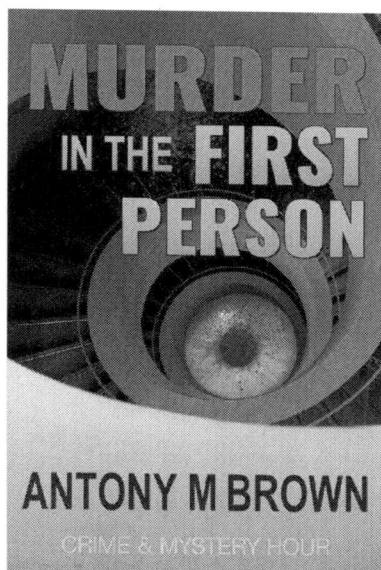

Includes *For Laura Hope* – shortlisted for the Margery Allingham Prize in 2021.

A collection of seven fictional short stories that have a common thread: they are written in the first person to impart immediacy and bring the reader closer to murder. Other than this, it is a diverse collection, providing a kaleidoscope of perspective from detectives to the perpetrators and victims. They span different eras, from the 19th century to the 21st, and raise a variety of philosophical issues, such as truth in the age of deep fakes, retribution and the blurred line between crime and entertainment.

Printed in Great Britain
by Amazon